Happy Rhythm

A Biography of
Hovie Lister & the Statesmen Quartet
Fiftieth Anniversary Collectors' Edition

DAVID L. TAYLOR

LEXINGTONHAUS
PUBLICATIONS

Typesetting, layout & design by LexingtonHaus Publications.

Litho negatives by Digital Printing Incorporated, Madison, Indiana.

Printed by BookCrafters, Fredericksburg, Virginia.

Library of Congress Catalog Card Number: 98-091671

International Standard Book Number 0-9639880-2-6

Printed in the United States of America

Acknowledgments

This biography is the culmination of years of effort. I want to thank everyone who assisted in making this Fiftieth Anniversary Collectors' Edition a reality.

When this project began in 1992 as the first edition of **Happy Rhythm**, Bill Gaither was influencial in bringing together a number of key elements. He made himself available, as well as a number of photos and resources. He also readily agreed to write the Foreword. The time, input and advice he has contributed have been invaluable. Simply put, the first edition of this biography, published in 1994, would not have been possible without the help of Bill Gaither and his ever-capable secretary, Carolyn Hall. She is a storehouse of patience and encouragement.

The Statesmen, past and present, and their families have been supportive. Hovie Lister invited me along on a weekend tour with the quartet; and spent time with me at concerts throughout the Midwest, in a hotel conference room in Atlanta, and during countless telephone conversations, providing information and personal insights. Jake Hess invited me into his home, sharing his views and recollections and offering much encouragement. Mosie Lister, Betty Rozell, Jack Toney, Jim Hill and Buddy Burton shared trips down memory lane. Elizabeth Wetherington, a dear lady and widow of the late Big Chief, provided photographs and shared a number of Statesmen and Melody Masters memories. She and the Chief's daughter, Diana Helton, were gracious in opening their home to me and providing valuable information, advice and encouragement. The Chief's nephew, Marc Wetherington, also shared photos and insights. Jerry Kendrick, son of the late Bervin Kendrick, shared pages from his father's ledger book from the early days of the Statesmen, which was a good source for personnel changes and when they occurred, concert dates and concert income.

Several gospel music personalities offered their views on the career of the Statesmen. Dr. James Blackwood was a valuable resource of information about the early years of gospel quartet music, and shared numerous thoughts on the years of the Blackwood/Statesmen team. Brock Speer, was a living resource of information regarding the singing schools and conventions. Brock gave input about the formation of Skylite Records and his years as producer for the company. J.D. Sumner also provided information about the Blackwood/Statesmen team, and shared stories about the zany antics of the late Cat Freeman. Vestal Goodman also took time to recall memories of Cat Freeman, her brother. Wally Varner contributed an enjoyable review of the career of the Melody Masters. Record producer Joel Gentry provided information about the later years of Skylite Records, and made available copies of later Statesmen releases on the label. Record collectors Bob Cobb, John Crenshaw, Bill Flack and Bob Holcomb shared numerous tidbits of information and rare recordings from their vast collections of quartet memorabilia.

Other information concerning Statesmen recordings came from Ronnie Pugh, Head of Reference at the Country Music Foundation in Nashville; and from Ed Rudisill and Harold Timmons, dealers in out-of-print gospel quartet recordings.

I want to recognize my brother, Standley Taylor, who first began attending gospel sings and bringing home quartet records in the early 1950s, and who freely loaned his extensive collection of Statesmen records and memorabilia during the writing of this book.

My wife, Cheryl, and children—Merilee, Melody and Davy—have been patient and supportive during both editions of this endeavor, as I poured countless hours of time and energy into research and writing. I love them with all of my heart.

To all of these I extend a very sincere "thank you" for contributing toward this biography. And finally, I want to express my sincere gratitude to the members of the Statesmen—those who are yet living and those who have gone on to sing around the throne eternal—for their story brings this volume to life.

...Dave Taylor

Contents

$\mathcal{F}oreword$

In any field of art, there is always a standard by which all other art is measured. In the southern gospel quartet field, most would agree that standard would be Hovie Lister and The Statesmen. Organized in 1948, in Atlanta, Georgia, The Statesmen established a level of excellence that would be difficult for other quartets to achieve for years to come. A bona fide original in any field is hard to find, but The Statesmen were truly originals in every sense of the word. They were inventive and disciplined and always in relentless pursuit of perfection in their harmonies, their stage performance, and their recordings. They consistently exhibited a level of professionalism unequaled in their field at that time.

Jerry Crutchfield, one of today's well-known producers — a young aspiring quartet hopeful back in the early '50s, remembers a friend saying in 1951, "I heard a new group last night in Jackson, Tennessee, called The Statesmen — trust me, life is never going to be the same in our field."

The appearance of these new "Statesmen" was to be the shot heard 'round the gospel world.

Hovie Lister and the Statesmen Quartet have always been — no matter which combination of personnel — a powerful team that southern gospel music lovers cannot forget. The Statesmen and their songs have lived on long after many of the singers have gone on to be with the One they sang about. The mixture of unforgettable showmanship, tight vocal harmonies, and heart within each of the men who took the stage will always be remembered.

Like myself, Dave Taylor grew up in a small Indiana town with a sincere love of gospel quartet music. **Happy Rhythm**, Dave's entertaining biography of Hovie Lister and the Statesmen, is an informative companion piece to our video in the Hall of Honor Series, "Bill and Gloria Gaither Present Hovie Lister and the Sensational Statesmen, An American Classic." His effort has been a labor of love. **Happy Rhythm** takes the reader beyond the concert and television appearances, and into the private lives of the Statesmen. I'm sure their inspiring story will be a blessing to you.

...Bill Gaither

Hovie Lister

Denver Crumpler

Jake Hess

Doy W. Ott

Big Chief

Prelude

The huge tabernacle stands majestically, resembling a behemoth Spanish mission which has been mistakenly deposited in the heart of a bustling Midwestern city. Street lights bathe three touring buses parked at the curb in front of the structure, casting gloomy shadows across the pale glow of the tabernacle's cream-colored, terra cotta exterior. Across the street a parking lot attendant enjoys brisk business as cars from all over Indiana, and many from surrounding states—Michigan, Ohio, Illinois and Kentucky—pour into the Hoosier State's capital city. A stream of people funnels into the front doors of the Spanish building. Many pause to admire the tour buses or to wait for the crowd to clear from the building's entrance. A few make small talk with the portly man who is unloading boxes of records and books from one of the buses and placing them on a handcart.

Anticipation written across each face, the people pour through the entrance and make their way to the ticket window. Two dollars buys an adult ticket. A child's admission is half the fare. One concertgoer buys a ticket for an old panhandler outside who, to little avail, has been working the crowd on the street. "A little singin' will be better for him than the bottle he'd buy if I gave him money," says the benevolent man to a lady in the ticket booth. It is a family crowd, a cross-section of ages and types, black and white alike, dressed in their Sunday best. Once through the foyer doors and into the main auditorium the crowd fans into four aisles until nearly every available seat in the tabernacle is filled. Most try to avoid the few seats from which steel support posts will obscure their view of the platform. For latecomers getting seats near the back, the only disappointment is with the view, for the acoustics are nearly perfect in any seat of the house.

It is late fall in Indianapolis. The common midwesterner turns his attention from John Kennedy's recent election to getting ready for the upcoming Thanksgiving holiday. On this Saturday, promoter Lloyd Orrell has brought Southern Gospel Quartet Music—none other than the most celebrated acts of the genre, the Blackwood Brothers and the Statesmen Quartet, complemented by "America's First Family of Gospel Music" the Speer Family—to the city's famous Cadle Tabernacle. And for the 10,000 quartet fans gathered inside, all is well with the world.

Orrell's son, Larry, leads the crowd in a couple of opening congregational numbers. A local pastor steps out to offer a word of prayer. At its conclusion bowed heads throughout the auditorium lift in anticipation of the music to come. A murmer of excitement ripples through

Cadle Tabernacle, Indianapolis, Indiana

the crowd as the elder Orrell brings on the opening group. A spotlight collects the Speer Family—G.T. and Lena Speer, known affectionately among the Gospel Music world as "Dad" and "Mom," their sons Brock and Ben, and Ginger Smith—as each group in this opening go-around enjoys the attention of the audience for about 30 minutes apiece. The Speers sing with such feeling and sincerity that members of the audience respond frequently to testimony and song with a loud "amen" or "hallelujah." Songs composed by Dad Speer—"The Dearest Friend I Ever Had," "Heaven's Jubilee," and "I Never Shall Forget the Day"—are a big hit with the audience.

Next up are the Blackwood Brothers, featuring Wally Varner, a virtuoso of the keyboard; popular tenor Bill Shaw, J.D. Sumner, the world's lowest bass singer; baritone Cecil Blackwood, and group leader James Blackwood. The latter is an articulate master of ceremonies who doubles as lead singer. The group is a huge hit with the audience almost from the moment the five men walk onstage. The Blackwoods score with the audience on such hits as "Crossing Chilly Jordan" and "Because of Him," songs written by Sumner, and "Dear Jesus, Abide With Me." Following the last encore of the Blackwoods' opening set, Orrell waits a few moments to allow the crowd to get calm.

"Now from Atlanta, ladies and gentlemen, would you welcome Georgia's Ambassadors of Good Will, Brother Hovie Lister and the Statesmen Quartet!"

Five handsome men, sharply dressed in navy blue, pin-striped suits, quickly make their way onstage. The audience reacts in a wildy enthusiastic roar of applause. Lister, flashing a toothy grin, pounds out a piano introduction and the group rips into its opening up-tempo song. This Statesmen concert, like all others, is a fascinating experience combining Christian ministry and entertainment. Statesmen concerts have been described variously as "high-spirited," "deeply emotional" and "wildly entertaining." Onstage, Lister is seated on the audience's right at a shiny, grand piano with his back to the quartet. A microphone on a short stand is conveniently placed at the piano for Lister's announcements and for him to occasionally sing along. Two other microphones grace the stage. The first tenor and lead tenor singers share the microphone to the far left while the baritone and bass vocalists share a microphone next to the pianist. "Each member of the group performs with an enthusiasm that can only be born of complete sincerity," Lister has often said, and the evidence is here tonight. The audience sways in time with the music, many sing along, most clap their hands or tap their toes with the rhythm. They respond thunderously at the conclusion of the opening number.

"Thank you very much, ladies and gentlemen! I tell you it's sure good to be back in Indianapolis tonight," Lister shouts over the microphone above another round of applause. "Ralph Goodpasteur wrote almost the sentiments of my heart in a song we'd like to do for you right now and it has blessed me throughout the days that we've sung it—'To Me It's So Wonderful.' "

Baritone singer Doy Ott smoothly interprets the opening verse of the song in his smiling, laid-back manner. Lead singer Jake Hess—eyes opened wide with a big smile playing across his face, the fingers of both hands fanned in front of him—delivers the next verse in his inimitable manner, each word phrased distinctly as only Jake can. Rosie Rozell, who sings the high tenor, takes command of the chorus, soulfully leading the quartet to the climax of the number.

Lister allows the applause to reach a crescendo and bursts into sermonette: "While the boys were singing that song my mind turned to a favorite subject of every man, woman, boy and girl—love. Love is a great word. God gave His only begotten Son, then His only begotten Son gave His life on Calvary. That was a love that supercedes all love that man has ever known. It's a love that gives me the joy and the happiness in my heart, and it's the love that makes me free tonight. Listen!"

The quartet then sings "Love Is Why," a song about Christ's

James Wetherington

death on the cross that features Hess and later James "Big Chief" Wetherington, the bass singer. At six feet-one, Wetherington is the tallest of the Statesmen. He commands the stage with his presence and his big bass voice. Chief and Hovie both sport pencil-thin, black moustaches, although many of the fans can remember when all five Statesmen wore moustaches. The audience accepts this song with as much enthusiasm as many of the up-tempo numbers. But again the applause doesn't have time to die down before the pianist/preacher is setting up the next song.

"You know, with love being so free, with God's Son dying so willingly, it always hurts me deep inside when I see folks that don't know him. Don't it you? (The audience responds with applause.) You know,

Jake Hess

Rosie Rozell

so many of us today all we think's necessary is to join the church and that's

Hovie Lister

Doy Ott

it. I know a bootlegger that done the same thing. And this old boy went down one Sunday morning, joined the church and was baptized and the next week he was bootleggin' again. But one night a dream came to him. In that dream he said he heard a million people crying out to God for mercy because it was the end of time. He remembered that he'd joined the church years ago and he went down to the Master and he said, 'Master, look at me. I been a member of the church for years. I'm all right, ain't I?' And he said the Master began to look through the Book of Life, page after page, and pretty soon the Master looked up to old Henkle and said, 'Henkle, I find no record of your birth, boy. Sorry, I

A capacity Cadle Tabernacle crowd enjoying an orchestra. The Statesmen and Blackwood Brothers enjoyed a similar view many times during the 1950s and '60s.

never knew you. Go and serve the one you served while on earth.' God had to bring him and show him that joining the church wasn't enough. We're going to sing this song. It's the entire dream and if it inspires you, let the boys know."

Midway through "Sorry, I Never Knew You," Big Chief begins to belt out the verses in a chanting recitation, haunting in its description of the songwriter's dream put to rhyme. The song ends with the writer awakening from the dream, and seeing his wife and children gathered around him, falls on his knees and begs God's forgiveness. This song, too, is met with enthusiastic response.

Lister, chording softly on the piano, paraphrases from the lyrics of the next song as he leads the quartet into the number. "You know, after hearing the boys sing that song I was just thinking. People often get religion but their heart ain't changed. They go to church and they testify. But you know it's an awful fate to find that they have no real salvation..." The quartet then launches into "I Believe In the Old Time Way" with the line "...but 'twill be too late." The song was written by J.D. Sumner, bass singer for the Blackwood Brothers. When the Statesmen offer an encore, Sumner and other members of the Blackwoods join them onstage in singing.

Sirens pierce the night on a nearby street as Hovie prepares the audience for the closing number of the opening set. "I'm tellin' you, I'm about to hot to death up here! Perspiration's runnin' off of me like sweat! Now ain't we havin' a time here tonight? I'd rather be here than in the best hospital in Indianapolis, tonight! You know, thinking about my childhood days, and thinking about children—we all have children. We're proud of 'em. Big Chief has a daughter. Doy has a little boy and a daughter. Jake Hess has ... you got two boys now, ain't you? We ain't been home in so long I forgot. And a girl. You know, children pray from the depths of their heart. Doy's little boy had a very sweet prayer that he always said with him. Doy, thinking about Little Joe and prayer time at home around the bed, he sat down and wrote the music to Joe's little prayer and it goes like this..."

Parents throughout the tabernacle hang on each word as Jake sings the child's prayer thanking God for the day, for his playmates, his toys and the many blessings received, asking God's blessings on Mommy and Daddy "and my sister, too. And watch o'er my doggy for I love him too..."

To close the set, Hovie stands, takes the microphone in his left hand, and with a sweep of his right hand, says over the resounding roar, "Have you really enjoyed Jake Hess tonight? How about it, ladies and gentlemen? How about the old Big Chief over to my left? How about Rosie Rozell? How about Doy Ott? The Statesmen Quartet!"

During the brief intermission, some fans slip out to a neighborhood coffee shop for a soft drink, popcorn, or other treats, while most crowd around record tables to purchase songbooks, gospel sheet music, souvenir booklets, photographs and the latest recordings by their favorite singers.

For some it is a brief opportunity to chat with their heroes and get autographs. Eavesdropping, we hear Hovie explaining to a reporter why all-night sings are so popular all over the country.

"There are folks out there," he says, with a sweep of his hand toward the audience seating area, "who would never go to a theater. They think theaters are sinful. This is almost their only form of entertainment. Others come to hear us, but never go to church! We get letters from men and women who find God here—they go home and fall on their knees after an all-night sing. And I've had them come backstage to pray with me."

A youngster beams as his older brother inspects Big Chief's autograph on the latest addition to the family's album collection. A graduate student and someday songwriter by the name of Bill Gaither makes small talk with Jake Hess near the record table. Rosie Rozell pulls change from a wad of bills for a woman who has purchased a songbook. A proud young mother wants Doy Ott to see her toddling twins. The panhandler recovers from his pocket a partially-spent cigarette he had found earlier on the street. Striking a match he prepares to light up, but noting that Reverend Hovie Lister is eyeing him, he drops the match and quickly hides the cigarette. Soon the crowd is seated again for the second round of moving renditions of traditional old hymns, spirituals and new songs of the faith.

Midnight is approaching when the Statesmen take the stage to close the concert. The audience may be tired but they remain electrified with enthusiasm. Onstage, the Statesmen are dynamic showmen. Their stage presence is a combination of exuberant singing, hand clapping, and energetic delivery while Lister attacks the keyboard and kicks his feet in time to the music. They burst into the fast-paced "Happy Am I," and songs written by the members of the group. Hovie, noting the quartet had received many requests during the intermission, introduces "I Believe in the Man in the Sky," an old Statesmen song many fans recognize.

Between songs Lister fascinates the crowd by alternately preaching, telling jokes and sharing the stories behind the songs. All too soon for the audience it is time to cap the evening with the closing song. "You know, sometimes the old devil can get us a little disappointed on the Christian road," Hovie observes. "Sometimes when we are striving to do our best and things aren't going just like we'd like for them to go, we look around and we see that the devil's crowd has all the attention. But one of these days the devil will have his run. There'll be a settling-up time. There'll be a payday for all those that's been faithful to the Lord. Yes, down here trials dark on every hand and we cannot understand, but we'll understand it better, praise God, by and by."

Slowly, soulfully, Rosie Rozell leads the group into the hymn "When the Morning Comes." The tempo picks up at the chorus and the audience jumps to its feet, clapping in sync with the vocalists. When Jake launches an encore with the verse that begins: "Temptations, hidden snares often take us unawares," the energy builds to a feverish pitch. The members of the group have scattered into the first few rows of the audience, shaking hands and inviting the spectators to sing along. At the conclusion of the encore, Hovie's "Have you enjoyed the Statesmen Quartet here tonight, neighbors?" is met with tumultuous applause that thunders on and on.

Eventually, the crowd is making its way to the exits. Some pause for a final purchase at the record tables, others express their appreciation to all the singers for the blessing they had received from the event. Young parents balancing sleeping babies and diaper bags, older couples walking hand in hand, teens on their first date—all of whom are uplifted on a wave of exhilaration—make their way back to their cars and the drive back to the routine of everyday life that awaits them at home.

1

Origins of Southern Gospel Music

From the time of the Old Testament and throughout church history, music has been an integral part of worship. Gospel music as we know it today, however, is an American institution. Early Americans, steeped in the custom of believing God would be insulted if mankind offered to Him songs other than those He had dictated in the Holy Scriptures, brought with them the songs of the Old World. Early colonists offered their praises from "psalters," hymn books containing the Psalms. In the eighteenth century, spawned by the first Great Awakening which was led by Jonathan Edwards, the use of "human composure" hymns during worship gradually became accepted among Americans. Eventually, gospel music became more personalized when a distinctly American form of hymnody—known as "gospel songs"—became popular.

Gospel songs—sacred folk songs that express emotions and convictions—are free in form, devout in attitude, evangelistic in purpose and spirit. Gospel songwriters compose lyrics that develop a single thought, rather than a line of thought. This central theme usually finds its supreme expression in a chorus or refrain which serves to bind the stanzas together in a very close unity. Gospel songs are more varied, intimate and spontaneous in expressing personal religious experience than liturgical traditional hymns.

Gospel music of this type was popular at camp meetings held as the frontier pushed the boundaries of our great country Westward at the dawn of the 19th century. Gospel was the dominant musical theme of our country before, during and after the tragic war that divided our nation in the 1860s. Two adversaries of that war later became partners in a business that published sacred and gospel songs. Ephraim Ruebush and Aldine Kieffer created an unusual system of musical notation featuring seven-notes. Each of the seven notes had distinctive shapes when printed in Ruebush/Kieffer Publishing Company songbooks. The concept was not new. Shaped-note singing originated in New England in the 1700s, and was introduced in the southern states by Ananias Davisson in the 1820s. While shaped-note singing soon died out in New England, it was kept alive in the South by people who revered it as a southern tradition. Prior to the seven-note system of Ruebush and Kieffer, songbooks throughout the South had been written in a four-note system popularly known as "Sacred Harp." With the shaped-note method of singing, pitch was indicated by the shape of the note. In the mid-1870s, the Ruebush/Kieffer system of shaped-note singing simplified sight reading so much that average students could learn to read a simple song in a convention book by the end of a two-week singing school. The two men opened a school to teach their method, thus helping to boost its popularity.

Singing Schools

The genre that is now commonly known as southern gospel quartet music had its roots in the singing schools and singing conventions that were held in courthouse squares and churches throughout the South. While these traditions began in the 19th century, the rural schools and conventions were extremely popular through the 1930s and continue to some extent today. For many singers, the only formal music training was the result of singing schools. Self-styled singing masters traveled the South organizing singing classes that often ran from two to three weeks. Some of the schools were sponsored by churches or Gospel songbook publishers. Pupils at the singing schools learned the rudiments of music—sight reading, marking time and how to sing harmony parts.

After the usual words of greeting and an opening prayer, the teacher passed out the rudiment books and prepared to introduce his pupils to an unusual notation system consisting of shaped notes. Mornings at the schools often consisted of developing sight reading and harmony skills. Class singing followed the lunch hour, giving pupils the opportunity to practice the skills they had learned in the morning sessions. The art of conducting group singing was included among the instructional curriculum of several of the schools. Often the schools would climax with a concert exhibiting the songs and skills that had been learned.

The late G.T. Speer, patriarch of the famous Singing Speer Family, supported his young family as a traveling singing-school teacher in the 1920s. As his son Brock remembers, the singing schools usually lasted about two weeks.

"Daddy would go to a community and a community leader would take subscriptions in order to raise the money. They'd charge so much a pupil—'a dollar a scholar,' they used to call it ."

The schools were very popular, sometimes attracting 200 to 300 pupils. Before the technology was developed that provided other forms of entertainment, singing provided an important form of community recreation.

"Folks didn't have TV back then," Brock emphasizes. "They didn't have radio, didn't have tapes and records, didn't have cars. If they'd had cars the roads were so terrible that you couldn't do much traveling. So what they did to amuse themselves they almost had to do at home or in their own local community. And learning to sing, and learning to read music—the shaped notes that we used to all learn back then—was a social gathering as well as a spiritual and musical event. It was a big, big thing back in the '20s and '30s and even some in the '40s."

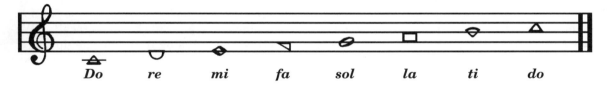

James Blackwood attended his first singing school with his older brother Doyle in 1929 at Clear Springs Baptist Church, about three miles from his boyhood home in Choctaw County, Mississippi. The teacher was Vardiman Ray, who represented the Hartford Music Company, in Hartford, Arkansas. Blackwood recalls little in the way of individual instruction. The emphasis at this school was on class singing.

Mr. Ray "didn't give any voice lessons. He was strictly teaching the rudiments of harmony, sight reading, ear training, and was quite efficient at it because at that school I learned to sing the shaped notes," Blackwood remembers. "He would have a blackboard and would put the diatonic scale—the do, re, mi, fa, sol, la, ti, do—with the shapes on a staff. And he would take a pointer and point to the various notes in the scale—no particular note, just jumping around— and you were to sound that note. This was the method that was used, I would say, by all singing school teachers of that era."

"Used to be," says Brock Speer, "I'd associate getting hot in the summertime—uncomfortably hot—with going to singing conventions and singing schools because the churches and school-houses where we used to go to singing conventions were usually packed and jammed, just crowded," he says. "You hardly ever see a building as crowded with people now as you did then, because the crowds are not as intense. But back then we mostly met in the summertime because in the winter time the dirt roads were so bad that even a horse and buggy or wagon had a bad time getting around. We sing in a lot better comfort now than we did then."

Singing Conventions

Singing conventions, often called "all-day singing and dinner on the ground," offered the opportunity for rural Southerners to gather and sing the old songs, visit and enjoy good eating. People who attended these singings, held at churches, schools and courthouses, prepared to spend the day and took along picnic lunches. These conventions attracted audiences from many miles around, folks who came not only to sing or enjoy the amateur and professional groups on the program, but to widen their circle of acquaintance. Young folks often attended the singing conventions for courting purposes. For most people the singings offered the pleasure of companionship with other people of similar status and interests.

The all-day singings offered rural Southerners a look at the latest convention songbooks. Companies like Ruebush/Kieffer Publishing Company, James D. Vaughan Publishing Company, Stamps-Baxter Music Co., J.M. Henson Music Co., R.E. Winsett Music Company and others produced the convention books.

"They published these books of songs in shaped notes," explains Speer, "and they taught the shaped-note notation music reading in singing schools. So it was making a market for the books, because after you would learn a song, you wouldn't necessarily be tired of it but you'd want to get to something else and practice your reading skills again. And so they kept the new books coming all the time."

Since these publications featured shaped notes, in many southern churches and singing conventions it was customary to sing the first chorus of a song through by singing the names of the notes ("fa," "sol," "la," etc.) instead of the words. As a youth Hovie Lister played piano at a number of singing conventions where this occurred.

"There would be a president or a presiding officer and he would call on different people to come forward and lead the singers in class singing. Sometimes, if it was a new song, they would sing the notes, the shaped notes," he says, chuckling. "That was a sight to behold and to hear, people singing four-part harmony, and maybe somebody'd be singing a 'do' and somebody else'd be singing a 'mi' and somebody'd be singing a 'fa' or 'la'—that sort of thing."

To people from other parts of the country, the result must have sounded like organized confusion. In later years the Blackwood Brothers Quartet would perform songs in this fashion to entertain their fans, "particularly when we were in Iowa in the 1940s," James recalls. "We were there about 10 years and that was very interesting and amusing to the people up there. They had never heard such a thing. The four of us would sing the sounds. We did four parts and, of course, each part would be saying a different sound at the same time. The people were quite amused by that. In fact it's still quite amusing. I think the Speers still do that some."

James D. Vaughan

Singing styles for the convention songs had begun to change after the turn of the century. Small group singing—usually done by a quartet—became popular. Prior to this time quartets had been composed of soprano, alto, tenor and bass. The male groups were organized with the melody on the top and all harmony below. Music publisher James D. Vaughan, a one-time student at the Ruebush/Kieffer music school, is said to have innovated the method of quartet singing in which the first tenor sang above the melody in the alto register. Shortly after the turn of the century, Vaughan founded a music publishing company in Lawrenceburg, Tennessee. Through the years the company grew into one of the largest publishers of gospel music in the United States.

Vaughan is thought to be the "inventor" of the gospel quartet. In 1910, Vaughan hired a male quartet of highly-trained professional singers to represent his publishing company, and later his singing school and Vaughan Phonograph Records. The Vaughan Quartet made appearances in churches, revivals, and singing conventions, giving concerts and promoting the songs of the Vaughan songbooks. The idea became so popular that by the late 1920s Vaughan had 16 full-time quartets on his payroll. The members of these sponsored quartets sometimes would each earn $12 to $15 a week. Appearing at singing conventions, these groups would sing selections from the books of their publishing company. In this way the groups promoted their sponsor and created a market for the songbooks. Travel was limited to each group's local region in those early years, until better cars and roads permitted more extensive road trips.

The Stamps Empire

One of Vaughan's employees, Virgil O. Stamps, founded the V.O. Stamps Music Company in 1924 in Jacksonville, Texas. In the same year his brother Frank Stamps put the first Stamps Quartet on the road. Frank Stamps' All Star Quartet was the first gospel quartet to record for a major label—Victor Talking Machine Company. That first recording, "Give the World a Smile," became the theme song for the quartets sponsored by the Stamps company. The company later moved to Dallas, and became the Stamps-Baxter Music and Printing Company in 1929. Like the Vaughan company, Stamps-Baxter soon was to sponsor numerous quartets across the country. Early in their career the Blackwood Brothers were affiliated with the Stamps organization. James Blackwood described the group's business arrangement with Stamps:

"Mr. Stamps would assist us with our booking arrangements and widen our field of operation; when needed, he would assist in securing and placement of personnel including pianists for accompaniment; he would immediately furnish a late model, dependable automobile for our business transportation as well as for our personal use...

"In return, we gave the Stamps company a percentage of our gross income after it had passed a stipulated amount. It was a very fair arrangement."

The Stamps brothers influenced the development of gospel music in numerous ways. They were the first to use piano accompaniment for professional quartets, the first to begin regular gospel quartet singing on radio and the first to use a theme song on radio. They founded what remains as the largest gospel music school in the country, staged the first all-night gospel radio broadcast in 1938 (over radio station KRLD, Dallas), and originated the all-night sing which became standard programming for gospel quartets. The idea for "all-night" sings came when a woman approached V.O. Stamps one night after a concert and said, "Mr. Stamps, I could

Brothers Frank (left) and V.O. Stamps

listen to your singing all night." He chose the huge Cotton Bowl in Dallas as the site for that first "all-night" sing in 1940 and 30,000 fans turned out. In time, other promoters jumped on the bandwagon and all-night concerts became a hit across the country. Of course, radio stations in nearly every major city of the South featured gospel quartets as part of their live programming. With radio beaming the music to the tune of 50,000 watts across the southern and midwestern states, gospel quartet music quickly grew beyond the boundaries of regional popularity.

Songwriter Bill Gaither was a teenager in Alexandria, Indiana in the late 1940s when he first became aware of the music via an Indianapolis radio station.

"There was a local quartet—I say local but a professional quartet—called the Dixie Four at WIBC (Indianapolis) that basically was our only local contact with the whole Southern Gospel field," Gaither says. "They were good, and they had quite a following in the area. I heard them first in 1946 or '47. That was my first contact with gospel music, and that's when I started buying the Stamps Quartet convention books. They would sing out of those books."

WHAS, in Louisville, Kentucky, was the home of the famous Rangers Quartet in the late 1930s. Other midwesterners could tune in to WWVA in Wheeling, West Virginia, where in 1949, the Sunshine Boys were very popular. The Blackwood Brothers had gained a huge following over KMA in Shenandoah, Iowa. Eighty miles away in Lincoln, Nebraska, KFAB boasted the Melody Masters. The members of this group included James Wetherington, Jake Hess and C.G.

"Cat" Freeman—all of whom would play prominent roles in the Statesmen Quartet.

Most of these groups broadcast one to three daily programs for the host radio station, then hit the road at night for personal appearances at churches, school auditoriums and other venues within a 250-mile radius of the radio station. In most of these performances, only one professional quartet was on the program. All that remained to bring gospel music into national prominence was to showcase several professional groups together in a concert setting and charge admission. While V.O. Stamps had introduced the "all-night sing" concept in Dallas in 1940, he did not take the show on the road.

On Friday, November 5, 1948, hillbilly musician Wally Fowler did just that. The idea came years before when he and the John Daniel Quartet were working for V.O. Stamps in Texas. V.O. once shared with Fowler that he wanted to travel the world promoting all-night broadcasts of gospel music. Stamps died before the realization of his dream, but the dream did not die with him. Wally rented Nashville's Ryman Auditorium—home of the Grand Ole Opry—and booked a large number of gospel acts, including the Blackwood Brothers, Gospelaires Quartet, Musical Millers Quartet, the Smile-A-While Quartet, the Speer Family, Frank Stamps and the Stamps Quartet, the Stamps All-Star Quartet, the Sunshine Boys, Kieffer Vaughan and the Vaughan Radio Quartet, Wally and his own Oak Ridge Quartet, and more to appear. He asked Jack Stapp, program manager of WSM radio, to broadcast the last hour of the concert live on the radio. Stapp consented only after Wally promised to have the Ryman at least half filled.

Wally Fowler

Wally and his quartet sold tickets door-to-door, and generated advertising to draw a crowd. On the day of the concert, Nashville was hit with a deluge of heavy rain. Stapp cornered Fowler at the old tabernacle where the latter was making final preparations for the sing.

"Wally, there's no way we can broadcast down here tonight!" Shaking the rain from his hat, Stapp continued, "You know you're not going to have any people here on a night like this!"

"Jack, 1,836 tickets sold in advance. These people will be here," returned Fowler.

Stapp was astounded. That was more than half the Ryman's available 3,214 seats. But common sense told him that even if 1,836 people had purchased tickets for "Wally Fowler's Gospel and Spiritual All-Night Singing" they wouldn't dare come out on a night like this.

But they did.

When the crowd began to pack the house, Stapp and others helped serve as ushers, filling all 3,214 numbered seats in the tabernacle's old pews. They arranged seating for another 300 on the stage, barely leaving room for the singers to maneuver, and still had to turn people away.

Three hours into the concert, WSM beamed the event to the entire nation east of the Rocky Mountains. WSM announcer Grant Turner, who appeared regularly on the Grand Ole Opry broadcasts, emceed the radio portion of the concert and announced that if listeners wanted to send in telegrams he would read a few of them on the air. By the end of the hour, Western Union had delivered more than 600 telegrams and the broadcast continued another hour. So great was the success that in 1949 Fowler's programs became a monthly event at the Ryman, and were regularly broadcast over WSM. Before long, all-night sings were packing the largest auditoriums in Atlanta, Birmingham, Fort Worth and numerous other southern cities.

According to Brock Speer, "The crowds soon outgrew church and school auditoriums and had to be moved to large city auditoriums and sometimes ball parks. Gospel singing programs grew geographically, too. From the Southeast, where they originated, they spread all over the United States and into Canada."

As *Saturday Evening Post* magazine would later report nationally, gospel music had "hit the high commercial trail."

2
Hovie Lister

Old-Fashioned Meeting

Greenville, South Carolina, was abuzz early that summer in 1941. Mordecai Ham, the fiery Southern evangelist of great renown, was to hold a city-wide revival meeting. Ham was a speaker in the mold of Billy Sunday and his meetings drew large numbers. Ham's revivals often involved the organizational assistance of pastors and laymen representing several churches and denominations in a community, much in the same way local organizers worked on a larger scale for the crusades of Evangelist Billy Graham in later years. In fact, it was under the preaching of Mordecai Ham that Billy Graham was saved during a revival meeting in Charlotte, North Carolina, in 1934. Highly literate and a man of intense convictions, Ham had once studied law. He made his living for a time as a traveling salesman, but after accepting the call to preach had served as pastor of the First Baptist Church in Oklahoma City. He had been a mighty protagonist for Prohibition. A stately, balding man with a neatly-trimmed mustache, what hair the evangelist had remaining had turned white by the time of the Greenville meeting. Ham wore spectacles and was immeccably dressed whenever he preached. He was a vigorously intense speaker. Sitting under his passionate manner of delivery, hearers were overwhelmed with the realization that Christ is alive. His bold, descriptive preaching was said to frighten people into heaven by dangling them over the fiery pits of hell.

Among the committee of local organizers for the revival was a Greenville businessman by the name of Kessler. A Baptist layman, he had for quite some time taught a Sunday School lesson every Sunday morning at the local jail. Each week he sent his driver to pick up a 14-year-old pianist to play for the jail services. It was an interesting experience for young Hovie Lister.

"Nowadays they call it the county correctional institute," Lister says, "but in those days they called it the county chain gang because everybody was put in leg chains even if they were just there for public drunkenness."

When Mordecai Ham arrived for the revival, organizers found they would need to provide a pianist for the congregational singing, someone who would also serve as piano accompanist for Mr. Ham's featured soloist, C. Austin Miles. Miles, a well-known songwriter, had composed the hymn favorites "In the Garden" and "Dwelling In Beulah Land." He was, at the time of the Greenville revival, in the twilight of his life, with only about five years to live.

"I had been going to the chain gang every Sunday morning with Mr. Kessler to play piano for his services," Hovie recalls. "So he immediately suggested to Mr. Ham that he had a young man that could play piano for the meeting. And my father volunteered my services to play for that city-wide revival. I didn't know the significance of who C. Austin Miles was. I didn't know he was the author of the great old hymn "In the Garden" and many, many other hymns that's in the hymnbook. But he was a fascinating man. He had shoulder-length, white hair. He had a chauffeur-driven Franklin automobile. I not only played for the congregational singing but I played for C. Austin Miles when he sang at the meetings."

When the Greenville meeting closed, young Hovie spent the rest of that summer traveling with Miles and Evangelist Ham in their many revivals. The regional notoriety the youngster enjoyed—a side benefit of the Ham experience—was self-gratifying to a degree, but it served to open doors for many valuable opportunities to share his developing talent with appreciative audiences.

Child Entrepreneur

Hovie Lister was born in Greenville, South Carolina on September 17, 1926, to William Herman and Renty Jo Lister. Both parents worked in a cotton mill. Cotton came in the door at one end of the factory in bales, and went out the other end as cloth. His father was the spinning department superintendent.

Hovie's childhood was heavily influenced by the Gospel. His paternal grandfather, A.J. Lister, traveled the country as a singing-school teacher. His mother's father, the Rev. E.N. Sanders, was a Baptist preacher. "I had been exposed all my life to preaching and singing," he says. Hovie was raised in the Holiness Baptist Church, which preached a doctrine akin to that of the Pilgrim Holiness, Nazarene and Wesleyan denominations.

Hovie's piano training began at the tender age of six, with lessons from A.E. Julian, "a man who came by my house once a week. My father sat in on all of the lessons and most all of the time he sat each day in the room while I practiced two hours a day for ten straight years," he recalls.

Hovie at age 5

Julian was well known in Greenville as a music teacher, according to the late E.O. Batson, who published the gospel music periodical *Gospel Singing World* in the 1950s. "Even so, in order to make a living, he drove a street car during the day," wrote Batson in 1955. "For some time, he walked four miles each Monday night to the Lister home to grapple with the job of instilling the fundamentals of music in the head of young Hovie. For this, he received 25 cents per lesson, which Father and Mother Lister managed to squeeze out of their meager earnings."

"My dad bought an old upright piano for $60. I'd pay for my lessons by collecting and selling bread scraps to a man who fed these to his hogs. All the neighbors would save their scraps and I'd sell them." The lessons cost 50 cents apiece. Hovie used any surplus earnings to purchase his music books.

It was but one of many such enterprises during his childhood. There was the summer when the government sent a crew of men to paint various buildings in his hometown. Hovie remembers it being hot and there wasn't a soft drink machine available for the workmen to refresh themselves. Though he was but a little shaver of five or six, "I got me a bunch of bottles, cleaned them up real good, bought me some Kool-Aid, borrowed the sugar from my gran'mama, iced the stuff up, put it in the bottles and sold it to those guys for 10 cents a bottle!"

By the age of ten, though he could barely reach the foot pedals, he was playing piano in church. In his early teens he was playing for the Lister Brothers Quartet. "My father and his brothers had a quartet. They were never professional but they did sing around Greenville and Pickens County, South Carolina," he explains. When he was about 14, Hovie remembers suggesting to his father that the group should sing on the local radio station. The elder Lister was skeptical. Hovie persisted, the only way to find out was to go down to the station and ask. Shrugging his shoulders, Hovie's father guessed there would be no harm in asking and took the boy to the station. Hovie went in, wearing old overalls, and asked for the manager. "I told him my dad had a quartet of gospel singers and we would like to do a program each week. I told him I'd sell the commercials for the program. He told me to bring the quartet in for an audition," Hovie says, smiling. Hovie's dad and uncles were dumfounded when they not only passed the audition but landed a "live," 15-minute program on Sundays in the process.

During the summer before he was to be a senior in high school, Hovie's father sent him to the prestigious Stamps-Baxter School of Music. By the mid-1940s the Stamps-Baxter Music & Printing Company was the most prominent and most active songbook publishing company in the growing gospel music industry. Each summer, Stamps-Baxter held a music school at the company's headquarters in Dallas, Texas.

"My father had been saving for some time, unbeknownst to me, enough money to send me," Hovie says. "I rode the train by myself from Greenville, South Carolina, to Dallas, Texas."

Hovie studied voice and piano for six weeks at the school—piano under the tutelage of Dr. Jack Hendricks, later the Dean of Music at Odessa University in Odessa, Texas. His voice teacher was W.W. Cones. At the conclusion of the six weeks, Stamps-Baxter asked him to go to Raleigh, North Carolina, to fill in with one of the company's quartets—the Lone Star Quartet—while the piano player took a two-week vacation. The Lone Star Quartet, managed by Milton Estes, was sponsored by Crazy Water Crystals on WPTF radio in Raleigh. The quartet apparently recognized Hovie's raw vocal talents and decided to get the most out of their temporary replacement—almost everyone in turn took a vacation. "I wound up playing two weeks and then singing tenor two weeks, singing the lead two weeks and singing baritone two weeks. So that spent my summer completely in school in Dallas and as a fill-in for the Lone Star Quartet in Raleigh, North Carolina."

Back in Greenville, Hovie completed his education at Parker High School. He would have liked to have gone to college but the family could not afford to send him. His parents had the needs of his younger brother and sister to consider.

"By that time I had been out almost on my own, so to speak. I had met so many people and I had ideas of playing piano for a gospel quartet and being in gospel music, since that's all I had known all my life. And college didn't really seem that important to me," he reflects.

Atlanta — A Gospel Music Mecca

After graduation, Hovie went to Atlanta to play for the LeFevres for a very short time. He became homesick and went back to Greenville.

Conner Hall called him soon after this, and Hovie came back to Atlanta to join with Hall, E.L. Landreth and Jim Waits in a group called the Southland Quartet. Conner sang first tenor, Hovie sang lead and played the piano, Landreth sang baritone, and Big Jim sang bass. Here began a friendship between Hovie and Waites which was to continue through the years. "Big Jim taught me more about quartet work and how important it is to love people than anyone else I have ever known," Hovie observes.

When that group disbanded, Hovie spent some time in Chattanooga, Tennessee, as pianist for the Sand Mountain Quartet. This quartet hailed from the Sand Mountain region in northeastern Alabama that would become famous for great gospel singers. The original Sand Mountain Quartet began singing in the 1930s. The group underwent several personnel changes during the ensuing war years. By the end of the World War II, personnel included Bobby Strickland, a great young tenor from Albertville, Alabama; Erman Slater, who would later gain notoriety as baritone singer with the famous Rangers Quartet; lead singer Alton Jolley, brother-in-law of Slater; and Irby Gardner, bass. "They were not full-time," Hovie remembers. "They all had jobs and we sang on the weekends. I taught piano lessons there at the Stamps-Baxter office in Chattanooga during the week." The Sand Mountain Quartet gained notoriety throughout south Tennessee and the northern sections of Alabama and Georgia via their daily radio broadcast on WDOD in Chattanooga. One of the members of the Sand Mountain Quartet, tenor Bobby Strickland, would play an important role later in Hovie's career. In the years to come there would be other singers from Alabama's Sand Mountain region who would be principal players in a group called the Statesmen Quartet.

Connor Hall's Homeland Harmony Quartet, shortly after World War II featured (standing, l-r) Connor Hall, first tenor; Otis McCoy, second tenor; James McCoy, baritone; and Big Jim Waites, bass; with Hovie Lister at the piano.

After about nine months, Conner Hall called Hovie and encouraged him to come back to Atlanta. Conner had been singing in the LeFevre Trio. When Alphus went into the

Hovie obviously enjoys himself as accompanist for a bass singing contest between greats Jim Waites (left), whom he worked with in the Southland Quartet, Homeland Harmony and LeFevres; and Arnold Hyles, with whom he worked in the Rangers Quartet.

Army and Urias to the Navy, the group had to break up. At this time the Homeland Harmony Quartet was re-formed. Members were Conner, Otis McCoy, James McCoy, bass B.C. Robinson, and Hovie, pianist. Robinson soon departed to return to the ministry. At Hovie's suggestion the group got "the great bass singer 'Pappy' Jim Waites" as Robinson's replacement. Waites today is remembered by many as the "dean of gospel bass singers."

Hovie today fondly remembers the great Waites and their years of working together back in the 1940s. "Big Jim Waites was my mentor. What I know about showmanship I learned from him. When I was with the Homeland Harmony he would slide down to get the low notes and he taught me how to go down the keyboard, like I was trying to find the note, and I would end up falling off the piano bench. If it was a grand piano, then I would crawl under the piano like I was embarrassed and they would have to coax me out."

Conner and the Homeland Harmony secured a radio time slot on WGST, Atlanta, their show sponsored by Chattanooga Medicine Co. The quartet would enjoy a great following for a number of years with the comings and goings of such personnel as Shorty Bradford, songwriter Lee Roy Abernathy, Aycel Soward, Wally Varner and Doy Ott, among others. Hovie spent two years with the group, making $20 a week, until the Rangers Quartet dismissed their pianist, Lee Roy Abernathy.

According to Hovie, Atlanta in the mid-to-late-1940s was very much a center for gospel quartet music. "At that time there were the LeFevres, the Homeland Harmony Quartet, and the Harmoneers had moved from Knoxville, Tennessee, to Atlanta. The Sunshine Boys were operating out of Atlanta. So we had quite a group of gospel musicians who were working out of Atlanta. Then the Rangers from Texas moved into Atlanta."

It is not surprising that gospel music should be so popular in the Peach State capital. Nearly 80 percent of Georgians in the late 1940s were affiliated with religious denominations, the overwhelming number being members of a Protestant church. About two of every three Georgians belonged to a Baptist church, with the Methodist Church being second in popularity.

In the early 1940s, the Rangers had been probably the state-of-the-art gospel quartet. From 1938 to 1948, the singing personnel remained unchanged: Denver Crumpler, tenor; Vernon Hyles, the lead singer who could sing down into the bass range; Walter Leverett, baritone; and bassist extraordinaire Arnold Hyles. For many years the Rangers worked only with guitar accompaniment. Among their big songs through the years were "Roll On Jordan" and "On the Jericho Road," songs which featured the deep bass of Arnold Hyles; and "My God Is Real," featuring the nonpariel lyric tenor of Crumpler.

Organized in 1935 in Luling, Texas, the quar-

Hovie, seated, with the famous Rangers Quartet, (l-r) Arnold Hyles, bass; Walter Leverett, baritone; Denver Crumpler, tenor; and Vernon Hyles, lead.

tet got its name after singing for the Texas Centennial celebration in Dallas in June, 1936. Texas Governor James V. Allred heard them and commissioned them Honorary Texas Rangers. The group was known for awhile as the Texas Rangers Quartet.

The Rangers set their sights on traveling to New York to appear on a talent contest broadcast nationally on radio. They schemed to pay their expenses to New York by scheduling concerts along the way. To create interest, the Rangers devised a promotion in which they would don cowboy outfits and ride bicycles to New York, billing themselves as "The Cycling Cowboys." They convinced Montgomery Ward to donate the bicycles. The Rangers barnstormed from Texas through the Midwest with bookings in Texas, Arkansas, Tennessee, Kentucky and Ohio, including an appearance on the Grand Ole Opry. Stopping in Louisville, Kentucky, for an appearance on powerful WHAS, the Rangers accepted a job offer. The job consisted of singing for two hours a day during the station's morning farm program. They never made it to New York for the talent contest. After several years at WHAS, the Rangers departed Louisville in January, 1939. They found receptive radio audiences first at 50,000 watt WBT in Charlotte, North Carolina, and later in Wheeling, West Virginia; Richmond, Virginia; and finally Atlanta, Georgia.

In those days groups frequently moved from radio station to radio station in search of greater opportunities. Even the Blackwood Brothers, one of the most successful gospel quartets of all time, moved their radio base of operations no less than seven times between 1934 and 1950, finally settling at WMPS in Memphis, Tennessee.

"As soon as the news was out that we were in need of a man, 'Little Hovie Lister' began wanting the job," wrote Vernon Hyles' wife years later. "He proved to be a master showman."

A few months after Hovie joined the Rangers in 1946, the group again relocated to Charlotte, North Carolina, for a regular broadcast over WBT radio, a CBS affiliate. "I went with them to Charlotte," Hovie says, "but was not completely happy and never really felt like I fit in in Charlotte. But I stayed there for about a year. I left them and came back to Atlanta."

"When we were asked to rejoin the staff of WBT," wrote Mrs. Vernon Hyles, "he left Georgia with reluctance and misgivings. He never liked North Carolina as a home very much, though the people in that section loved him, and after making every effort possible to adjust himself to the change, decided he wanted to go back to Georgia."

By 1947, Hovie had settled in with the LeFevres once again. A well-established family group—Urias LeFevre and siblings Alphus and Maude began singing in Middle Tennessee in 1921—the LeFevres were based in Atlanta, Georgia. The group used traditional string instruments in its performances. As is common in gospel singing, the personnel of the group had changed frequently through the years. Eva Mae Whittington married Urias and joined the singing group in 1934 as pianist and vocalist. Eva Mae took brief respites from the road to have five children. The LeFevres helped launch the careers of numerous gospel singers, including Jim Waites, Troy Lumpkin, Bob Prather and Conner Hall, over the years. Several of these Gospel Music personages filled in when the trio was scrambling for personnel during the war years as both Urias and Alphus LeFevre served in the military.

While with the LeFevres, Hovie became

Hovie with the LeFevres in the late 1940s. Standing are (from left) Eva Mae, Urias and Alphus LeFevre.

Hovie (at right) with his parents, William Herman and Renty Jo Lister.

host of a gospel radio show on WEAS in Decatur, Georgia. Warren Roberts, who one day would become station manager of WEAS, sat in the control room spinning the records and handling the engineering aspects of the show. Hovie selected the music for the show and sat in the studio making introductory comments between platters. In this role, Hovie could hone his skills as a speaker in preparation for the day when he would be master of ceremonies for his own group. Although much of the programming on radio was live during those post-war years, many shows played recordings of popular music on the air. But at the time, Hovie believes, no one played gospel records exclusively. "We have researched that pretty thoroughly. I think I'm the first gospel disc jockey in America," he says.

During the years he had served with semi-professional and professional gospel groups in Raleigh, Atlanta and Charlotte, Hovie had been obsessed with a dream. "All the while I'm doing this, I'm thinking in the back of my mind, 'When you get a few more years on you, you're going to organize your own group.' So I became active during my years in Atlanta with lots of people who were not connected with gospel music, such as becoming good friends with Barry Howell."

As Chairman of the Board of the *Atlanta Constitution* newspaper, Major Howell, Barry's father, was among the most influential men in Atlanta. The acquaintance proved to be fruitful for young Hovie Lister.

3

In the Beginning

Atlanta's two major newspapers, now merged, were separately-owned entities in 1948. In addition to publishing a newspaper, *The Atlanta Journal* also operated WSB radio in the city at that time. Often in the early days of radio and television, broadcast stations came into being as new ventures of an existing newspaper publishing company. Not to be outdone by the chief competition, the stockholders of the *Atlanta Constitution* voted to open a new radio station to claim a share of the broadcast advertising pie.

Hovie Lister, serving as a gospel disc jockey on a Decatur radio station and as pianist with the LeFevres, saw the new radio station as an opportunity to put together a gospel quartet of his own. "I had big dreams," he recalls. "I knew that I was going to have a group of my own. Back in those days, that's the way you got to be known. You got a radio program and then, through that radio exposure, you could tell people that you were available for concerts and that sort of thing. That's where you got your dates, your 'be-ats.' That's where you told the people where you were going to **be at**. I was following in the footsteps of how the other groups had done it."

When Hovie's good friend Barry Howell, whose father was Chairman of the Board of the *Atlanta Constitution*, told him about the newspaper's plans to open a radio station, Hovie shared with young Howell his dream of having a quartet. "Well, Pop will put you on the station," Barry said, confidently. Not yet 22, a determined Hovie was armed both with the brashness of youth and a proven knack for salesmanship. Perhaps the radio sales pitch on behalf of the Lister Brothers Quartet in his childhood was still vivid in his memory. A month before radio station WCON was to go on the air, Hovie gathered all the grit he could muster and went with his friend Barry to see the Chairman of the Board, Major Howell.

"I explained to him that, since they had a brand-new radio station, I'd like to organize my own group and I asked him for radio time," Hovie fondly recalls. "I told him we would need a radio program so we could get known, and we could have people calling for concert dates. I was just happy that he even consented to hear my request."

Not only did Major Howell grant Hovie an audience and hear the request, his reaction was favorable. "Yes, we'll give you time. When do you want to be on the air?"

Hovie was shocked at how easy this had been. Struggling to mask his surprise, he replied that six o'clock in the morning would be just fine. "I told Mr. Howell I'd like to be on at 6 a.m. and 12 noon. So he called in the manager of the station and asked him to bring his program log with him and asked if he could work us in. He said he could. Now I began to get very nervous at about that time because I didn't have a quartet. All I had was an idea."

The elder Howell then asked, "How are you boys going to eat?"

"Oh, we'll get concerts. People will call in and book us. That's the way we intend to make our living," Hovie replied, in a matter of fact sort of way.

"Well, what about the station paying you guys $50 a week apiece?"

Hovie nearly fainted! "Now that just wasn't done then. That was God workin', brother!"

Hovie knew few of his friends in any of the other gospel groups were getting paid to appear on radio. Most were permitted to announce their concert dates, but earned their living on the road. Suddenly, a horrible thought came to mind: "I don't even have a group! What am I gonna tell him now? I've got all the radio time I asked for, plus he's gonna pay us $50 a man a week."

Fearing the worst, Hovie faced the issue head-on with the gruff old businessman: "I have to be up front with you, Mr. Howell. I right now don't have the men. I have them in mind, the ones I want. But it will take me a month or two to get everybody together."

The silence was deafening.

"He looked at me with one of those corporate office frowns," remembers Hovie, "and I quickly bounced back by saying, 'Oh, I can play records, gospel records, until I get the men together.' Of course, he had never heard of such a thing."

But Hovie's salesmanship and enthusiasm had won Howell over. In August, WCON went on the air and for the next two-and-a-half months Hovie worked as a gospel disc jockey in the time slots which had been assigned to the yet-to-be-organized quartet. He spent the rest of his time on the telephone bringing together personnel for his new quartet.

Hovie Lister, Gospel Disc Jockey

The Original Statesmen

Hovie dreamed of having some real heavyweights in the gospel field as members of his quartet, established stars like the Rangers' Denver Crumpler, and Harley Lester, who was a traveling teacher in the Stamps-Baxter Music Company. James Blackwood as an adolescent worked to pattern his singing style after the popular Lester. "He was a great singer," Blackwood recalls today. "In fact, he could've sung opera if he'd wanted to, but he chose to sing gospel music."

"I had several names in my mind," Hovie explains, "but me being so young, I thought, 'You're only 21 years old. These men are older than you and they're not going to listen to you. They'll think you're a kid and don't know what you're doing.' Now this was before I went to the owner of the newspaper and the radio station and knew that I could get something this good. But I had quite a big stick when I went to Mr. Howell and he granted my request—more than my request. Stamps-Baxter wasn't paying their men that kind of money."

Hovie didn't have to go far to find a lead singer. Songwriter Mosie Lister lived in Atlanta and was tuning pianos at the big Rich's Department Store, which was just across the street from radio station WCON's studios. Mosie had some previous quartet experience, having sung with groups in Tampa, Florida. The two Listers, who are not related, had met while Hovie was with the Rangers and Mosie was singing with a group called the Melody Masters.

"In 1946, I was with a group called the Sunny South Quartet," recalls Mosie. "James Wetherington was in that group along with Lee Kitchens and a man by the name of Horace Floyd. Then, after a while, Wetherington and Lee and I left and formed our own group called the Melody Masters. After about a year, that group left town. I stayed in Tampa and was replaced by Jake Hess. Incidentally, I was also replaced by Jake Hess when I left the Sunny South Quartet."

A native of Cochran, Georgia, Mosie once attended a summer singing school at the James D. Vaughan Music Company in Lawrenceburg, Tennessee, under the instruction of Adger M. Pace and G.T. "Dad" Speer. Speer recognized the raw talent in the youth, telling the students that one day they would hear a lot more from Mosie. "I predict that he'll make a name for himself in music," Speer had said.

"I was about 18 years old, I guess," says Mosie. "I studied harmony under Dad Speer and it was Dad Speer, really, who gave me confidence to start writing. He convinced me that I had a knack for melody and really pushed me strongly toward writing gospel music, and I've always loved him for it."

Having secured a lead singer, Hovie tracked down the highly-talented tenor singer he remembered from his short hitch with the Sand Mountain Quartet in Chattanooga. During the time it took Hovie to go through the series of playing for the LeFevres, Homeland Harmony and Rangers, then back to the LeFevres in Atlanta, Bobby Strickland had left the Sand Mountain Quartet to sing tenor with the Harmoneers. Based in Knoxville, the Harmoneers were featured on WROL radio and recorded for RCA Victor. By 1948, Bobby had moved back to Alabama.

"So I called Bobby Strickland and I told Bobby about Mosie," Hovie remembers.

"We've got a lead singer and we'll need a baritone, a bass and yourself," Hovie told the tenor.

"He came up with Bervin Kendrick, from Birmingham, as baritone; and Gordon Hill to sing bass," Hovie says. "So the very, very original group that went on the air was Mosie Lister, Hovie Lister, Bobby Strickland, Bervin Kendrick and Gordon Hill."

Like Strickland, Kendrick was a seasoned veteran in quartet work. Born February 28, 1910, Kendrick had worked with the Ideal Quartet in Birmingham and the Radioaires in Topeka, Kansas, among other groups. All of the Statesmen quickly relocated to the Atlanta area.

The Statesmen Quartet debuted on WCON in October, 1948, broadcasting at 6:45 o'clock a.m.,

Hovie Lister and the Statesmen Quartet, 1948. Bass singer Aycel Soward, lower left, posed for the group's first publicity photo, although he would not be available to join the group for a few months. Tenor Bobby Strickland is at lower right. Standing (l-r) are Bervin Kendrick, baritone; Hovie Lister, pianist; and Mosie Lister, lead.

11:00 a.m. and 1:00 p.m., immediately after the noon hour news. Following the Statesmen each morning on WCON was a young comedian who was just beginning to make a name for himself—Dick Van Dyke.

Hovie wanted a special name for his new quartet because he had great ambitions for the group. With so many professional gospel acts taking to the road this group wouldn't be just another gospel quartet. It had to be something "that would stand above and beyond and be an example in gospel music—something that other groups coming along would want to strive to emulate. I was striving always to make gospel music a little bit above just the average bunch of men that would get together and sing, because we rehearsed a lot, as you well know." To Hovie, the group's name should set this special quartet apart from the crowd. "I wanted something that would denote class, confidence. I thought about Senators. And the reason, I guess, I began to think in terms of politics is because I have always, from my high school days, been involved and interested in politics," Hovie explains.

But the more he thought about the name Senators, the less he liked the idea. After all, the Senate is an elective office. What does a senator become after he leaves office? An elder statesman. STATESMAN! Ahh, that's it! One who is wise or experienced in government is an elder statesman.

"Someone that sets an example becomes a 'statesman.' He no longer is in politics. He's now appointed because of his ability, because of his knowledge, because of his class, because of his background and setting examples throughout his earlier life, maybe in politics or whatever particular field he might be in. He becomes a statesman after awhile, for that sets him apart from the others," Hovie reasoned.

Hovie was an acquaintance of Governor Herman Talmadge and, in fact, had worked in Talmadge's late father's gubernatorial campaign. He remembered that Talmadge printed a newspaper called *The Statesman*. So, Hovie marched right up to the governor's office and asked Talmadge if there would be any objection on the governor's part if he called his gospel quartet the Statesmen. Governor Talmadge, who remembered the young musician, was delighted.

"He said he'd be honored to make us Colonels on his staff and commissioned us to be Ambassadors of Good Will for the State of Georgia," says Hovie. "So that's where the name came from."

Hovie Lister and the Statesmen went right to work learning material and developing their blend of four-part harmony. A few years would pass and some changes in personnel would occur before that blend developed into what is now remembered as the "classic Statesmen sound." Early on there was little that distinguished them from many other good quartets on the airwaves, but the sound of that original quartet was pleasing to the ears, nonetheless.

Among the songs that became early favorites with their radio audience were quick-paced numbers like "Christ Is Keeping My Soul" and "Heaven Is Singing In My Soul," and a slow number that featured the low range of young Gordon Hill, "I'm Glad My Savior Was Willing."

Being young, the men adapted with little problem to the routine of rising early to prepare for their daily 6:45 a.m. radio broadcasts. Coached by Mosie Lister, the group rehearsed frequently and exhaustively to build a repertoire. They constantly had to have new material to remain fresh for their growing radio audience. The ability to read shaped note music was essential for they often performed material straight from the songbooks during the radio show.

Says Hovie, "When we started the Statesmen if you couldn't read music you didn't have a job!"

"We all used to study," Brock Speer says of the gospel quartet fraternity during those pioneer years. "We thought you had to do it, you know. It was almost a reproach if you didn't know how to read music at least a little bit."

Mosie Lister

Within a few months changes began to occur. Mosie Lister, who, Hovie says, was "just beginning to come into his own" as a songwriter, "didn't want to go out on concert dates, didn't want to be away from home. He wanted to concentrate on songwriting and arranging."

As a youth Mosie had been urged to pursue a career in country music. He was often asked to write secular music, he says, "but I just never could quite get my heart into that, so I just didn't do it." His chief motivation has always been to compose gospel music.

Music didn't always come easy for the Georgia native. When Mosie was a child his parents thought he was tone deaf when he had difficulty distinguishing pitches. Violin lessons, begun when he was 12, greatly improved his sense of pitch. By his late teens, Mosie had become a country music fiddler and was winning fiddling contests all over Georgia. He also had taken up the guitar. Mosie's only downfall in his studies was in his writing. Communicating his thoughts on paper was a struggle. That is, until he became a Christian at the age of 17. "I realized that God had a plan for my life and that plan involved my being able to create gospel music," he says. "I write music because I've always felt, as a friend of mine used to say, a Divine imperative," Mosie says, reflecting on his career. "I felt called—genuinely called—to write songs when I was 17. And I still feel that same urging."

Statesmen founder Hovie Lister had met the aspiring songwriter in 1946 when he was playing piano for the Rangers. "My impression of Mosie Lister the first time I met him was that he was a very smart, astute, and yet very reserved musician," he says. "He throught through all the songs he wrote. He thought through the theology of the songs, the harmony—he was very careful about everything he did. I think that stemmed from a lot of things: from his personal relationship with the Lord; his extreme knowledge of music; and the fact that Mosie was a perfectionist."

Though his stint as a singer with the Statesmen was brief, he and the group continued to enjoy an excellent working relationship through the years. His valuable contributions to their success came through his arranging and songwriting expertise. Many of the great Statesmen hits through the years are products of the pen of Mosie Lister. In time his songs would be recorded by most major gospel groups, including the Blackwood Brothers, Oak Ridge Quartet, LeFevres, Rebels, and George Beverly Shea, among countless others; and by many top country and popular music artists, such as Loretta Lynn, Porter Wagoner, Jim Reeves and Elvis Presley. His songs have blessed untold millions.

"Listen, if God had not led me," he says, "my world's work would have meant nothing. Absolutely nothing! I've always asked Him for wisdom and I've asked Him to give me ways to say what I need to say. Somehow, He's always done that. I don't know how it works but I know why."

Mosie stayed with the Statesmen long enough for Hovie to find a replacement. He recalls that he had suggested that Hovie call Jake Hess, Mosie's replacement with the Melody Masters. "I don't want him," said Hovie. "He sings like a girl!" But later, in a routine telephone conversation with his father, Hovie casually mentioned that Mosie didn't want to sing and that the group needed a new lead singer. The elder Lister remembered a young man that had been with the Melody Masters when that quartet was based at WFPC in Greenville. The group had long since left Greenville for Birmingham, then had moved to Lincoln, Nebraska. Hovie's father suggested that his son call this young lead singer, whose name was Jake Hess.

"So I called Jake," Hovie remembers. "I don't know, but he probably called my father to see what I was up to because I didn't know Jake that well. I had just met him one or two times. Anyway, he came. The rest is history."

4

Jake Hess

The Great Depression was the longest and deepest economic setback that Americans have ever had to endure. Farm prices fell by 53 percent from 1929 to 1932. During the same four-year period, 11,000 banks failed in the United States, unemployment rose from 1.5 million to about 15 million—with millions more working less than full time. Marginal farmers saw their mortgages foreclosed. Tenant farmers often were replaced by machinery—"tractored off their land." Literally tens of thousands migrated hopelessly to other parts of the country.

Growing up in Haleyville, Alabama, Jake Hess learned early the value of hard work. To say the Great Depression was a struggle for his parents, William Stovall Hess and his wife Lydia, is a great understatement. Jake's father, a sharecropper, earned a few extra dollars as a songwriter for the Athens Publishing Company, and in the spring when the crops were planted he taught singing schools. But he and Lydia made sure their seven sons and five daughters had a happy home life. They were poor, but then, so was everyone else.

"We were sharecroppers and we'd work our crops, and when we had finished we'd work with everybody in the community. We had a pretty good work force there for awhile," Jake remembers. "We kids, we didn't know it was rough."

Jake was born the 12th child of this family on December 24, 1927, in Athens, Alabama. With his father being a teacher of the shaped-note singing schools, and the family being Southern Baptist, gospel singing was the order of the day around the farm as Jake grew up. "I don't remember when I learned to read the shaped notes," he says. Learning them at such an early age, reading music seemed second nature to him in later years. His older brothers already had a quartet, the Hess Brothers. Eventually, as the oldest brothers left home, little Jake took his place in the quartet. The Hess Brothers often sang at area churches and singing conventions.

"I can't remember a time in my life that I didn't want to sing in a quartet," he says. "That's all I ever wanted to do."

In those days the Speer Family lived only 20 miles away in Double Springs, Alabama. "Jake lived in the same county that we lived in. We've

Grand Ole Opry stars, The John Daniel Quartet. Standing (from left): John Daniel, 16-year-old Jake Hess, Troy Daniel, Ottis Williams and Lonnie Williams. Seated: Everett Buttram, pianist.

known Jake Hess ever since he was just a child," recalled Brock Speer years later. "We used to go to singing conventions together. He and his brothers used to sing. Back then as a child—I mean a little boy—he had a beautiful voice. Oh, he could sing! So he hasn't known anything but being a good singer all of his life."

"Well, I don't know. You can get by with a lot when you're a child," says Jake laughing. "G.T. Speer and my dad were friends years ago. Back in those days at the all-day singing conventions the churches would start at 9:30 or 10 in the morning, break for lunch and then go back and sing that afternoon. I'd sing with my brothers. There were seven boys there and we managed to keep a quartet most of the time."

As a teenager, Jake sang for a few months on WLEY radio in Sheffield, Alabama, with a country band—Lloyd George and the Rhythm Rascals. "I was 'Curly'," he laughs. His next group was the Haleyville Melody Boys. But soon he hit the big time singing with the John Daniel Quartet, one of the big names in gospel music in the 1940s. "At that time it was THE name," he stresses.

John Daniel had worked for both the Vaughan and Stamps-Baxter music companies. In 1940, his self-named gospel quartet had become regulars on WSM radio's Grand Ole Opry in Nashville. Signed to Columbia, the John Daniel Quartet was among the first gospel quartets to record for a major recording label. It was during World War II that the quartet enjoyed its greatest popularity, via a portion of the Grand Ole Opry that was broadcast on the NBC radio network. Thousands of Southerners had relocated to other parts of the country, either in the armed services or to work in defense plants. They took with them their love of the Gospel Music they had enjoyed so much in their native South. The John Daniel Quartet had a great following among these listeners. People from other parts of the country, many hearing this type of music for the first time, found they, too, enjoyed the gospel quartet sound.

The Sunny South Quartet

After a short while with John Daniel, Jake rejoined his brothers who were by then based in Lakeland, Florida. This opportunity lasted only a few months and Jake returned to the John Daniel Quartet. In 1945, he got a call from Tampa's Sunny South Quartet, whom he had met while singing with the Hess Brothers. When Jake came to them as lead singer the group was based at WFLA radio and sponsored by the Dixie Lily Company, a large milling company in Florida. Group personnel included Horace Floyd, manager and tenor singer; Joe Thomas, the baritone; J.D. Sumner, bass; and pianist Quentin Hicks. According to Sumner, on Jake's

The Sunny South Quartet. Pictured at left are (l-r): Horace Floyd, tenor; Lee Kitchens, lead; Mosie Lister, baritone; James Wetherington, bass; and Quentin Hicks, pianist. After Kitchens, Lister and Wetherington had departed, the new personnel included (right photo, l-r) Jake Hess, lead; Roger Clark, baritone; J.D. Sumner, bass; Quentin Hicks, pianist; and Horace Floyd, tenor.

The original Melody Masters in Tampa, 1947: Wally Varner, piano; Alvin Tootle, tenor; Lee Kitchens, lead; Mosie Lister, baritone; and James Wetherington, bass.

Below (l-r): Calvin Newton, Lee Kitchens, Alvin Tootle and James Wetherington. Wally Varner is seated.

When Mosie Lister left the group later in 1947, Alvin Tootle moved to baritone. Calvin Newton became the new tenor. He would be replaced by Cat Freeman later in the year. Soon after this photograph was taken, Jake Hess replaced Lee Kitchens as lead singer.

opening night with the Sunny South, the group drew 16 people at a church in Auburndale, Fla. Jake, perhaps feeling he had joined a group that was fast going nowhere, feigned to flee. "Which way is Haleyville from here?" he jokingly asked Sumner. Over the next few months they made little in the way of money but had a lot of fun. A rival group, the Melody Masters at WSUN in St. Petersburg, saw to that.

As Mosie Lister has stated, the three founding members of the Melody Masters—Mosie, Lee Kitchens and James Wetherington—had previously sung with the Sunny South Quartet. Pianist Wally Varner recalls the formation of the Melody Masters.

"They called me and got a fellow by the name of Alvin Tootle and we went to butting heads with the Sunny South. We were probably a little better than they were. It just so happened that way. However, they probably thought they were the best. But, anyway, we had a lot of fun."

Sumner recalls that the two groups "fought tooth and nail for popularity in that area. Back in those days we tried to out-sing one another and tried to out-do one another."

One Sunday, the Melody Masters found themselves without a place to sing. They knew that the Sunny South had a singing date, but they didn't know where. They suspected which direction their friends would be traveling and decided to wait for them along the highway outside Tampa. When the Sunny South came by, Wetherington pulled in behind them and kept pace. Sumner, who was driving the Sunny South, figured out the game and tried to outrun his fellow bass singer. But Wetherington stayed right with him at speeds of up to 90 miles per hour. When the Sunny South pulled in at their baritone's house in Wauchula, Fla., the Melody Masters pulled down the road to wait for them, unaware there was a back way out. Unseen, Sumner, Hess and their comrades escaped and made their way, minus the Melody Masters, to the singing convention at Arcadia in plenty of time for the dinner-on-the-ground.

Wally Varner remembers another wild ride during the Melody Masters days with Wetherington: "I was riding with him once from Lakeland down to Tampa, and there was a state patrolman in the middle of the road with his flashlight and flags signaling traffic to stop. Lo and behold, we just kept on going! Chief was just kind of lying back in that seat and holding the bottom of the steering wheel as if he didn't have a care in the world. Finally, he slammed on the brakes just about 50 yards before he got to that policeman, and slid right up to the feet of the policeman who jumped out of the way. Chief got out to say he was sorry. The policeman calmed down when he saw who got out of the car. 'Oh, so it's you. It's a good thing I know you, Wetherington, or I'd have put you under the jail!' "

Shenanigans continued to fly between the Melody Masters and Sunny South quartets. Jake and his friends pulled one on their rivals during a singing convention in Lake Okeechobee, Fla. The Sunny South group purposely arrived late forcing the Melody Masters to sing first. When the Melody Masters were just hitting their stride with the audience, the members of the Sunny South Quartet marched down the center aisle, periodically stopping to shake hands with members of the crowd. When the Sunny South's fans saw them come in, they erupted with applause. Needless to say, any momentum the Melody Masters had going was quickly erased.

"One time we were both at the Hillsboro County Singing Convention," Sumner recalls. "We sold the Stamps Quartet Music Company songbooks, they sold the Stamps-Baxter songbooks. Frank Stamps was down there and they were up on the stage singing, making a big hit. So Frank got up and accidentally hit the cord to the P.A. set, which unplugged the P.A. set, which made the P.A. go dead. It just ruined their stand. We used to do all kinds of foolish things like that."

The Melody Masters Seek New Horizons

In an interesting turn of events, Jake eventually left the Sunny South Quartet to sing lead with the Melody Masters. He and Sumner parted company but remained great friends thereafter. Other changes were in store for the Melody Masters. Over the next few months, Lee Kitchens departed, Alvin Tootle moved from tenor to baritone and Calvin Newton moved into the tenor spot. Months later, C.G. "Cat" Freeman replaced Calvin Newton as tenor. The quartet developed a great sound but they were barely making a living in Florida. After looking around for other opportunities, they eventually landed a job with WFBC radio in Greenville, South Carolina.

"We were invited to Jacksonville to be on the program with the famous Rangers Quartet," recalls Varner. "Now that was something big to us because we had never seen the Rangers Quartet!"

Hovie Lister was playing piano for the Rangers that night. According to Varner, Hovie was impressed by the Melody Masters.

"Look, men," Varner recalls Hovie telling them, "I'm from Greenville, South Carolina. If you want to move somewhere else, I believe you could make it well up there."

They went but, unfortunately, Greenville was no answer to prayer. "We didn't do well in the way of putting groceries on the table, but we did get exposed to a lot of other groups," says Varner. At one point the Melody Masters had to steal fruit to keep from starving.

"We didn't have anything to eat," Jake explains, "so we went out and borrowed some peaches over in Paris Mountain, out from Greenville there. They had some beautiful peaches so we ate peaches there for a couple of days until we could get something. Then we started singing at this restaurant there in Greenville called the Pantry. We'd sing for our dinner. We got one good meal a day that way."

All could have found jobs in another line of work and would have had more comfortable lives in those years, but the Melody Masters and many other fledgling young gospel quartets struggled on. They loved singing, believed in what they were doing, and were determined to succeed. "I just wanted to sing. I just figured I'd make a living somehow," Jake says.

Still looking to improve their lot, the Melody Masters moved temporarily to Birmingham.

"We thought we'd go over there and get rich," says Varner. "We got over there and didn't make it. It was really tough. By then, Cat Freeman was with us. The Freemans lived up on Sand Mountain, and in order to keep food a-goin', they would invite us up there. So we got to know them pretty well. Cat was kind of a mama's boy. They thought the sun rose and set in Cat."

Still determined to sing, the Melody Masters sent radio transcription recordings to several radio stations all over the South and Midwest hoping for a better opportunity. They heard the Blackwood Brothers had found some measure of success out in Iowa, so they sent transcriptions to stations in that part of the country. "We got three job offers off of that, and the best was at KFAB" in Lincoln, Nebraska, Jake recalls.

"When we saw that we were about to break up, all the food was gone and we had no money," says Varner, "we got a call from a 50,000 watt radio station out in Lincoln, and that saved us. We went out there and kept the ball rolling."

The Blackwood Brothers had started their singing career in Mississippi, and worked out of Shreveport, Louisiana, for a time before being sent by their sponsor, the Stamps Music Company, to Shenandoah, Iowa. During the war years the quartet was forced to disband temporarily. They regrouped in San Diego, California, worked in an aircraft plant and sang part-time. After the war, the Blackwoods returned to their KMA radio program in Shenandoah.

"Our broadcasting up there was very effective," James Blackwood remembers. "We were doing the best we had ever done financially, having the best crowds and making the most money, so we just stayed. We had been so successful up there and the news got around. Other stations wanted to cash in on it and other singers from down south wanted to get in on it. The Melody Masters were actually in the same market we were in. It was only 80 miles from where we were in Iowa. There was another group, called the Radioaires, a quartet from down south that came to Topeka, Kansas, which was just 145 miles from us and within our radio range and concert range, also. Another group, the Rushing Family Gospel Singers, came to St. Joseph, Missouri, and went on the radio there which was only 100 miles from us."

At KFAB, the Melody Masters joined 32 staff musicians that worked out of studios in the Sharp Building in Lincoln. Unlike the Blackwood Brothers and most other gospel quartets that worked on radio in those days, the Melody Masters were paid entertainers on the staff.

"We were not actually paid on the staff," Blackwood explains. "We reserved the right to announce our personal appearances and sell songbooks and records on our radio program."

Jake and the guys sang in three KFAB shows a day, and traveled to concerts at night. "We did a gospel show at 6 o'clock, a variety program at 9 o'clock, and another gospel show at 12," Jake says. "Then we had time to get to our date that night. We worked every night and had to get back at 6 o'clock in the morning and do that early morning radio show."

The quartet worked very hard, not only on polishing their sound, but also their stage presentation. Since many of the audiences of Nebraska had not seen or heard gospel quartets previously, the group had to sell itself through good song selection, a good quartet blend and showmanship. Jake explains: "A lot of places out in that area you would go in and sing and you would get no reaction from the audience whatsoever. But then, when that last song was over, why they'd nearly tear your clothes off! I mean they were the most excited people you had ever met. I guess the Melody Masters were one of the wildest organizations, for the lack of a better word, that I've ever worked with."

"I used to turn flips and things like that," laughs Wally Varner. He recalls a concert in Montgomery before the Melody Masters moved to Nebraska. "The Harmoneers ate that crowd up, and we couldn't turn a trick for nothing at all. After intermission, we went out and I turned a big flip on the stage and almost got a standing ovation. From then on we just tore 'em up. In those days gospel music wasn't as spiritual, it was more entertaining. We had a rambunctuous type of program, but we also had some beautiful singing that we would settle down to."

"They were very—what's a good word—daring in trying new sounds," Mosie Lister says of the Melody Masters. "I sort of walked into that spirit of daring and I wrote some arrangements that for that day were extremely advanced. They learned them and sang them. Some of them worked and some of them didn't."

"Mosie is a songwriter," says Varner. "I am too. The difference is I don't care to write and he loves it. That's his first love. He would take a pen or a pencil and jot down everything. He and I did work in conjunction with each other and we put together some beautiful five-part harmony and some modern harmony and it was years before its time. We thought just by shoving it out there, beautiful and real modern and real good that would get it, but there's a little more to it than that. These other guys, like the Sunshine Boys and the Rangers, they had never heard anything like it. Hovie was impressed by it and later the Statesmen got into some of that."

The Melody Masters worked mostly church dates. While a number of their appearances were at school auditoriums, those events likewise were sponsored by churches. Since the all-night sing phenomenon had not yet become the norm, the Melody Masters seldom appeared in concert with other known groups. "We didn't see anybody out in Nebraska," Jake laments. "In fact, we

The Melody Masters were paid entertainers on the KFAB radio staff in Lincoln, Nebraska in 1948. Gathered around a studio microphone are (l-r) pianist Wally Varner (seated), Lane Shaw, alternate vocalist; tenor Vernon Bright, who had replaced Cat Freeman; Jake Hess, lead; Alvin Tootle, baritone; and James Wetherington, bass.

never worked with the Blackwoods. Occasionally, we'd be working in town there somewhere and they'd come in and we'd get a chance to run out and see what they were doing."

Amid their busy schedule the quartet took time to make a recording for White Church—a small, exclusively-gospel recording label. "We didn't settle down long enough to do another," Jake says. "We did radio work and concert work at night and just had a good time." Like the Blackwoods, moving to the Great Plains had improved their lot. But when Hovie Lister made a single telephone call from Georgia in the fall of 1948, it would be the beginning of the end for the Melody Masters.

"I didn't know Hovie too well," Jake says. "We were good for a few laughs now and then when I'd see him around over the country, but I knew his dad, Herman Lister, real well. Hovie called and after he hung up, I called his dad to see what was goin' on. His dad says, 'Yeah, you'd better get down there, boy. They're gonna have a good quartet!' "

The Melody Masters secured Ben Swett, an uncle of James Wetherington, to take Jake's place. Further departures, however, were imminent. Within a few months Wally Varner got a call from Atlanta to play piano for the Homeland Harmony Quartet. Wally later was accompanist for the Deep South Quartet and eventually the Blackwood Brothers. Cat Freeman, who had already departed the Melody Masters to sing with the Blackwood Brothers, later would serve two tenures with the Statesmen. James Wetherington would soon join the Statesmen and become widely known under a moniker derived from his Indian ancestry.

Returning to Georgia was a bittersweet experience for Jake. He and the Melody Masters had become great friends during those hard months of struggle, then success. He had heard about Wally Fowler's successful all-night concert at the Ryman and felt that gospel music was about to happen in a big way back home. "I wanted to come back to the South and I wanted to be around the other quartets. The only ones we ever heard out there was the Blackwoods and RadioAires and I wanted to get back to see what was going on."

5

James Wetherington

When Jake Hess came to Atlanta late in 1948 to assume the position of lead singer for Hovie Lister and the Statesmen Quartet, he moved in with Bervin and Bessie Kendrick and their family, until he could afford an apartment of his own. Jake's singing style was still in the process of transition. Not quite 21 years of age, Jake was already a seasoned quartet veteran and loved the quartet life. However, his was not yet the distinctive lead voice which later became synonymous with the "sensational Statesmen sound."

"I was accustomed to hearing a much stronger, much more commanding lead voice," Hovie says. "I am, and always have been, of the opinion the melody in any quartet should be the outstanding voice in the group and the harmony should compliment the melody. When Jake got there he had been used to singing kind of a thin, soft-type singing."

Jovial tenor Bobby Strickland, who never met a stranger, took the newcomer under his wing. Pulling Jake aside one day, Strickland told him Hovie felt Jake's voice was too thin and it was only fair to tell the new lead singer his job was on the line. Hovie wanted a big sound and Jake had better find a way to deliver. Jake felt the pressure. Departing Nebraska he had felt he was leaving what he considered the best job in the whole quartet field. Now he was being told his singing was inadequate.

While with the Melody Masters, Jake had admired the style of Ernest Braswell, a singer with the Radioaires Quartet. The Radioaires had worked out of Birmingham when the Melody Masters were there, and were later based in Topeka, Kansas, after the Melody Masters had landed at KFAB in Nebraska. Bervin Kendrick had also been a member of the Radioaires.

"I guess he influenced me more than anybody," Jake says of Braswell. "He had a real freedom there that the other singers didn't have. If he wanted to, he'd change a line and interpret, throw his own style in there. I think I probably learned more from Ernest Braswell than anybody else."

"I wanted something boistrous and something commanding," Hovie recalls. "I wanted something sensational."

Being on the bubble filled Jake with resolve. He became serious about improving his vocal technique, widening his tone and becoming the best he could be at his art. He enrolled with one of the premiere voice teachers of the South, Dr. John Hoffman, director of the Atlanta Civic Opera, and from him took voice lessons faithfully for years until Hoffman retired. In addition to helping Jake develop more power in his delivery, Hoffman preached

Hovie Lister (seated) with the Statesmen late in 1948. From left: Bobby Strickland, tenor; Jake Hess, lead; Gordon Hill, bass; and Bervin Kendrick, baritone.

the importance of good diction. He based his teaching on the simple premise that "singing is talking on key with expression." This training echoed some of the instruction Jake had learned at the knee of his father years before.

"My dad was a great influence on me," Jake recalls. "He thought that if you had to choose between hitting the pitch just right or say the word just right to be sure they understood what you were singin' about. That influenced me quite a bit. It stayed with me all my life."

"Jake developed into, of course, as we all know, the greatest lead singer that's ever been," claims Hovie, "and Jake Hess did not copy his style from anyone. Jake developed that style."

Aycel Soward

On March 3, 1949, shortly after Jake had settled in with the Statesmen, Aycel Soward replaced Gordon Hill as bass singer. Soward, like Hovie, was a veteran of the Homeland Harmony Quartet and The LeFevres. Aycel had worked with Bobby Strickland previously when the two were members of the Harmoneers in Knoxville. Like Hill, Soward's stay with the Statesmen was brief. Hovie had dreamed from the beginning of having Soward as the bass singer for the Statesmen and still considers him one of the great basses of all time.

The Statesmen in early 1949 included (clockwise from left) Bobby Strickland, tenor; Jake Hess, lead; Bervin Kendrick, baritone; Aycel Soward, bass; and Hovie Lister, piano.

Orphaned at an early age, Soward had grown up a Catholic. When Aycel was 12, the superintendent at the Protestant orphanage where he was living took him to a Billy Sunday revival in Nashville, Tennessee. As a teenager, Aycel committed his life to Christ and became a Missionary Baptist. At 16, he received his first formal music training under the tutelage of Otis McCoy in Cleveland, Tennessee. Soward continued to hone his talents, studying voice at the Cincinnati Conservatory of Music. He was a quartet workhorse. Whenever a quartet needed a bass, Soward was there to fill the gap until a permanent replacement could be found. The six-foot Soward, somewhat older than most of the Statesmen, had a wonderful personality.

Soward studied with Lee Roy Abernathy when the two were working together in the Homeland Harmony Quartet. A few years before his death Abernathy praised Soward as the "best bass singer ever in the gospel quartet business without a doubt! If he didn't hit a note just right, he would work on it again, and again, and again. He would work for hours, days or weeks—I'm talking about working to place the tone just right—before he ever sang a song," Abernathy observed. "He was a well-educated man. He had the most beautiful handwriting you ever saw, and his diction was perfect if you ever heard him speak."

Soward was not a flashy singer. He had a big bass voice, and every quartet he ever sang with sounded big because of the superb vocal foundation he provided. He was a very humble man and occasionally when the leader of a quartet he was singing with gave him a chance to say a few words during a concert, Aycel capably gave a touching testimony of his faith.

"Friends," he once told a Memphis audience, "I often wonder in these 15 or 16 years that I have been in the singing business why large crowds as you do come out to our singings. You must have the love of God in your heart because we feel it ourselves when we sing. And it is wonderful to stand up and sing the praises to God in song to you wonderful people. It does us good. Right now I'm so overwhelmed with joy I can hardly talk. It really does me good to give the praise and glory to God in Heaven because He deserves all the credit."

While with the quartet, Soward floated a loan to purchase the first matching suits the Statesmen ever wore. Not only were they a great-sounding quartet, but snappily dressed also.

For several months after the Statesmen went on the air at WCON, Hovie continued to host a daily, 15-minute deejay show, sponsored by Adams Motor Company, of East Pointe, Georgia. This exposure helped him become widely known within listening range of the station. Almost everyone knew the young radio personality as "Little Hovie Lister." Promotional materials, distributed to advertise Statesmen appearances, often made reference to "The Statesmen Quartet with Little Hovie Lister of WCON, Atlanta, Georgia."

Such was the case on the group's first venture to Montgomery, Alabama, on December 4, 1948. In the years following World War II, Americans were obsessed with victory. People used the word victory for many things, such as in the process of naming their businesses or even the products their companies manufactured. G.T. "Dad" Speer sensed the trend and seized upon an opportunity. He rented the city auditorium and hired several professional gospel groups to appear on a program with the Speer Family.

"Daddy began to sponsor a Victory All-Night Singing, he called it," says Brock Speer. "It was a takeoff on victory in the war. The first big concert that the Statesmen played, and Hovie has confirmed this several times with me, was at our concert in Mongomery, Alabama—the Victory All-Night Singing."

Also appearing that night in a program billed to last until 4 a.m. were the Homeland Harmony Quartet with Big Jim Waites, the Happy Hitters of Birmingham, the Harmony Boys from Montgomery, the Dixie Rhythm Quartet of Dothan, Alabama; the Sunshine Boys, and, of course, the Speer Family. The price of admission was a dollar, plus 20 cents tax.

Capitol Records

Shortly before Aycel Soward left the quartet, Hovie signed the Statesmen to a contract to record for Capitol Records. Capitol was a relatively new company in the 1940s, but had a good base of operations in Atlanta. The recording sessions for the quartet's first records for the new company—78 rpm singles—were not held in a typical sound recording studio, but rather in the WCON radio studios in Atlanta. The group's first platter featured Soward on "Hide Me, Rock of Ages" on one side, and tenor Bobby Strickland singing "Heaven's Joy Awaits" on the flip side. Eventually, the company released record "albums" by its artists. Albums released by Capitol and other major recording companies in those days were actually collections of 12 songs released on six 78 rpm discs. These were packaged together in six sleeves bound with a hardback cover. The package resembled a thick photograph album, hence the name. Later, when collections of songs were released on one long-playing, 33-1/3 rpm record in a single sleeve and jacket, the term "album" was retained.

Songwriter Bill Gaither, then a teenager in Alexandria, Indiana, had read about the Statesmen in a Stamps Quartet newspaper. On learning of their recordings on Capitol Records, Bill ordered one from Joe's Record Shop in nearby Anderson.

"The first time I heard the Statesmen was on a Capitol record, and the song was 'Led Out of Bondage,' by a writer by the name of Bob Prather, and it featured the Big Chief (James Wetherington) chanting," Bill says, smiling at the memory. "They might even call that rap music today, because he wasn't singing in melody. He was just speaking words, very fast and rapidly in the speaking tone, belting it out like Phil Harris would. On the other side was 'Wait 'Til You See Me In My New Home,' which was the first time I had heard groups change keys in the middle of songs. That song was written by Joe Parks and was basically a convention song rearranged by the Statesmen."

"I was still working with them as a writer," recalls Mosie Lister. "In fact, they had me on a small retainer for a few years and I worked very closely with them. I was in the studio when they did their first Capitol recordings. A man by the name of Ken Nelson produced those cuts. He had a long, long career of producing."

James S. "Big Chief" Wetherington

After a period of time, Hovie realized that Soward, although a great, robust bass singer, was not compatible with the direction the Statesmen were going musically. Soward was not a showman nor a rhythm bass singer, and up-tempo songs were predominant in the Statesmen repertoire. To replace Soward, the Statesmen called in Jake's former Melody Masters cohort, James Stephen Wetherington.

He was born October 31, 1922 to Luther and Ida Vesta (Swett) Wetherington, on the farm where his mother grew up near Ty Ty, Georgia. When their parents divorced in 1925, James and his older brother Austin were taken in by their grandparents to be raised on the Swett's 198 acre farm. Ty Ty remains today much as it was then, a bucolic community of 300 residents intent on raising their crops and their families. Wetherington's grandparents, Soloman and Hester Swett, had not yet finished raising all of their own children, with three still at home. Everyone pitched in to help with the chores, as farm families do, but soon the Great Depression forced everyone to struggle to make ends meet. The Swett farm produced peanuts, cotton, corn, hay and tobacco during those years. The labors may have been long and difficult at times, but young James developed a healthy work ethic that would serve him well in his adult years.

Grandpa Swett supplemented his meager agricultural earnings as a traveling teacher of singing schools. Soloman Swett was also an ordained Methodist minister, and frequently served as guest choir director for touring evangelists—including the great Billy Sunday.

James found he had a song in his heart at a very early age. Austin Wetherington recalls his younger sibling singing in church at the tender age of seven. By the age of 10 he sang all the time. "James just loved to sing, he'd sing around the house, or when plowing the field, or just walking down the road," Austin would later say.

When their chores were finished, the Wetherington brothers found time for fishing, and for hunting and trapping game, usually opossum, raccoon or rabbit. Young James also found time for athletic achievement. A mishap while pole vaulting during his junior or senior year at Tift County High School resulted in the loss of his front teeth, and they were capped thereafter.

James Wetherington

James began honing his singing talents in his late teenage years with a weekend quartet in Ashburn, Georgia. "Daddy worked in the grocery store on Saturdays and spent the night there in order to sing with the quartet on Sunday," says his daughter Diana Helton. "He then was taken back home to go to school during the week and went back to Ashburn the following Saturday. Even after Dad moved to Florida, he took his vacation time to go back to Ashburn and sing any bookings that his former employer had set up for the week."

It was during a trip with the grocery truck to Miami, that James stopped in Lakeland, Florida to see his mother who had taken up residence there with her second husband and three younger children. He hadn't intended to stay in Lakeland but his mother's entreaties persuaded him otherwise. Not long after James settled in Lakeland, he and Austin began singing together on radio and in a few shows here and there, billing themselves as the Jolly Boys. Although Austin would like to forget the name, he recalls the days of the Jolly Boys well. "We would sing three 15 minute shows per week on local low-power radio stations in Lakeland and Tampa," he says. "We would fill in for a

James and Austin Wetherington
The Jolly Boys, 1940

singing country family, whose name escapes me, and would be paid $30-35 per week. That was some kind of money for a couple of poor farm boys!"

"They were good," recalls Wally Varner, who later worked with James in the Melody Masters. "It was low-sounding but it was super good. They were just doing singing conventions and things like that."

"I did not like the road," Austin relates, "and I used to get livid with James when he would schedule two shows back-to-back, 50 miles away with an hour to get there, driving an old model-T, then later a model-A. I never knew if we were going to make the show or not, and I always felt bad when we were late. When I married Evelyn, that was pretty much it for me, I wanted to settle down and start a family."

James, meanwhile, had a love interest of his own. A couple of days after his arrival in Lakeland, he attended services at an inter-denominational church in town. It was there an attractive young lady with fiery red hair caught his eye. He and Elizabeth Hughey dated for three years and continued to attend the inter-denominational church where she served as pianist and he became choir director. "He'd been singing ever since he was knee-high to a duck but I didn't know him then," says Elizabeth, whom he married in July of 1942. "He had sung most of his life with weekend groups before he went to the Sunny South, and then the Melody Masters, and then the Statesmen. He was my choir director for about three years before we married."

"Elizabeth is a sweet, quiet, almost timid lady," says Varner. "She was very neat, very orderly and pretty intelligent. The two were very different. He was flamboyant and flashy, and she was kind of reserved."

The Wetheringtons attended weekend singing conventions throughout Florida, meeting a number of people and making numerous contacts. James never lacked for an invitation to sing. At one of these conventions he met a man by the name of Taylor who was the head of personnel of the Atlantic Coast Line Railroad (ACL). Mr. Taylor also was a deacon at the First Methodist Church in Lakeland. He struck a deal with James to stay and be a soloist at the Methodist Church and he would give him a job with ACL. Wetherington had been working on a dairy farm near Lakeland since arriving in town.

World War II interrupted Wetherington's quest for a career in gospel music. The United States had been at war for nearly a year when James enlisted in the Navy in November 1942.

He first served on a tanker, the USS Beaconoil. After a shakedown cruise to Beaumont, Texas, the ship and crew prepared to sail for England. The USS Beaconoil set sail for England minus one sailor. James Wetherington stayed behind in a naval hospital in Brooklyn battling an altogether different foe, a severe case of tonsillitis. While recovering in the hospital, James received word that the Beaconoil was bombed at sea. When he was well enough to return to duty, James was assigned to a supply ship, the USS Belgium. Bosun's Mate Wetherington and his fellow crewmen sailed to England several times during the next two years, and sailed twice to Russia, although they were not permitted to land either time.

In 1944, Wetherington enjoyed his first leave since boot camp. When he returned to duty he was reassigned to Virginia Beach for amphibious training and trained as a gunner. Elizabeth went to Virginia Beach to stay, so the couple could be together on weekends. Their happiness was short-lived, however; as James was assigned to LST 673 and his unit shipped out for the Pacific Theatre of the war. "They left for the Pacific by way of major riverways and exited the states in Mobile, Alabama so they wouldn't need assignment to a convoy," says his daughter Diana. "When the convoy gathered they went on to the Phillipines where he was stationed until the end of the war. They took one island at a time until shortly

On leave from the Navy in 1944, James Wetherington relaxes with wife Elizabeth beside Lake Mirror in Lakeland, Florida.

after Hiroshima was bombed. He was in the first convoy to land in Japan."

Following the war, Wetherington returned to his job with the Atlantic Coast Line Railroad, "but it was clear that he wanted to pursue his music," Elizabeth says. "He wanted to sing and I gave him my blessing."

The Melody Masters (Again)

The contacts he had made in Florida prior to the war quickly paid off for Wetherington. In 1945, he was invited to join the Sunny South Quartet in Tampa. This group had organized before the war but was forced out of existence when Uncle Sam presented higher priorities. Mosie Lister, Lee Kitchens and Horace Floyd were anxious to reorganize the Sunny South Quartet, and in addition to Wetherington, secured the services of Quentin Hicks as pianist. On the strength of a radio show sponsored by Dixie Lily Flour on WFLA, Tampa, the members of the Sunny South Quartet saw fit to leave their jobs behind and become singers by profession.

Lister, Kitchens and Wetherington, as stated previously left the Sunny South to form the Melody Masters. With Wally Varner and Alvin Tootle aboard, the Melody Masters "turned out to be an almost magical combination," Lister would say years later. Although he eventually left the group, Lister continued to write new songs and innovative arrangements for his pals.

Hovie had met Wetherington when the latter was singing with the Melody Masters, and recalls that the lanky bass singer had later visited Hovie and the Rangers in Atlanta:

"When I was playing for the Rangers Quartet in Atlanta, James Wetherington came to our noontime radio program and introduced himself to all of us. Most of the guys in the Rangers were courteous enough to speak to him but they didn't give him much time as far as what he was there for. Me being single and interested in what was going on in the quartet world, I went out to have a sandwich with him. He told me he was with the Melody Masters Quartet out of Florida, and that they were looking for someplace new to locate their quartet. He had a radio transcription of one or two of their radio programs with him, and he wanted to know if I thought Atlanta would be a good place for them to locate. We went back to the radio station and I listened to their singing on this record transcription, and they about blew me away. I hadn't heard quite that good of harmony and the arrangements were way ahead of their time. They not only could sing gospel, they could do pop, they could do country. It was just amazing what they sounded like. I thought to myself, 'I don't want this group in Atlanta, especially if I'm fixing to organize a group of my own somewhere down the road. We've got enough gospel groups in Atlanta. I don't want this kind of competition here.' So I suggested that he let me call the manager of WFBC in Greenville, South Carolina. When I was growing up I played for some local groups there, including my father and his brothers. So I put him in touch with the manager of WFBC in Greenville and he talked with him on the phone. The Melody Masters finally moved to Greenville."

The Melody Masters, of KFAB, Lincoln and Omaha, Nebraska, in 1947. Seated are Alvin Tootle and Wally Varner. Standing are future Statesmen Cat Freeman, James Wetherington and Jake Hess.

While undergoing an occasional change of members, the group stayed awhile in Greenville, then moved to Birmingham, and ultimately Lincoln, Nebraska. There, Cat Freeman, Jake Hess, Alvin

Tootle, James Wetherington and Wally Varner took the midwest by storm, thanks to KFAB radio. Wetherington was the group's spokesman, his job on radio made easy in that his comments were scripted by KFAB staff writers and all programming back-timed to allow no "dead-air" or silence in the broadcast. Even their transcribed 15-minute shows were scripted and carefully timed, with James doing the song introductions and announcing "BE ATS."

Life was exciting in Nebraska. In the middle of their hectic schedule of radio shows and road engagements, the Melody Masters once joined with the 32 staff musicians at KFAB in a Omaha concert with singing cowboy and movie star Gene Autry. The boys from the deep south also experienced at least one harsh snow storm while traveling on the plains. Wetherington's daughter heard her parents speak of this storm often.

"The drifts stranded (the Melody Masters) so they got out and 'ran with the wind,' because it was the only direction you could go in," says Diana. "They could only tell they were on the road by running beneath the electrical wires and listening for the 'hum' the wires made. They finally located a large barn with a rope tied from the barn to the house and followed it to the door."

Taken in by the farmer, the Melody Masters found themselves stranded for a few days. They paid him well for what they ate and the lodging by means of cash and chores for several days. They did all of his milking, egg gathering and cooking for the time they were there. They also kept him well supplied with cigars for many years, according to Diana.

The Blackwood Brothers had two quartets on the road in Nebraska that evening. Attempting to return to their home base in Shenandoah, Iowa, they found themselves stranded in a snow drift near Hastings, Nebraska. They were preparing to dig their way out through a pasture when a farmer appeared with a double-barrel shotgun.

"What are you people fixin' to do?" he inquired gruffly.

"We're trying to get around this drift," James Blackwood replied. "There's no other way."

"Well, friend," growled the farmer, drawing a bead on the intruders, "if there ain't no other way to do it—then you just ain't a-gonna git it done!"

Some Nebraska folks could be most hospitable, others could be most cantankerous.

"After Jake left us in Nebraska," says Elizabeth Wetherington, "he just wasn't satisfied until he had talked Hovie into getting Jim to come to Atlanta to sing bass with the Statesmen."

On Wetherington's first day with Hovie and the gang in July, 1949, the Statesmen were performing in a baseball park in Atlanta. Aycel Soward, in his typically gracious manner, insisted on introducing his successor to the audience.

Although he was on the verge of suffering a nervous breakdown when he took leave of the Statesmen, Soward remained active in gospel music. Soward sang with a number of groups in his career—Lee Roy Abernathy's Miracle Men Quartet, Wally Fowler's Oak Ridge Quartet, All American Quartet with former Melody Masters Vernon Bright and Lane Shaw, Church of God Quartet with Cat Freeman, Friendly Five Quartet, The LeFevres, The Harmoneers, The Statesmen and in two different hitches with Homeland Harmony. Soward was singing with the Homeland Harmony Quartet until his battle with lung cancer forced his untimely retirement from singing. "You don't realize how hard this work is, folks," he told an audience in 1951. "Quartet work is really hard. I nearly had a nervous breakdown two years ago because I worked so hard singing." He was only 42 years old when he died on Easter Sunday, April 1, 1956, in Canton, Georgia. He left a wife, Dorothy, and two very small sons—Joe and Dwight.

Aycel Soward, 1955

The "Big Chief"

Shortly after Wetherington joined the Statesmen in 1949, the quartet worked a concert in Donalsonville, Georgia, with Lee Roy Abernathy and Shorty Bradford—the Happy Two. While getting the sound system set up and making other necessary preparations before the concert, Abernathy inquired about the new addition to the Statesmen Quartet and was told the new man's name was James S. Wetherington.

Abernathy noted the dark complexion of the newcomer and in casual conversation was told that one of Wetherington's ancestors had been Cherokee Indian.

"Man! How are you going to introduce him as James S. Wetherington?" Abernathy inquired of Hovie. "How many people do you think are going to get that? He needs a different name. You should call him something like 'The Big Chief!' "

"Chief, you know, was real dark complected. He was just something different," Jake says, laughing, "and I don't know whether we took it as just a joke or what. It started that week and it just stayed with him."

"As to the moniker 'Chief,' when Dad first had it hung on him by Lee Roy Abernathy it came as quite a surprise but there were never any negative feelings connected to it," observes his daughter

Hovie and the Statesmen with James Wetherington on board in late 1949. Wetherington would spend nearly 25 years as a member of the Statesmen.

Diana. "It amused Dad to think that Lee Roy would come up with such a thing for publicity, but the results have nearly always been positive."

Elizabeth had never thought much about her husband's Cherokee ancestry. "She had often thought he was part gypsy—as much as he traveled and they moved," says Diana.

"I'll guarantee you," says Hovie, "three-fourths of the people who've known him don't even know what his real name is, except for Big Chief."

Georgia Governor Herman E. Talmadge presents the Statesmen with a proclamation naming them "Georgia's Ambassadors of Good Will."

6
Doy Ott

Life On The Road

"We are the Statesmen, Ambassadors of Good Will. We're bringing a message of hope and cheer and our voices ring glad and free. Music is in the air, music is everywhere, that's the way 'twill always be. So come and sing along and help us swell the song 'til it covers the land and sea."

This musical introduction signaled to gospel music fans within reach of their broadcast the beginning of the daily radio programs of the Statesmen Quartet. By late summer of 1949, the popularity of the quartet—Bobby Strickland, Jake Hess, Bervin Kendrick, James "Big Chief" Wetherington and Hovie Lister—had grown substantially through their broadcasts on WCON. Additionally, *The Atlanta Constitution* ran the group's picture nearly every day, advertising their two daily radio shows. Not only were they spreading joy over the airwaves, but their faces were becoming well-known through the efforts of the newspaper. The result was a growing

The Statesmen in late summer of 1950.

demand for personal appearances. Hovie's estimate that the quartet "has probably sung in every courthouse in the state of Georgia, and a lot of the country school houses" is probably no exaggeration. But the group's ability to meet the demand for concerts was limited by two factors—transportation and the radio show that had created the demand in the first place.

"Back then you had to do that radio program," Jake says. "That's where you got all your personal appearances—churches and schools. We worked a lot of schools back in those days."

"We filled as many requests for appearances as we could," Hovie explains. "Of course, we were limited by the fact that we had those live radio broadcasts and our distance from Atlanta out. We couldn't leave until after our noontime show, and after we got through with our noontime live radio broadcast we could maybe go 50 or 60 miles out at night. We'd drive back and do our programs, except for the weekends. On Saturday nights and Sundays we could be out a little further."

So, for much of the first year of the group's existence, the Statesmen sang primarily around Georgia and Alabama with an occasional venture into other surrounding southern states. Eventually, the group began to tape some of the radio programs which gave them more freedom for traveling longer distances to engagements. "Basically, because we traveled in a Plymouth coupe with our sound system and songbooks and everything," Jake says. "It would have been pretty rough to go very far back then, for a year or so."

Hovie concurs: "The first vehicle we had was a Plymouth coupe with a mother-in-law back seat—three of us in front, two in the back. Cars were fairly hard to come by because 1948 wasn't too long after the war. Then we graduated to a four-door sedan, a brand-new Hudson."

SING ALONG WITH THE STATESMEN

HOVIE
LISTER,
Pianist

BOBBY
STRICKLAND
1st Tenor

BERVIN
KENDRICK
Baritone

JAKE
HESS
2nd Tenor

JIM
WETHERINGTON
Bass

6:45 A. M.-1 P. M. Daily

WCON

FIRST IN ATLANTA AT 55 ON YOUR DIAL

THE CONSTITUTION STATION

A 1949 advertisement in The Atlanta Constitution promoting Statesmen radio program on WCON.

Hovie and the Statesmen in concert at a Wally Fowler All-Night Sing at Nashville's celebrated Ryman Auditorium in 1949.

Among the radio transcription recordings that have survived from that era is a show that was broadcast on April 9, 1949, during which Hovie lists the quartet's schedule for the upcoming week: "Tonite, we go down to be with our friends in Piedmont, Alabama, yessirree! Piedmont, Alabama tonight, Saturday night, April 9. We're looking forward to a big time. Old Hap Strickland and the girls travel club and that bunch say they've really got it told around that the Statesmen are coming down. So we'll be looking forward to a big time with all of our friends and neighbors in Anniston—I mean Piedmont, Alabama, tonight. Excuse me for 25 miles again, boys. But right now I want to tell you that next Thursday night, April the 14th, we'll be up at Oakwood, Georgia, in the Oakwood school auditorium. That's Thursday night, April 14th. Then, Friday night, April 15th, Central Park Auditorium, Birmingham, Alabama. Saturday night, April 16th, Sylacauga, Alabama, and then on Sunday—on Easter Sunday—we'll also be in Sylacauga, there in the school auditorium for a big time with all of our friends there."

Occasionally, while traveling to a singing engagement, the Statesmen played a favorite game—taunting their enterprising pianist/manager into getting them instant radio appearances. "Bet you can't get us a radio show at this next town," they'd say. Rising to the challenge, Hovie would answer, "We'll find a radio station!" On finding a station, Hovie would go in and give his well-rehearsed sales pitch to the manager or announcer on duty. "I'd come back to the car and tell them to come on. We'd go in and do a 15-minute radio show on the way to a concert." It was a friendly game of dare, Hovie claims.

"Hovie, I hate to let you down like this but we bet in the back seat," Jake says with a wink and a laugh.

Beginning with his first anniversary concert on November 4, 1949, the Statesmen began to frequent Wally Fowler's All-Night Sings at Nashville's Ryman Auditorium, portions of which were broadcast to most of the nation on WSM. The Statesmen were paid $150—$30 per man— for their initial Ryman appearance. Fowler boosted their take to $200 a show in 1950.

While the demand for their services at these events was a testimony to their success, the long days and nights of traveling were a hardship, often exhausting. Here were five men sandwiched together into a coupe—bodies contorted in search of comfort or as restful a sleeping position as was possible in the small amount of space available, heads resting on each other's shoulders, elbows jabbing each other in the ribs, legs and knees cramping in the tight confines of the speeding car—struggling to rest despite the jostling of the vehicle. At times, a sudden swerve of the car or a hard application of the brakes by whichever group member was driving would jolt his comrades from their fitful sleep. On the rare occasion when the quartet members were able to enjoy a night of sleep at home, they would sometimes dream they were on the road and suddenly, terrifyingly, awaken with a start, convinced they were on the verge of catastrophe.

There were other sleeping peculiarities, as well. The Big Chief, James Wetherington, was frequently known to hum or sing whole songs in his sleep. This nocturnal trait was made even more entertaining by the subconscious habit of the sleeping singer to keep time patting his foot in bed. "You just get used to it," his wife would say.

Bobby Strickland

Several changes were in store for the group during the next couple of years. Like Hovie, Bobby Strickland had a dream. He had worked with several groups through the years and now, at age 30, wanted to form a group of his own. Bobby worked his last date with the Statesmen on September 1, 1950, then left to form The Crusaders Quartet. Returning to his native Alabama, Bobby handled the Crusaders' booking duties as well as arranging the music and stage choreography. In July, 1951 the Crusaders were ready to go to work and quickly created a demand for themselves, thanks in part to a daily radio broadcast on WVOK in Birmingham.

Tragically, Strickland's career would be cut short at the age of 33. On September 24, 1953, Bobby died in a violent automobile crash that occurred near Trussville, Alabama, while the Crusaders were returning home from a revival meeting in Chattanooga. He left behind a young widow and three small children. Only a short time before the accident, Strickland had felt impressed that God wanted him to preach the Gospel and had been making preparations to embark on this Divine calling.

Those who followed his career remember Strickland as one of the finest tenors of his era. Members of the Sand Mountain Quartet, the Harmoneers, the Statesmen and the Crusaders fondly remember him as one of the jollyest and friendliest men with whom they ever worked.

"When you went around him with a long face it couldn't last. A few minutes after being exposed to a man whose smile was as gay as an April morning sun, why the corners of your mouth just kind of turned up automatically and before long, you'd forgotten what you were all cloudy about. Bobby's smile was famous—I remember we used to kid him about gettin' Ipana for a sponsor," recalled Herschel Wooten, who sang bass with the Crusaders.

Bobby Strickland

"Bobby was with us a little over two years and he was an inspiration as well as a great teammate," wrote Fred C. Maples, of the Harmoneers, after Strickland's death. "He thrilled the hearts of thousands with his singing... Bobby was a good mixer and a great friend maker wherever he went."

"He was a big man with a big heart," said Buddy Parker, another of Strickland's Crusaders. "He loved God calmly and completely. When he died thousands of people lost a friend."

Claris Garland Freeman

On Strickland's exit from the Statesmen, Claris Garland "Cat" Freeman got the call to fill the role of tenor singer. Now three former Melody Masters were reunited. In fact, Jake Hess says the Melody Masters had once tried to get Hovie to join them before they went to Nebraska.

"It was amazing how we almost had the Statesmen at one point," Wally Varner says of the Melody Masters. "It was only natural that when Hovie Lister formed his new quartet in Atlanta that he would certainly call the guys that he had been so impressed by only a year or two earlier."

Freeman—born March 11, 1922 to Gordie McKinley Freeman and Maebelle Maddox Freeman—hailed from Fyffe, Alabama, where he grew up singing in the Highway Church of God. Singing was a family trait. His sister, Vestal, married Howard Goodman and gained a huge following with the Happy Goodman Family.

"Growing up, he was the oldest one in the family," Vestal says. "There were five girls and Cat was our brother. With Daddy it was a law at our house that you study music. Cat went to all of the singing schools way off. Daddy would send Cat, and then Cat had to come home and teach us. He was a great voice teacher."

In the late-1940s, there were two Blackwood Brothers quartets, based in Iowa. Here are the personnel of both quartets. Top row (l-r): Warren Holmes, Hilton Griswold, Doyle Blackwood, James Blackwood, R.W. Blackwood, Billy Gewen and Roy Blackwood. Bottom row: Bill Lyles, Calvin Newton, C.G. "Cat" Freeman and Johnny Dickson. Cat Freeman sang with the Blackwood organization for about a year before succeeding Bobby Strickland as tenor for the Statesmen.

Freeman had worked with a number of part-time quartets in and around Alabama. His first professional singing experience came with The Bama Boys Quartet, based in Chattanooga. Good-looking, jovial and dark haired, Cat was extremely popular with the gospel singing crowd because of his extremely high, distinctive, tenor voice, and because he was a clown onstage. Occasionally, in holding out long notes, or sliding between notes, his voice faintly resembled a feline wail, hence the sobriquet "Cat." A short while before Jake had left the Melody Masters to join the Statesmen, Cat had left to sing with the Blackwood Brothers Quartet in Iowa. He had spent about a year with the Blackwood Brothers when, like Jake, he jumped at the opportunity to sing with the Statesmen.

"Cat Freeman was a fun guy, one of the craziest guys you'd ever want to work with and he kept you laughing all the time," says Jake.

The Blackwood Brothers Quartet #1 in the studios of radio station KMA, Shenandoah, Iowa in 1948. From left are pianist Hilton Griswold, Cat Freeman, tenor; James Blackwood, lead; R.W. Blackwood, baritone; and Bill Lyles, bass. Cat Freeman was the only individual to sing full-time with both the Blackwood Brothers and later the Statesmen quartets.

"He was a cute, funny, funny guy—one of the funniest guys in the world," recalls Varner. "He was highly talented. He was a great guy."

"Cat was a very strong tenor," Hovie recalls. "He was one of the easiest guys to get along with there ever was. Lots of fun, loads of fun. A little negligent, irresponsible to a certain extent, but nothing serious. He was one of the funniest guys, but Cat had figured a way to be so entertaining on the stage that, if it was a hard note to hit or it was a difficult song, he clowned his way through it. That was not what I wanted. I wanted singing. I didn't mind the clowning at the right time."

"He was not only the family clown," says his sister, Vestal, "but he was THE clown, a very big clown. But he was one of the most precious people and loved people so much."

Doy Willis Ott

The next personnel change in the group involved its founder. Hovie was called for service in the U.S. Army late in 1950. The United States was at war in Korea and Hovie answered the draft, leaving Big Chief to manage the group and serve as master of ceremonies in his absence. Boyce Hawkins, an alumnus of the John Daniel Quartet and who had been with the Oak Ridge Quartet briefly in 1949, came to play piano for the Statesmen. After a few months, he returned to Nashville where he eventually became a successful announcer and weatherman on radio and television. He also found time to work as a session musician for recording companies in Nashville. Interestingly, he appeared as organist on numerous Statesmen recordings for RCA Victor through the years, including the last sessions the quartet recorded for RCA in 1967.

On Hawkins' exit, the Statesmen secured as their pianist Doy Ott, who was already in Atlanta playing for the Homeland Harmony Quartet and attending college at the University of Georgia. He had, in fact, followed Hovie in two previous keyboard assignments, as pianist for the Rangers Quartet and Homeland Harmony.

When Hovie left the Rangers in Charlotte to return to Atlanta, "Doy Ott joined us then, along with his wife, Joyce," wrote Mrs. Vernon Hyles. "They remained with us until we had finished a year's work with a radio station in Topeka, Kansas. Doy is, we think, one of the finest musicians in the business today and his playing was an inspiration to all."

Born on April 28, 1919 in Haywood, Oklahoma, Doy Willis Ott could trace his lineage to three Indian tribes: Choctaw, Chickasaw and Cherokee. As a youth he had been exposed to the Stamps Quartet broadcasts on KRLD and developed a great love for gospel music. Doy began his study of the piano at the tender age of nine. For several years his summers were filled with music studies—piano, music theory, accordian and voice. By the late 1930s, he was pianist for such groups as the Stamps-Baxter Melody Boys (featured on the Mutual Radio Network) and the Hartford Quartet, sponsored by the Hartford Music Company.

Doy studied a year at Southeastern State College in Durant, Oklahoma, before entering the Army. During World War II he received training

The Stamps-Baxter Melody Boys (l-r): pianist Doy Ott, tenor Pat Garner, baritone Clarence Heidelberg, lead Art Bowman, and bass Ernest Lindsey.

in the then-new technology called radar, radio engineering and radio-controlled aircraft. He spent 18 months overseas and participated in the invasion of Normandy in 1944. In his four years of active duty, Ott earned five battle stars.

Following the war, he played accordian briefly with Otis Echols and the Melody Ranch Boys, later moving to Little Rock, Arkansas to rejoin the Melody Boys Quartet. While with the Melody Boys, Doy returned to college, to finish his pre-med work. Unable to get into medical school, Doy put aside his dreams of becoming a doctor. Instead he studied accounting, and left the Melody Boys to become accompanist for the famous Rangers Quartet.

At age 32, Doy was already married with a young daughter, and as Jake recalls, a

The Melody Ranch Boys, featuring (l-r) multi-talented Doy Ott on the accordion, Jimmy Wardlow, Otis Echols and Jimmy Jones.

"tremendous musician" when he came to the Statesmen as pianist in 1951. He eventually earned a degree in business administration which would prove beneficial in the operation of several Statesmen business ventures in the future.

A flurry of personnel changes occurred next. In the summer of 1951, Bervin Kendrick wanted to return home to Alabama and join his old friend Bobby Strickland in Strickland's Crusaders Quartet, and Cat Freeman dropped out briefly. Temporary replacements included tenor Earl Terry and baritone Troy Posey. When Hovie returned to the group upon completion of his military hitch, Doy Ott stayed on, moving from the keyboard to baritone. As 1952 commenced, the group's personnel consisted of Cat Freeman, Jake Hess, Doy Ott, Big Chief and Hovie Lister.

Doy Ott brought with him excellent skills as a music arranger. This was to become a tremendous asset, as Mosie Lister, on retainer to the Statesmen as arranger and songwriter, was soon to leave Atlanta and move to Florida.

"Mosie did a lot of the arrangements in the early days of the Statesmen, inasmuch as he was there," Hovie says. "I would say that each man in the quartet contributed to those arrangements. Say, for instance, that one guy could hear a certain note in a certain chord. Mosie could figure that chord out and could write it down very quickly and very easily, and we had written-out arrangements."

Mosie met with the quartet every day at the WCON studios following their morning program for rehearsals and to help with arrangements. The quartet rehearsed very hard. It was not enough to merely sing a song well. There are several elements to a perfectly executed arrangement, and the Statesmen worked at perfection in every musical aspect of each song. They began with four-part harmony—the coincidental combination of notes in the triad. When each individual was comfortable with his part, the quartet worked at melding the voices into a perfect blend. They practiced diction, ensuring the song lyrics were enunciated properly and with correct tonal quality in order to be understood. They worked hard at phrasing, ensuring that all four singers were synchronized as they sang each phrase of every song. Attacks and releases were rehearsed, so that all singers attacked the beginning of each phrase together and ended the closing note of each phrase at the same time. As they polished each arrangement, it was important for the Statesmen to pay heed to dynamics—the degrees of loudness and softness in music.

Temporary Statesmen lineup while Hovie was away in the Army (l-r): Jake Hess, baritone Troy Posey, James Wetherington, pianist Doy Ott and tenor Earl Terry.

"A lot of the songs I wrote for them I arranged in such a way that they were kind of tailored to their voices, and that made it not very easy for other groups to pick up and sing," says Mosie, because the song exactly fit the collective voices of the Statesmen.

"There were some similarities," says Mosie, between the sound of the Statesmen and the Melody Masters. Of course, Jake, Chief and Cat had sung with the Melody Masters, and Mosie had done much of the arranging for that group as well as the Statesmen. "When the Statesmen started, I used some of those same ideas and started developing some sounds for the Statesmen. The Statesmen," Mosie observes, "developed into a much stronger group vocally."

"Any time they would do a new song or learn a new

song they were excited over it," says Elizabeth Wetherington. "If it didn't sound special they just didn't do it. There are songs and then there are songs. There were songs that might fit some other group that would not fit ours. They would not fit the voice range. When you don't feel a song, there's no sense in doing it. When they found a song that they particularly liked and worked it up, they were always excited over it."

"Doy was a great arranger," states Hovie. "He knew how to figure out chords, how to structure chords and how to say, 'This is your part, that's your part and that's your part,' and so forth. Doy was a great help in later years with arrangements after Mosie became more involved with his songwriting career and his choral arranging."

Occasionally, Hovie would have a vocal solo during the group's radio programs and concerts. Doy would take over the piano in mid-song so Hovie could take the microphone. Well-rehearsed, the keyboard transition was a smooth operation.

"We had an ideal situation," Hovie stresses, "in that Doy was such a great musician and a great piano player. If we were rehearsing and an important phone call came or I needed to book a date or check on something, I'd just leave them with him and they'd go right on."

Often, when the group would arrive at a church, concert hall, or courtroom in some little Georgia county seat, they'd set up their record table and sound system, then find a piano and start singing to kill time. Sometimes after a concert Hovie would have to settle with the promoter or collect payment. The rest of the group would pack up the car, then go back inside to gather around the piano and sing until Hovie was ready to leave. They had desire.

"We just loved to sing," recalls Jake. "That was the singingest group you've ever been around. And, whether we were working together that night or not, we were just together singing all the time; and singing as much as we did we just developed our own style. To my knowledge we didn't pattern after anyone."

Bervin Kendrick's singing career with Bobby Strickland's Crusaders Quartet was short-lived. In the same automobile accident that claimed Strickland's life, Bervin suffered a broken back. "Subsequently, he was unable to do a lot of traveling with a quartet," says his son, Jerry Kendrick. When he had recovered sufficiently from the injuries, Kendrick took a job with Southern Electric Steel in Birmingham until he retired in 1977.

"He followed the quartet business quite a bit," says Jerry Kendrick. "He went quite often to the concerts when the quartets were in Birmingham. When he was in quartet work he had never been able to participate in his local church, which was the Midfield First Baptist Church in Midfield, Alabama. He was ordained a deacon, and he was very proud of that. He sang solos at church and was a member of the choir. I was the Minister of

Bervin Kendrick

Music and I was very proud that my Dad was a member of my choir. The last solo I remember him singing at church was 'The Longer I Serve Him the Sweeter He Grows.'"

Following Bervin's retirement from the steel mill, he and wife Bessie moved to Bainbridge, Georgia. It was there that Bervin Kendrick died on February 13, 1991, two weeks shy of his 81st birthday.

7

Happy Rhythm

A Vast Collection of Songs

The rigors of two daily radio shows demanded a vast repertoire of songs. The quartet sang a number of old, soul-stirring hymns, songs the members had learned as youths in Sunday School. They sang selections from the singing convention books, songs like Albert Brumley's "Jesus Hold My Hand," J.M. Henson's "Happy Am I," Luther Presley's "In The Sweet Forever," E.M. Bartlett's "Everybody Will Be Happy Over There," Bob Prather's "Roll On Jordan," and many others.

"When you're singing as many songs as quartet people used to do back in those days, you'd just luck up on songs," says Jake. "You had those radio programs so you had to keep fresh material. Singing and rehearsing for those programs you'd luck up on several good little songs. Of course, we were like a lot of other groups, when a song got popular we wanted to sing it. Well, you **had** to sing it. People requested that you sing whatever was popular!"

"When I got ready to go into the service," Hovie remembers, "we gathered around a microphone and recorded 13 weeks of radio transcriptions just the day before I went into the Army. I emceed from the piano and they sat around a table. They had songbooks piled all over that table."

Bill Gaither has been a student of the gospel music industry for years, both as a fan and later as one of its brightest stars (he still is a fan, too). While reflecting on the gospel quartets he loved and learned from as an adolescent, Bill noted that in the late 1940s and early 1950s the groups began to look beyond the hymnals and singing convention books for some of their material—songs that became great favorites among the following the quartets had accrued.

Early in 1953, the Statesmen's Packard automobile was involved in a traffic accident. Doy was the only member of the quartet injured, requiring surgery to repair his injured nose. During his recovery period, Mosie Lister filled in on the baritone, since he was writing the group's arrangements and knew all the parts well. Pictured are (l-r) Cat Freeman, Jake Hess, Mosie Lister, Big Chief Wetherington (being featured on a solo) and Hovie Lister.

"What happened, back with the Statesmen and those early groups is they started singing what they would call 'spirituals,' which meant that they were going and beginning to get some of their material from the black gospel groups. One of their early hits was 'You Sho' Do Need Him Now'. In fact, that is public domain. Nobody knows where that came from. It came out of the black tradition. 'Peace in the Valley' is a Thomas Dorsey song that came from the black tradition. So many of their early hits began to stray away some from the southern, singing convention style—the music that was coming out of Stamps-Baxter—and basically were coming out of the black tradition."

White men singing black music: The same phenomenon would occur in the mid-1950s with white secular artists—such as Elvis Presley, Pat Boone, Ricky Nelson and others—recording black rhythm and blues and taking it to the broader white audience. This practice excited gospel music fans in the late 1940s and early 1950s, and young popular music fans of the early rock and roll era, much as it had excited minstrel show audiences a century earlier. This time, however, no black makeup was involved. It was straightforward delivery by whites of spirituals or R&B material in the black style.

"We'd hear different records back in those days," Jake says. They'd always have a few programs over the country that played black spirituals and we heard some of those. But I guess our favorite group back then, black group, was Golden Gate. We liked the Golden Gate Quartet quite a bit. We didn't do too many of their songs. But I guess we used more of their type stuff than any other group."

"They were classy," Hovie says of the Golden Gate Quartet. "They were real good. They were showmen."

Songwriters

Another source of material for the Statesmen came from specific writers who began starting their own publishing companies at that time, Gaither observes. Writers like Mosie Lister, Ira Stanphill, V.B. "Vep" Ellis and former cowboy singer Stuart Hamblen. Mosie, unlike many other popular writers of that time, published his own songs rather than placing them with established gospel publishing houses.

"But he was a good enough writer to do that," Gaither says. "His songs found their way to the top whether or not they were in a book collection or not. He was one of my early models as a writer. Mosie did it and so some other writers started coming along. Bill Gaither did it because he saw Mosie do it. Ira Stanphill published his own songs. Stuart Hamblen published his own songs."

"I had never known a gospel songwriter who did nothing but that," says Mosie. "All of the songwriters that I knew did something else. They were editors and they were singers and they were quartet people, and so forth. But I had plans to just write and just to give my life to the Lord and do that. It took, I guess, an awful lot of faith to do it. I really did not know a publisher that I felt I could trust to take my music and publish it just as it was, so I started my own publishing company."

The Statesmen were singing Mosie's songs from the very beginning. By 1952, they were getting good response out of "Land Where Living Waters Flow," "Reap What You Sow," "Way Out Yonder," "Trouble," "Sunday Meeting Time," "Bound for the Kingdom," and "On Revival Day."

"Happy Rhythm" was another of Mosie's songs that proved to be a big hit for the Statesmen. Although the tempo of their original arrangement of the song was moderate, they eventually re-arranged the song with a quicker tempo to suit Big Chief's love of rhythm. No up-tempo song ever fit Wetherington as did "Happy Rhythm." The quartet was to record the song many times through the years.

"When I wrote 'Happy Rhythm,'" says Mosie, "it was one of those spontaneous ideas and I took it to them and they learned it. That is a song that featured Chief all the way through the chorus and it was really tailored for his voice. It was created for his style. You see, I had been working with him for so long that writing for him became almost second nature. He had a way that he could anticipate certain notes and sort of lean into them. He had such a marvelous voice and a marvelous way of presenting his voice. The song did speed up in later years. In the earlier version what rhythm was there was probably what was in Chief's voice, and it was a little slow. But that's the way I felt it and that's the way they learned it."

It is interesting to note that the term "rock and roll" had not yet become a part of popular music culture, yet here was gospel composer Mosie Lister incorporating the phrase "there's a happy rhythm keeps a-rockin' and a-rollin' " into a rollicking, boogie setting.

No longer a vocalist with the Statesmen, Mosie enjoyed riding along with them to engagements occasionally. He happened to be traveling with them on the night they presented "Happy Rhythm" in concert the first time. It was at a high school auditorium in Griffin, Georgia. "Hovie introduced it with his usual boistrous fanfare. Then they sang that song and people yelled and screamed and whistled and stood up in their chairs—a standing ovation! I had never seen anything like that," Mosie recalls. "I didn't know what was going on. They had to sing that song over and over. It became a very good stage song for them."

Ira Stanphill committed his life to Christ at the age of 12. As a child he traveled with his family in a covered wagon from Arkansas to New Mexico, and later to Oklahoma and Kansas. At 17 he

was writing songs and began traveling with evangelists, playing the piano, organ, ukelele and accordian. Stanphill answered the call to preach when he was 22 years old, ministering first as an evangelist and later serving pastorates in Florida, Pennsylvania and Texas. Possibly his most popular composition is "Room At The Cross," written when he was 32, in 1946. The song has been a favorite of Statesmen fans for years.

Vesphew Benton "Vep" Ellis, like Stanphill, was a preacher of the Gospel. In addition to his ministry as pastor and evangelist, Ellis was also a soloist and wrote powerful songs, more than 500 in all. Early in their career the Statesmen were stirring heart strings with "Heaven's Joy Awaits," and "The Love of God," among other Vep Ellis compositions.

When he began to flood the gospel music public with his songs in the early 1950s, Stuart Hamblen had only recently become a Christian, although he had been raised in a Godly home. His father was a Methodist preacher in Texas. Stuart had written and

Vep Ellis, top right
Stuart Hamblen, above
Ira Stanphill, right

recorded a country hit, "Out On The Texas Plains," some years earlier. In 1949, when the Rev. Billy Graham began an evangelistic crusade in Los Angeles, Hamblen was the host of a daily radio program in the city and was the leader of a dance band on Saturdays. His life as a successful race horse owner, gambler, heavy drinker and hypocryte was about to change. Urged by his Christian wife to meet Graham, Hamblen was charmed by this fellow southerner and invited the preacher to be a guest on his radio program. The publicity generated by the interview helped boost attendance at the tent revival held in the "Canvas Cathedral," on the corner of Washington Boulevard and Hill Street.

Hamblen attended the meetings, and soon fell under conviction. The cowboy began to feel that Graham's preaching was aimed directly at him, as the preacher charged that someone in the audience was a "phoney" and leading a "double life." Finally, after the meeting had gone three weeks, Hamblen rose during one fiery sermon, shook his fist at Graham and stormed out of the tent. He tried to calm his fury by stopping at several bars on the way home. But God had a hook in his jaw and wouldn't let go. When he arrived home he aroused his sleeping wife, and not in a gentle manner. "Let's pray," he told her. But he wasn't able to "make connections." At 2 a.m., he called Billy Graham at his hotel, and at the evangelist's invitation, joined Graham and other members of the evangelistic team in Graham's suite. They prayed all night until Hamblen, with God's touch, became a new man. On his radio program that day he testified to his conversion. Eventually, he was fired from his $1,000-a-week program because he refused to advertise beer. His friend, actor John Wayne, one day inquired if it was true that Hamblen had given up drinking. "Tell me truthfully, Stuart, haven't you wanted one?"

"No, John. It is no secret what God can do."

The Duke suggested, "You ought to write a song with that line 'It is no secret what God can do.'" Hamblen did just that and found his new calling in life. The Statesmen were to record a number of Hamblen classics through the years, songs like "First Day In Heaven," "This Ole House," "Until Then," "Known Only To Him," "Teach Me, Lord, To Wait," and many others.

A Room Full of Excitement

The group's delivery of their material in personal appearances earned them the nickname "Sensational Statesmen" over the years. A journalist in one southern city once wrote that when the Statesmen walk onto a stage, "they come on like Gangbusters. Hovie Lister and the Statesmen have proven themselves capable of taking a town as forcefully as Sherman took Atlanta."

"Their delivery was exciting and dynamic. Their electrifying performance captivated me along with the audience," was how a writer for *Billboard* magazine described his first Statesmen concert experience.

"We went out to have fun," Hovie admits. "We went out there fully aware that we had a goal to reach and that was to entertain those people. And we were going to do it whatever it took. If it meant Jake getting up on the piano bench, we did it. You worked at it."

"When I was on top of the piano bench, Hovie was on top of the piano," Jake laughs.

"If it takes shaking my hair down, beating a piano like Liberace or Piano Red to keep these young people out of beer joints and the rear seats of automobiles, I'll do it," Hovie told a *Saturday Evening Post* writer in the mid-1950s. "The devil's got his kind of entertainment. We've got ours."

"The first time I saw the Statesmen was in the Ryman Auditorium, the old Opry House in Nashville," Bill Gaither recalls. "The personnel then was Jake, Hovie, Doy and the Chief, and Cat Freeman was singing tenor. That was the most exciting thing I had ever seen, because they were just such good performers. The crowd just went crazy when they came on! I mean they liked the other groups but, boy! When the Statesmen came on—you've been in those kind of settings when the thing was just about out of control the excitement was so high."

What was so different about their presentation at that time from other groups?

"I think the word is called showmanship," Gaither says. "I just think the showmanship was at such a high level compared with the other groups. The other groups kind of just stood around the mike and sang. But I think both when the Statesmen and Blackwoods came around there was a lot more of what we call showmanship. I suppose now it wouldn't mean that much but gospel music has always

Jake Hess, Cat Freeman, James Wetherington, Doy Ott and Hovie Lister: the Statesmen lineup from 1951-53.

followed what happened out in the pop field, you know. And the church has always had a hard time accepting that because it looked a little bit 'worldly' up front."

The Statesmen, the Blackwood Brothers and a few other quartets were not content to just stand and sing. They really believed in what they were singing. The message of the Gospel was worth getting excited about. Popular music phenomenon Elvis Presley once told an interviewer that as a child in the local Assembly of God Church he noticed that, although the singers sang well, nobody responded to them. The preachers, however, would cut up and move around all over the platform. The audiences loved them. Veterans of several years in quartet work, the members of the Statesmen had learned—like the Assembly of God preachers that electrified a young Elvis—what it took to get the audience to respond.

"First of all the voices were, I think, superior to the other voices that were out there at the time," Gaither believes. "And their ability to sing together as a unit was a lot better, I think. Jake tells me, and I believe it's true, they must have done a lot of rehearsing to get the sound that good. The sound was good. It sounded exciting!"

"We were very cognizant of the fact that you had to have good material, number one; number two, you had to have good arrangements; number three, you had to be good singers and sing on pitch, and to also have good stage presence," Hovie says. "I'm not alluding to being in show business, but you had to give the people more than just standing up there and singing. You had to be very professional and to entertain the people in a Christian way, have fun, and yet have very much a good Christian atmosphere along with your singing. I make no apology, none whatsoever do I make any apology for the entertainment side of the Statesmen Quartet. I think God's people like entertainment. If it's clean, and it's fun, and it's enjoyable, and at the same time it's getting the message across, then I'm for it!"

"I guess the word excitement is overused so much in our whole field," reflects Gaither. "But music was pretty routine and pretty regular, and when the Statesmen came along there was a buzz. There was some excitement. There was **something** going on! And, obviously, young people are very impressionable and at my young age that something was a wonderful alternative. It kept my attention focused on the church, so that couldn't be all bad. And it was through that music that later led me to Christ. So in my case it wasn't bad at all."

In addition to the showmanship, the Statesmen were among the few groups of the era who visibly ministered in their programs. According to Jake, the group did not build into its programs any pre-planned testimonies or preaching. "We didn't sing one song and then say, 'Hey, you give your testimony here,' another one, 'You give your testimony there and if that don't get them, then we'll do so and so.' We didn't do that. I'm a Christian. I love the Lord. I want to do what God would have me do. Our prayer before we got up on stage was for God to use us that night or that day, whatever the situation called for. But as far as having a built-in place where you preach here, you do this there, we didn't do that."

Hovie, who always served as the master of ceremonies during the quartet's concert appearances, had a talent for setting up the next song, whether it was holding the audience spellbound with the story of how the song came to be written, telling a joke in his inimitable way, giving the song a Biblical basis, building up the individual singers in the Statesmen Quartet, or outright preaching.

"Hovie sold himself by selling us," says Jake. "By telling an audience how good I was, or Chief was, or Denver or Doy, he made us feel better about ourselves and we sang better. He was a great motivator."

"I think they were one of the first gospel groups to come along and tie spiritual, theological things in their chatter to what they were doing," says Gaither. "Up until then the groups would say, 'Now for our next song we're going to slow down the tempo, or speed up the tempo.' Hovie came along and gave us some Bible tie-in to what they were singing. And James Blackwood did also with the Blackwood Brothers."

"I was just blessed. That was a God-given talent," Hovie reasons. "I didn't do research, or any sort of thing. It was just from knowledge, going to church, reading the Bible, from hearing so many various preachers, seeing how they did things and just being alert. It's a gift that God gives you in the way of knowing and reading an audience and being able to have the right timing."

Parson Hovie

Hovie's emceeing was enhanced by the fact that in 1951 he had answered an Almighty call to preach. He was ordained as a Southern Baptist preacher at the Oak Wood Baptist Church in Anderson, South Carolina, where he held his membership at the time. Shortly thereafter, in September 1951, he accepted the pastorate of a little country church, Mount Zion Baptist, near Marietta, in Cobb County, Georgia. For a number of years the Statesmen Quartet's singing schedule was arranged to enable Parson Hovie to be in the Mount Zion pulpit each Sunday, even if it meant driving all night after a Saturday night concert 1,000 miles away. Due to Hovie's diligence and commitment, Mount Zion did not remain a "little" country church for long.

"Of course, me being on TV and being in the newspaper quite frequently, I was pretty well known and people would come out to hear me preach," Hovie reasons. "We had a lot of visitors who later became members. The church grew, enlarged, and went from a country church to a suburban church."

It is true that Hovie was widely known in the greater metropolitan Atlanta area, and his popularity likely attracted many to Mount Zion. But what made them return again and again, and ultimately to make commitments spiritually and unite with the church was due in large part to Hovie's inspired, dynamic delivery from the pulpit. Following are excerpts from one of his sermons on prayer, based on The Gospel According to St. Luke, chapter 9, verses 28 and 29.

"And it came to pass about eight days after these sayings, he took Peter and John and James and went up into the mountain to pray. And as he prayed the fashion of his countenance was altered and his raiment was white and glistering."

"One time when I was over in Fort Jackson, South Carolina, I was trying to find a place to pray. I said I would find me a place to kneel alone with Him. I went out into the woods and found me a great big tree. A symbol of His strength and assurance. A great big pine tree. I don't know if I ever found the top of it, but I sure did find the roots. And I thought, if I could humble myself and kneel on this old root of this pine tree that has stood straight and strong and has weathered the storm and has stood for many years, if I can be a symbol of its strength on my knees before the Lord Jesus Christ, I want to pour out my heart to Him. And there I had many blessings come my way. Sometimes I would kick up the straw that had fallen from last year's pine needles, and I'd have myself a shouting good time, but the Lord always managed to meet me there every time, when I knelt in humble prayer to Him.

"Listen, I want to tell you, if you are not a praying Christian, you are not a happy Christian. If you're not a praying Christian, you don't know what it means to have the full joy of salvation, because it only comes when you talk to your Master. When you're on your knees in prayer, you can really get on the line and feel the tugging. James Blackwood once told the story about a little boy who was flying a kite. The little boy was standing out holding this kite by the string and some men came along and said, 'Sonny boy, what are you doing?' He said, 'I'm flying a kite.' They looked up into the clouds and said, 'We can't see anything. How in the world do you know you're flying a kite? How do you know you've got anything on the string?' He said, 'Because I feel the tugging on the line.' I can feel the tugging on the line and, my friends, if you will get on the line that leads to glory, there is no charge. There are no interruptions, there is no party line. You've got a straight and driect line to go with, and there is always an operator on the other end, and His name is the Lord Jesus Christ. He'll pick up the phone. He'll listen. He'll talk to you just as long as you want to. He'll hear your prayers and give His all and full salvation if you want it.

"Listen, I want to tell you that the only way that you can have real, old-time, heart-felt, Holy Ghost-filled religion is to pray constantly to the Lord Jesus Christ. Who are we not to pray if men like Peter, James and John, even if Paul had to pray, even if my Lord Jesus Christ had to pray.

What about you and me? We must be of all men most miserable if we are not constantly in touch with the Great Redeemer.

"...If during the week you have become dirty and smutty, if during the week some of the world has rubbed off on you, and if during the week you have been in the flesh pots of this world and your crown is not shining, if your stars are not blinking, if your light is kind of covered up because you have become smutty with the forgetfulness of prayer, won't you kneel down and let the Lord change your countenance and cause your raiment to be white and glistening? He'll do it, and only will He do it when we come to the place and to the realization that prayer and only prayer is the only thing that will bring us face to face with the Master.

"...I believe in people, when they come to the altar of prayer, getting on their knees and telling God what they want and not the preacher, or somebody else. I'm not interested in what you want. I'm interested in you getting something from prayer that will absolutely make your soul so thrilled that you won't hardly know where you are."

Hovie's preaching was characterized by a fiery, exuberence of delivery—a byproduct of his Holiness Baptist upbringing. No one could be accused of sleeping during his services. With the help of the Lord, Hovie made the experience of attending church interesting, entertaining and inspiring—all at the same time.

Sunday morning in the early 1950s at Mt. Zion Baptist Church, in Cobb County, Georgia, where Rev. Hovie Lister served as pastor for 12 years.

8
Climbing Higher and Higher

Teamwork

The entertainment world is rife with successful partnerships: Hope and Crosby, Abbott and Costello, Burns and Allen, Laurel and Hardy, Martin and Lewis, and the list goes on. Since the gospel music industry has often followed trends established in secular culture, it was only natural that a successful combination of gospel acts would develop. It had become common practice in the field of gospel quartet singing for two groups to join together for a double-header concert. The teaming of Hovie Lister and the Statesmen Quartet with the Blackwood Brothers Quartet occurred purely by accident as a result of a single concert of this type in 1952. Surviving members of both groups forget today where that initial pairing of the two quartets occurred, but the success of the program warranted serious consideration of an ongoing working relationship.

By 1952, the Blackwood Brothers and Statesmen had become the most popular among the many quartets actively capitalizing on the success of the post-war gospel music boom. For the Blackwood Brothers, it had been a long climb. The group was first organized in 1934 by brothers Roy, Doyle and James, and R.W., Roy's son. This Mississippi family quartet had known years of struggle before finding success in the open plains of Iowa via Shenandoah's powerful radio station KMA. At the time they were one of many quartets sponsored by the Stamps brothers' growing operation in Dallas, Texas. Then came World War II, and the Blackwood unit was forced to disband temporarily. Reunited in San Diego, California, the group worked in aircraft factories and sang part-time until the great world conflict was settled.

Following the war the Blackwoods returned to Iowa and, due to the great demand for their services, operated two quartets for a period of time. Eventually, Roy and Doyle tired of the rigors of the road, leaving James and R.W. to carry on with a series of support personnel. In September 1950, the Blackwood Brothers Quartet said goodbye to its 10-year association with KMA in favor of a regular radio spot on WMPS in Memphis, Tennessee, just across the state line from the founding members' native Mississippi. By 1952, the personnel of the quartet consisted of Bill Shaw, tenor; James Blackwood, lead; R.W. Blackwood, baritone; and Bill Lyles, bass. Their accompanist was a young keyboard whiz by the name of Jack Marshall.

By contrast, the popularity of the Statesmen had been achieved in an amazingly-short four years. It helped, of course, that Atlanta was a mecca for gospel music during the group's formative years. The members of the Statesmen were very dedicated to their craft, following the principle that the harder one works the better his opportunity for success. Most importantly, the group credits their success to God's hand in their career. "If you're called by the Lord, if you're ordained by Him to do His work, then you just hope that you can be as big as you can be for Him, in Him, and by Him," is Hovie's observation.

"It can be stated with certainty that the Statesmen gained popularity, prominence and financial success more quickly than any other quartet in the history of gospel music," was the assessment of *Billboard* magazine, in a 1965 publication devoted to the gospel music industry.

Brock Speer, whose family had worked concerts and other appearances with many of the top gospel groups, saw the magic formula in the teaming of the Blackwoods and Statesmen:

"First, these two top gospel groups drew capacity crowds," he would write years later. "The Blackwood Brothers Quartet had a loyal following, built up through many years of singing in person and on records, to draw from. The Statesmen had a new style and quality of gospel singing that was making ardent fans of everyone who heard them. Very soon, about all that was needed to fill an auditorium for a gospel concert was the announcement that, 'the Statesmen and Blackwoods will be there.'

"Then, the programs put on by these two quartets were second to none. Both groups maintained their individuality in style and presentation and both knew what to do to please their audiences and keep them coming back month after month to the regular singings."

James Blackwood remembers that each group "had a good following and their own fans. Each group was good, but different. We both were popular and we were different in our singing in style and approach. And we thought perhaps if we would team up or sing together that the Statesmen would draw their fans, we would draw ours and by combining them we thought it would be a surefire thing to have a good crowd."

After discussing the issue at length, the two organizations decided to try the idea at Central High School in Birmingham, Alabama, another of the South's many gospel music strongholds of that era. The concert was so successful the school auditorium was sold out. And to the great satisfaction of group managers James Blackwood and Hovie Lister, each quartet's contingent of fans enjoyed hearing the other quartet sing.

"That proved our idea was right. We had something there. So we formed the team in 1952 and for a good number of years we did probably a majority of our appearances together," says Blackwood.

Their joint engagements included the unheard of practice of playing monthly concerts in several southern cities. W.B. Nowlen, who promoted gospel singings in Texas, booked the Blackwood/Statesmen combination in engagements at the Will Rogers Auditorium in Fort Worth every month for five years. Wally Fowler hosted the Blackwoods and Statesmen, along with several support acts, at his monthly hymn sings at Nashville's Ryman Auditorium, and city auditoriums in Birmingham and Atlanta for many years.

The Blackwood Brothers in 1952, clockwise from top: Jackie Marshall, pianist; Bill Lyles, bass; R.W. Blackwood, baritone; James Blackwood, lead; and Bill Shaw, tenor.

"No type of entertainment performers had ever tried such a thing," stresses Blackwood. "Most singers, pianists, musicians or orchestras, or whatever, would not play the same town more than once a year. They figured to retain their drawing power. Nobody had ever done that before."

After a few years, however, the two quartets cut back on the amount of their exposure in certain cities. Eventually, they would play only four times a year in Birmingham. One of these bookings became an annual New Year's Eve tradition at the Birmingham City Auditorium.

"I don't remember for how many years, but every year that was an annual thing," says Blackwood. "Wally Fowler, of course, would book more than our two groups in the bigger places like Atlanta and Nashville and Birmingham, but on New Year's Eve he would have just the Blackwoods and Statesmen and it was always sold out."

The two groups had been averaging about $250 per group for a performance at the all-night sings around the country. With the success of the team, they were able to command higher fees. Soon promoters were more than happy to pay the combined team $1,000 to $1,500 for an appearance, because the appearance of the team insured drawing power, as Brock Speer had said.

Teaming as they had was probably the one move more than any other that influenced the upward mobility of the Blackwoods' and Statesmen's careers. Appearing together night after night as they would for many years, their competitive nature forced each group to work harder at their craft, honing arrangements, polishing their stage presentations, striving to be the best they could be. Despite the competition, James Blackwood says the rivalry between the two groups was very friendly, unlike some other quartets in the business at that time.

"There was (a rivalry) to the extent that we each did the very best we could on a program but we never really pulled dirty tricks on each other because of our partnership and working together. We had our own separate groups and, of course, the money was all separate. But we had formed this team and because it was so successful—if for no other reason than our pocketbooks—we knew it was to our advantage to get along. And we were friends, good friends. We even took our vacations together."

The strong bond between the two groups would manifest itself again and again, through times both good and bad, in the years to come.

A Legendary Outpouring of Emotion

Beginning in 1941, the Speer Family was featured in a live, 15-minute radio show weekday mornings at 6:15 a.m. on WSFA in Montgomery, Alabama. Following the Speers each day was a popular, up-and-coming local favorite in Montgomery—Hank Williams. At an early age Hank had taught himself to play guitar, and when he was 14 organized his own band—Hank Williams and his Drifting Cowboys. For 11 years, beginning in 1937, the band was featured in its own radio program on WSFA. National stardom came in 1947 when the young man began to record his brand of country and western folk songs, most of them self-penned, on MGM Records. From 1949, when he joined the cast of the Grand Ole Opry, until his death less than four years later Hank Williams dominated the country music scene. He scored hits with such songs as "Hey, Good Lookin'," "Jambalaya," "I'm So Lonesome I Could Cry," and others. But he also penned several religious songs, including the ever popular "I Saw the Light." Despite his overwhelming success, or perhaps because of it, Hank Williams became a tortured man, burned out by months of alcohol and drug abuse. On January 1, 1953, just a few months after being fired by the Opry, Hank passed quietly from life to legend. The end came while he was sleeping in the back seat of a car enroute to another of an endless stream of one night stands. Hank Williams was 29 years old.

Some of Hank's friends from the Grand Ole Opry—Roy Acuff, Red Foley, Ernest Tubb and Carl Smith—were invited to sing at the funeral. A planeload of country and western entertainers flew from Nashville to Montgomery to pay their respects. During the funeral, Hovie Lister and the Statesmen Quartet, the lone group representing the gospel music industry at the somber proceedings, offered their interpretation of "Precious Memories."

"It was a song requested by Hank Williams' mother. That's why we were there, she requested us to be there," Hovie recalls. "Then we backed Red Foley singing 'Peace In The Valley.' We were the only quartet there. Red asked us if we knew 'Peace In The Valley,' if we could back him up on that and we did."

Jake recalls with a smile an incident that occurred during preparations for the funeral. "Roy Acuff wanted us to sing 'I Saw the Light.' We didn't know 'I Saw the Light.' "

"You know 'Peace in the Valley,' " Acuff said. "Why don't you know 'I Saw the Light ?' Anyway, that's Hank's song!"

"He really got concerned about us not knowing 'I Saw The Light,' says Jake."

The funeral, held at Montgomery's city auditorium, drew an estimated crowd of 20,000 mourners. A newspaper account of the event called it the "greatest emotional orgy" in the city's history.

Television

Not long after the Statesmen began their careers on WCON, Atlanta's two major newspapers, *The Atlanta Constitution* and *The Atlanta Journal*, merged. When the two papers became one corporation its leaders were faced with unloading one of its two radio station licenses. *The Journal* owned WSB, which had pioneered radio broadcasting in Georgia in 1922. Of course, WCON, the broadcasting entity of *The Constitution*, had joined the airwaves in 1948. According to regulations of the Federal Communications Commission, a corporation was not permitted to own two radio stations in the same city.

"So WCON was sold, since it was the newer station," Hovie explains. "We were transferred over to WSB, which was a 50,000 watt, clear-channel station. That's where our careers really began to blossom."

The Statesmen continued to produce a radio show for WSB for several years. Eventually, Hovie says, they pre-recorded programs to sell to other radio stations, developing a Statesmen radio network of sorts. By 1955, the programs would be airing in 36 radio markets across the U.S.

"We made some programs, 15-minute radio shows, and had them pressed onto 33 1/3 records. My secretary and I would time those programs out where the necessary spots would be there, and I would simply say, 'We'll be back in just a moment.' Then the local station could put their spot there and it was timed so that if they were on time and on the ball the whole program, including the commercials, came out to 15 minutes. We hired a man to go about and sell radio stations into buying the programs."

On weekdays, the Statesmen continued to broadcast two daily programs—early morning and noon—for some time on WSB. Additionally, they initiated a Saturday night broadcast called "Singing Time In

Dixie." On the strength of WSB's 50,000 watts, the gospel melodies of the Statesmen were filling the airwaves in several surrounding states. "Singing Time In Dixie" soon became a household word throughout the South and Midwest.

"We could get WSB" in central Indiana, remembers Bill Gaither. "In the mid-'50s, I did hear a lot of stuff coming out of WSB, Atlanta, and the 'Singing Time In Dixie' shows. I could get them on Saturday nights. Those were fun."

Television was the next medium for the group to conquer in spreading its message across America. That door opened soon after they moved to WSB radio. The Statesmen were offered a program at 5 o'clock every Monday evening on WSB-TV. The live program was sponsored by Westinghouse for several years. In time they acquired a new sponsor, the National Biscuit Company, better known as Nabisco. The company had a very large bakery in Atlanta which supplied most of Nabisco's crackers and cookies for distribution throughout the southeastern United States and Cuba. Nabisco sponsored the Statesmen locally on WSB-TV for nearly a year. When Nabisco executives began to review the growing numbers on their sales charts in comparison to the popularity of the Statesmen program, they developed a promotional plan that would eventually place the Statesmen on television in about 150 markets across the country.

Denver Crumpler

Preparing a television series for national syndication meant the group would be rehearsing even more than their existing regimen of exhaustive practice. The group wanted to be at the top of its game for the television series. After all, no gospel quartet had ever been featured in its own national television series. No gospel quartet had ever secured a national sponsor.

One hitch developed, however, before the television series became a reality. Cat Freeman wanted out.

"Cat had gotten to where he didn't really care too much about singing," says Jake. "We were right in the middle of a local television show there and just fixing to go into the Nabisco series and Cat didn't like to rehearse. Now Cat was one of my dearest friends. I dearly loved him. But he just let you know right quick, 'You get your part and I'll take care of mine.' And he did. Somehow he'd get by. But he didn't like to rehearse at all. And Cat didn't care if we got another tenor. He didn't leave mad. But Cat just didn't care to rehearse and we needed somebody that was on the ball all the time."

It had always been Hovie's dream to have Denver Crumpler, the Rangers' great Irish tenor, as a member of the Statesmen Quartet. He had wanted Denver when the group organized in 1948. Back then, Denver would have been ill-advised to leave a well-established group like the Rangers for a brand-new group of upstarts managed by a 21-year-old. Hovie and Doy Ott had both worked with Denver in their separate stints as pianist for the Rangers Quartet some years before. They remembered him as a gentleman, courteous and very thoughtful. Big Chief had met Denver on his visit with the Rangers in Atlanta some years before. Jake had been a Denver Crumpler fan for years, having heard him on Rangers broadcasts from all over the country. The group was convinced that Denver was the man they wanted as Cat Freeman's replacement. All that remained was for them to convince Denver he wanted the Statesmen. The assignment of doing the convincing went to Hovie Lister, the group's ever-capable salesman. On one of the quartet's trips to Fort Worth to sing for W.B. Nowlen, Hovie and Doy "went to Denver's home in Texas and more or less talked him into coming with us," says Hovie. By then the Statesmen/Blackwood team was taking the gospel music business by storm. The Rangers were no longer the strong quartet of yesteryear, due to a traffic accident that had seriously interrupted their work in 1951. Hovie offered to rent a house in Atlanta for Denver and his family. When the Statesmen returned to Atlanta, that's exactly what he did.

Crumpler was 40 years of age when he moved to Atlanta in 1953 to join the Statesmen. Music had been his life. Born into a family of musicians in Arkansas, Denver was the youngest of seven children. It has been said that he learned to play guitar when he was too small to even hold the instrument. He had to lay it flat on a bed to play it. Even as a child he was blessed with a remarkable singing voice, and would lead congregational singing at his uncle's singing conventions. At the age of 20, Denver traveled to Dallas, Texas, to study voice under the tutelage of the renowned Virgil Stamps. His professional quartet experience began with The Stamps Melody Boys, sponsored by the Stamps brothers' company in Dallas.

By 1953, Crumpler had been singing with the Rangers Quartet for nearly 16 years. In the late 1930s and early 1940s, the Rangers had been one of the top quartets—if not the best—in the nation. Though the group originated in Texas, they were later based in Louisville where Denver met his wife, Frances "Frankie" Harper.

For more than 10 years, from 1938 to 1948, the personnel of the Rangers, with the exception of their pianist, remained the same: Arnold Hyles, bass; Walter Leverett, baritone; Vernon Hyles, lead; and Denver Crumpler, tenor. For several years their only accompaniment was guitar. Then came a succession of keyboardists: Lee Roy Abernathy, Hovie Lister, Doy Ott and David Reece, among them. With the death of Leverett, on June 1, 1948, Ermon Slater became the new baritone. The Rangers continued their broadcasts from Charlotte, and later Raleigh, North Carolina, for a few years before returning to Texas. Following a concert in Mount Pleasant, Texas, on the night of January 12, 1951, the Rangers were returning to their homes in two cars when a grinding collision occurred. Outside of the town of Atlanta, Texas, an intoxicated driver who was later convicted of murder with a motor vehicle, slammed head-on into the automobile containing Ermon Slater and Arnold Hyles. Slater's injuries proved fatal. For the better part of a month doctors held little hope for the recovery of Hyles. He survived, but the next couple of years would bring numerous follow-up surgeries and painful rehabilitation. This period was a difficult one for the Rangers. The quartet eventually disbanded in 1955, although pianist David Reece formed the Rangers Trio some years later.

Tall and handsome, Denver Crumpler's graceful, easy style of singing and stage presence fit well with the good looks of the Statesmen. And that voice: Unbelievably high, clear as a bell, no hint of false tones, and no strain!

"I was so excited about Denver" coming with the Statesmen, recalls Jake. "I could hardly wait to get on the stage with him. He was just the epitome of a pro in gospel music!"

Hearth and Home

Denver and his family moved to Decatur, Georgia, and settled in with the extended Statesmen family—by 1953 all of the group had married except Hovie. Denver and Frankie Crumpler had three children, daughters Dale and Charlotte, and son Bobby. Doy and Joyce Ott had married in their native Oklahoma long before Doy came to Atlanta to attend the University of Georgia. Their daughter, Delores, born in 1942, was the oldest of the Statesmen offspring. Big Chief and Elizabeth Wetherington were the parents of little daughter Diana. Jake and Joyce Hess were the newlyweds, having tied the knot on October 5, 1952.

Despite frequent personal-appearance tours and their heavy schedule of radio, television and recording engagements, the Statesmen relished their time of relaxation at home with family and friends. In their spare time the men enjoyed hunting, fishing and gardening. While all of the men golfed, Jake and Denver especially enjoyed spending time together on the links regularly when not on the road. All faithfully served their churches and Sunday Schools. Big Chief served his home church as director of the choir. Denver served on his church's finance committee. Pastor Hovie, of course, took great interest in the spiritual needs of his growing congregation at Mount Zion Baptist Church.

The life of a quartet wife was one of sacrifice. When the quartet began pre-recording their radio shows in lieu of live daily broadcasts, it became commonplace for the Statesmen to be away from their families for several days at a stretch during an extended concert tour. According to Hovie, "The wives knew this was our living, this was our calling, this was our work, this was what we were going to do. When we were home and not on the road we rehearsed, just about every day at least two or three hours a day. And that was accepted by the wives."

The Statesmen (standing, from left): Hovie Lister, Denver Crumpler, Jake Hess, Doy Ott and James "Big Chief" Wetherington receive their commissions as Lieutenant Colonels on the Georgia Governor's staff from Governor Herman E. Talmadge.

9

His Master's Voice

Cadillac, Cadillac, Cadillac Style

In the early 1950s, the Statesmen had forsaken the Plymouths and Hudsons of their early days in favor of a larger, more comfortable mode of travel. As they began to spend more time on the highways and their destinations became more and more distant, the quartet opted for an automobile that offered more room and comfort for the exhausting travels success demanded of them.

"We began to buy Cadillac limousines which had a jump seat in the back," Hovie says. "If it was a long trip the guys could put their hips in the jump seat and their backs in the back seat and kind of stretch out. The three in the back would take turns about with the other guy that wasn't driving sitting in the front. On the long trips we pulled a trailer to carry our clothes and our records in."

Jake tends to downplay the discomfort: "Of course, we try to make it sound a lot worse than it really was. It was much worse back then than it is today. A Cadillac pulling a trailer, that wasn't the worst way in the world. You had a big limousine, and had a lot of room. We didn't suffer too much."

Even a seven-passenger sedan can become cramped with the addition of the cargo required for a successful quartet to travel. Each member of the quartet needed more than one suit available for personal appearances. Their sound system required a considerable amount of space in the trunk. Items for merchandising at concert record tables needed to be stored effectively, also. The Statesmen acquired a little trailer from a country music band, and utilized it to carry extra clothing as well as records, songbooks and other merchandise to sell at their concerts. They fondly nicknamed the little vehicle "Elmer."

By the mid-1950s, the Statesmen were averaging 1,000 miles a week on the road in meeting 250 engagements a year. But, regardless of the long trips and loss of sleep, they always arrived smiling and in good voice, ready to spread sunshine and inspiration with their songs of faith. It was a life of success, but not necessarily one of comfort.

The Statesmen defined a work ethic that most gospel music artists, with the exception of the Blackwood Brothers, had not known in the early 1950s. To some people of that era, singing in

a gospel quartet was not seriously considered to be real work. These people would look at gospel quartets in the manner of: "That's okay, but what do you do for a day job?"

Quartet work was both a day AND night job. A typical day for the Statesmen meant getting up at 4:30 in the morning and going down to the local radio station to perform on a live 6:30 radio show. After getting breakfast at a local cafeteria they would return to the radio studios, find a spare room and rehearse hard until time to do another radio show at noon. In the afternoon they would get in the car and travel to their evening singing engagement. They might get home at 11 p.m. or midnight for a few hours of shut-eye before getting up the next morning and beginning the whole routine over again.

"You can't say that's lazy in any stretch of the imagination," stresses Bill Gaither. "In fact, I wish some current artists today would understand that kind of work ethic. And that carried over to the day when they finally were in their stretch Cadillacs for awhile and put up their own sound set. It carried over into the days when they were in their buses, carrying their own records, doing their own bus driving—did all the work. I think they left a wonderful work ethic behind. If you look at most of those guys, they were pretty skinny. And they were skinny for a reason. They worked very, very hard. And I'm not so sure it didn't tell on some of their health. I'm not so sure that's why three of them are already dead and gone, you know."

Two New Voices in the Heavenly Choir

By the summer of 1954, the Blackwoods and Statesmen were working the majority of their engagements together. For some time the Blackwood group had been traveling by airplane to their appearances, while the Statesmen continued driving in their luxurious sedan. The Blackwood Brothers owned an airplane and, at first, hired a pilot to fly them everywhere. Later, R.W. Blackwood had earned his pilot's license and became pilot for the group. Bill Lyles, the group's bass singer, served as navigator.

On June 30, both groups were scheduled to sing for the Chilton County Peach Festival in Clanton, Alabama. The concert was to be held in an aircraft hanger at the municipal airport. Members of the festival committee had arranged for a sound system to be set up in the hanger. The concert had been well publicized. All was in readiness for the big event in this small, central Alabama town.

The Blackwood Brothers' plane glided onto the Clanton airport runway at about noon. A large reception committee was on hand to welcome them, and congratulate them on their success in winning Arthur Godfrey's Talent Scouts on CBS television just 18 days before. The Blackwood Brothers obliged the fans by giving a short, informal concert, answering requests of the assemblage. The formal concert was scheduled for that evening. The Statesmen arrived by late afternoon.

Since the Blackwood schedule called for them to fly home to Memphis that night, R.W. Blackwood and Bill Lyles decided before the evening concert to make a practice takeoff in the daylight to be familiar with the unlighted field in the darkness. They were joined by young John Ogburn, Jr., whose father was the founder of the Peach Festival. The takeoff went well, but R.W. aborted his first attempt at landing on the short strip. On the second landing attempt, the plane bounced hard and R.W. gave it full throttle, apparently realizing he would have to get the plane back in the air and try again. Suddenly, as if it were a toy on the end of a string, the plane's nose jerked upward in a vertical climb, the propellers beating the air fiercely and creating a horrible wracking sound. Slowly the vehicle's upward momentum stalled. The plane hung suspended momentarily, before gracefully dipping away and diving savagely into the ground. The three passengers died on impact.

The remaining members of the Blackwood Brothers Quartet, along with the Statesmen and many of the fans who had arrived for the concert, witnessed the horrible accident. Jake Hess had to forcibly restrain James Blackwood from trying to get into the burning wreckage in what would have been a futile—perhaps fatal—attempt to rescue the victims. Hovie Lister and the Statesmen stepped in to take charge of their bereaved comrades' lives, one of the group even going to the funeral home with the gruesome assignment of identifying the bodies. The Statesmen drove James Blackwood from Clanton home to Memphis that night, checked into a

Clanton residents erected a monument (left) in memory of R.W. Blackwood, Bill Lyles and Johnny Ogburn near the site of the airplane crash. The Clanton airport hanger (above) where the Blackwoods performed a brief concert just before the plane crash is still in use today.

Memphis hotel, cancelled immediate engagements and rearranged their heavy schedule of appearances. Hovie & Co. had determined they would be close at hand to help their friends in their hour of need. Hovie took charge of contacting promoters across the country, cancelling some of the Blackwoods' upcoming dates. He made dozens of calls, sent dozens of telegrams and handled the business affairs of the Blackwood Brothers Quartet during the 24-hour period following the crash. Denver, Jake, Doy and Big Chief made themselves available to the Blackwood family to help in every way they could, including taking long-distance telephone calls and handling telegrams from all over the country as condolences poured in.

Thousands of grieving fans poured into Ellis Auditorium in Memphis for the funeral service in memory of R.W. Blackwood and Bill Lyles. With the auditorium stage filled completely with flowers and floral designs, the Statesmen and Speer Family each sang during the service. The subdued sobs and somber, tear-stained faces of the audience seemed foreign to the huge auditorium—its halls had echoed with the joyous laughter and applause of so many great Christian concerts through the years. Concerts that had featured the now-stilled voices of Lyles and Blackwood.

Statesmen alumnus/composer Mosie Lister penned a song—"Two New Voices in the Heavenly Choir"—in memory of the fallen friends. The Statesmen learned the song quickly and sang it in a number of memorial concerts held in the weeks following the tragedy. They recorded it on a single, backed, fittingly, with "Known Only To Him," the great Stuart Hamblen composition that opens with the phrase "Known only to Him are the great hidden secrets..."

The Blackwoods and Statesmen, since forming their partnership, had begun the practice of scheduling their vacations at the same time, during the last two weeks of July. The Blackwood Brothers resumed their singing schedule within a few days after the funeral with the intention of hiring new vocalists for the baritone and bass positions during the vacation.

"In the appearances we had between the plane crash and the time that we reorganized our quartet," James Blackwood recalls, " Big Chief filled in and sang bass with our quartet and my brother Doyle sang baritone up until the time of our vacations. And then, during our vacation period when neither quartet was singing was when I selected J.D. Sumner to sing bass and my nephew, Cecil Blackwood, to sing baritone. Our first appearance back, the Blackwoods and Statesmen sang in Clanton, Alabama, in the same place where we were supposed to have sung that night when the plane crashed."

James has always been appreciative of how the Statesmen stepped in to help at the time of the tragedy. More than a decade later he would write: "Their friendship was a priceless aid, in our greatest trial."

RCA Victor

The Statesmen had continued to record for Capitol until early 1953. The label issued four singles by the quartet in 1951, including such songs as "Hide Me, Rock of Ages," "Peace in the Valley " and "Sho' Do Need Him Now." Four singles followed in 1952. The "A" sides of these records were "On Revival Day," "Stand By Me," "Rock A My Soul" and "The Love of God." The four songs released on two singles in 1953 were "How Many Times," "Someone to Care,""One of These Mornings" and "When You Travel All Alone."

Sometimes the label was slow to release material. In fact, "The Love of God" was released nearly a full year after the session occurred during which it was recorded. The Statesmen needed more recorded product to meet the demand of their growing number of fans. During their association with Capitol and from the time they had parted company with Capitol Records, the Statesmen continued to make records, releasing these recordings on their own custom "Statesmen" label. These records were what is now called "table product," meaning they were not sold in stores (unless stores specially ordered them directly from the group), but were sold from the quartet's record table at its appearances around the country. The group sold these recordings in both the 78 rpm and 45 rpm vinyl disc formats with one song on each side of the record. The 78 rpm format was the standard of the day in the late 1940s and early 1950s. The smaller, 45 rpm records soon became the product of choice for most Americans since they were easier to handle and store, and didn't break as easily as the bulkier 78 records. Columbia Records developed the longer-playing 33 1/3 rpm records in 1948. Other major labels soon began producing long-playing records, but it would be a few years before most gospel recording artists would have product available in this format.

In the early 1950s, there was no major record label dealing exclusively in the business of recording and distributing product for religious artists. Smaller companies, such as White Church and others, provided this service for a number of gospel groups and singers, but generally only on a regional basis. Many quartets, if they had any records to sell at all, sold custom records on their own label.

The Blackwood Brothers had made records on the White Church label, and produced custom records before signing a recording deal with RCA Victor in 1951. Due in part to the company's success with the sales of records by the Blackwood Brothers, and also because of the rapid rise in popularity of gospel music, RCA Victor began adding new artists to its religious roster. George Beverly Shea, soloist with the Billy Graham Crusades, along with Cliff Barrows and the entire Billy Graham team, began recording for the label, as well as Tony Fontane, Stuart Hamblen and others.

The Statesmen signed with the elite label during the summer of 1954. RCA scheduled them to begin work on their first recording release in the label's New York City studio facilities. During their initial session as RCA Victor recording artists—a three-hour time block on the afternoon of August 24, 1954—the quartet recorded "This Ole House," a song that would ultimately sell more than 100,000 copies, along with "I've Been With Jesus," "Move That Mountain" and "If God Didn't Care." "This Ole House," backed with "I've Been With Jesus," was the quartet's first single release to be issued by RCA Victor. The relationship with a major company of the stature of RCA Victor ensured greater distribution of Statesmen recordings, even on an international scale, for RCA does business throughout the world.

Radio Corporation of America (RCA) was born during the days when the broadcasting industry was still in its infancy. Founded in 1919 for the purpose of manufacturing radio sets to meet the increasing demand for such instruments, the company grew very quickly. RCA's sales during the three-year period between 1922-24 amounted to $83.5-million. It has been estimated that by 1924 there were three million radio sets in use across America. The company ventured into broadcasting, first by owning and operating radio stations, then by forming the National Broadcasting Company (NBC), the nation's first major radio network. RCA eventually expanded its operations to include television and other enterprises. RCA also established itself as a leader in the sound recording industry, adding Victor to its name when the company purchased the Victor Talking Machine Company.

By the early 1950s, RCA Victor had established a stable of top recording artists. This was especially true in the field of country and western music, for they had signed such personages as Eddy Arnold, Chet Atkins, Homer and Jethro, Pee Wee King, Jim Reeves, Roy Rogers, Hank  Snow and the Sons of the Pioneers, among others. The man responsible for building the company's enviable C&W roster was Steve Sholes. Sholes had begun what was to be a 40-year association with RCA Victor when he was in high school in New Jersey, where the company had facilities in Camden. As RCA Victor's Artist and Repertoire Director, Sholes was one of the first record producers to see the potential of Nashville as a recording center for the company. He was the guiding light behind recording sessions at RCA Victor's studios at 1525 McGavock Street in Nashville, and later facilities in the Music City.

It was Steve Sholes who signed the Blackwood Brothers. Sholes and James Blackwood developed a good working relationship. After the Blackwood/Statesmen partnership developed in 1952, Blackwood began to urge Sholes to consider signing his friends the Statesmen to the growing RCA Victor roster of gospel artists. However, James was less than pleased with one aspect of the Blackwoods' arrangement with RCA. The Blackwood Brothers were having to buy their records at the distributor price from their local RCA record distributor. When the expiration date of the Blackwoods' initial contract drew nigh, Sholes wanted to re-sign them.

"Well, Steve, I can't afford to buy the RCA records from the local RCA distributor, then sell them retail. I don't make enough profit," James told him. "We just can't afford to pay what we're paying for records."

"Well, if I set you up as a distributor and you could buy records at the distributor price, would you re-sign?" offered Sholes.

James agreed and penned his signature to the new deal. "I had a record shop already and was distributing records all over the country," he explains, "so it was a natural tie-in. I began distributing for RCA and buying records at the distributor cost. And then when the Statesmen signed with them, they bought their records through me. I let them have them at just a few pennies over what I paid for them so they, too, did not have to pay the dealer price for their recordings. They for many, many years bought their records through me."

While Sholes scheduled and directed most of the Statesmen's earlier recording sessions, renowned guitarist Chet Atkins served as producer of many of the group's early records. Atkins also played guitar on many of the sessions, surrounded by a combo of Nashville's top session instrumentalists who specialized in providing backup music for recordings. When you were signed with a company like RCA Victor, you worked with the very best! Complemented by these musicians and the ever-capable keyboard stylings of Hovie Lister, the RCA Victor recordings of the great Statesmen vocal arrangements of that era are still a treasure these many years later.

Blackwood remembers the bulky, middle-aged Sholes as "a fine man. He was a great influence in country and gospel music. He was the one who bought Elvis's contract from Sun Records."

Long before he met Steve Sholes, Elvis Presley knew the Blackwood Brothers and Statesmen. Living in Memphis, he occasionally attended the same Assembly of God Church of which the Blackwoods were members. In the early 1950s, young Presley was attracted to the big, all-night gospel quartet concerts which were promoted monthly by the Blackwoods and Statesmen at Ellis Auditorium in Memphis. From time to time they would have other groups—the Speer Family, Blue Ridge Quartet, Oak Ridge Quartet, and more—as guests.

"Elvis always came," James Blackwood remembers. "He was just a teenager and we would let him in. We'd let him in the back door, in the stage door, or wherever he wanted to go. One time he came and none of us were around, and whoever was in the box office did not know him and didn't know that we always let him in. So he bought a ticket. I remember tickets were a dollar and a quarter at the time. I found out about it later and wrote him a note and sent him a check for his dollar and a quarter. I've been told that he kept that and it's still at Graceland somewhere now."

At eighteen, Elvis auditioned for James Blackwood's nephew, Cecil, for an opening in the younger Blackwood's Songfellows Quartet. Then the lad who had left the group changed his mind. Elvis was disappointed, but still hung around and sang with the group during rehearsals from time to time.

Despite his close friendship with the Blackwoods, it was Jake Hess of the Statesmen whom Elvis most admired as a singer. Some years later, pop singer Johnny Rivers told of visiting Elvis at Graceland:

"One of his idols when he was young was a man named Jake Hess, who was the lead singer for the Statesmen Quartet. If you'll listen to some of their recordings, you'll hear some of that style that is now Elvis Presley's style, especially in his ballad-singing style. He was playing some of their records one day and he said, 'Now you know where I got my style from. Caught—a hundred million records too late.' Jake and the Statesmen and the Blackwoods. He played all kinds of records, but mostly it was gospel music..."

It must have filled Elvis with a sense of pride when RCA issued his first release, to see the logo of the dog and phonograph with the inscription "His master's voice" on the label. That same logo for years had appeared on previous records he loved so much—those of the Blackwoods and Statesmen.

"I think the whole RCA Victor label thing was no big deal to the Statesmen," observes Bill Gaither. "You know, today if a person leaves a Christian label to go to a secular label, they're considered bad. But they were on a secular label back in '48 or '49. I never thought that was bad. It couldn't be bad if it led me to the Lord. It was through a gospel group on a secular label that I found the Lord. I think they paved a lot of ways in that."

August 24, 1954: The Statesmen rehearse in RCA's New York studios during their initial recording session for RCA Victor. The rhythm guitarist is studio session musician Art Ryerson. Phil Kraus accompanied on drums, and Charles Green played the upright bass.

At left, the Statesmen listen intently to the playback of a "take." The quartet's first single for RCA, recorded during this session, was "This Ole House."

Arthur Godfrey's Talent Scouts

Arthur Godfrey for many years was the only personality in television history to have two top-rated shows running simultaneously in prime time for an extended period (8 1/2 years). In the 1950s, he was the host of two hit shows for CBS: "Arthur Godfrey Talent Scouts Show," a 30-minute talent contest which aired on Mondays at 8:30 p.m.; and "Arthur Godfrey and His Friends," a 60-minute variety show on Wednesdays at 8 p.m. Godfrey's ratings were superb. In 1953, the shows were the second and third most popular programs for the season behind "I Love Lucy." On the Talent Scouts program, agents who worked for the network scouted the country for exceptional talent to audition for the show. These scouts would bring their discoveries on the show to perform before a live national audience. Since most of these discoveries were aspiring professionals with some prior experience, the quality of the acts was quite high. Winners for each show were chosen by an audience applause meter. Among those who made a Talent Scouts

appearance on their rise to stardom were Tony Bennett, Pat Boone, Roy Clark, Patsy Cline, Rosemary Clooney, Connie Francis, the McGuire Sisters, and many others.

The scouts were known to make a mistake now and then. For example, two rising stars—Elvis Presley and Buddy Holly—failed to pass their auditions to get on the program.

The Blackwood Brothers won Arthur Godfrey's Talent Scouts on June 12, 1954, becoming the first gospel quartet act to make an appearance on the program. Arnold Shaw, of Hill and Range Publications, was familiar with the requirements of the Talent Scouts auditions and arranged an audition for the Statesmen. The audition went successfully and in September, 1954, Hovie Lister and the Statesmen were set to fly to New

The Statesmen at the Atlanta Airport as they prepared to board the airplane for the flight to New York City for their winning appearance on Arthur Godfrey's Talent Scouts in September, 1954.

York City to make their live debut on one of the nation's major television networks. By this time the Statesmen, because of their Westinghouse and Nabisco programs in Atlanta, had become quite at ease with television.

The song they chose as their competing selection for the Godfrey program was "This Ole House," a Stuart Hamblen composition, the up-tempo arrangement commencing and culminating in the refrain of "When the Saints Go Marching In." They had recorded the arrangement for RCA Victor release only days before. The clever arrangement and its high-energy delivery by the handsome group proved to be an unstoppable combination when the Statesmen sang it on the Godfrey program on Monday, September 6, 1954. The Statesmen overwhelmed the audience with their performance. After winning, the Statesmen were invited by Mr. Godfrey to appear daily during the following week on his live, CBS television and radio network shows. Also appearing with them on these programs were the McGuire Sisters, who had become regulars on Godfrey's broadcasts.

On the day following the Statesmen's winning appearance on the Godfrey Show, RCA Victor scheduled them to another recording session at the label's New York City recording facilities. The quartet committed four songs to tape that day, including Bob Prather's "Led Out of Bondage," Stuart Hamblen's "Known Only to Him," "Everybody Will Be Happy Over There" and "I Believe In The Man In The Sky." They sang "Led Out of Bondage" on one of the Godfrey appearances later that week. In fact, their entire weeklong stand in New York City was an overwhelming success.

Immediately, the Statesmen were approached with contract offers. They entertained an offer to appear regularly on a nationwide TV program. The powerful William Morris Agency wanted to sign the group to a personal management contract and guide their career. William Morris had the contacts, financing and expertise necessary to make the Statesmen one of the most successful acts in all of the entertainment industry. Each of the offers involved a fabulous salary. The serious down side was, each of the offers involved a change of direction that was contrary to the course these Christian men had charted for themselves.

The nationwide TV offer called for them to sing popular, not gospel, tunes. The William Morris Agency was ready to book the Statesmen in showrooms at Las Vegas if the group would opt for popular music over gospel. They offered to furnish coaches and choreographers. The agency was prepared to spare no expense in taking the Statesmen to the top.

"We very politely and very diplomatically declined," says Hovie. "The seriousness of our work would not let us accept."

According to Jake, "We never gave it a second thought because we were working every night. We had all we could do."

Hovie is convinced that the Statesmen, had they forsaken gospel music, would have been very successful in secular music. He cites as an example the Oak Ridge Boys, a gospel group that enjoyed immense success after crossing over to country music two decades after the Statesmen said no.

"Four-part harmony is definitely acceptable and likeable, and very much in demand in any form of music," he says. "But once you're a gospel quartet, you can't be wishy-washy. You can't be pop this week and gospel the next. You can't be country this week and gospel the next. You've got to stay with what you're going to do. That's why when the William Morris Agency heard us on the Arthur Godfrey Show, they knew they had something if they could just get us to go over into a different field. We had the voices. We had the charisma. We had the class. We had the look they wanted. We had everything they wanted—except we were singing Gospel Music and they wanted us to sing something besides gospel.

"The Statler Brothers started off as a gospel group and starved to death. They couldn't make big bucks. The Oak Ridge Boys were popular in gospel music but they wanted to make the big bucks, so they went country. I could name you any number of big groups that their background is gospel. I could name you any number of black artists whose background was in church choirs and in gospel. But to become a superstar, or to become known more widely and to make the big bucks, they had to go into jazz, pop, or something of that sort. For instance, our good friend Elvis Presley—he loved gospel music better than he did the kind of music he sang. But it didn't make millions of bucks. And it still doesn't make millions of bucks. You have to draw the line somewhere."

The Statesmen and McGuire Sisters on the Arthur Godfrey set in the CBS studios in New York. The photo was taken during a joint appearance on one of Godfrey's daily radio programs during the week following their winning appearance on the Talent Scouts show.

10

Merry Melodies Coming Your Way

Nabisco

For several months the National Biscuit Company (Nabisco) sponsored the weekly Statesmen program, broadcast live on WSB-TV, in addition to the quartet's radio broadcasts in Atlanta. During this time Hovie became good friends with the southeastern general manager of Nabisco Products, a man by the name of Fryerson. It was through his efforts that the company developed a promotional plan to feature the Statesmen in a syndicated television program in several markets across the country. Fryerson met with the President of Nabisco in New York and lobbied the sales manager at WSB, selling both on the idea.

"One day the sales manager came in and asked me to come to his office," Hovie recalls. "He told me that Nabisco wanted to work out a deal" to put the group on a syndicated network of 35 television stations. "I asked him, 'Do you know what this is going to entail? We're going to have to film these programs.' "

At that time videotape had not been developed for the television industry. The programs would have to be filmed on 16 millimeter, reel-to-reel film. The quartet would have to film each show as if they were making a movie. Hovie worked out the details concerning where the Statesmen and Nabisco could secure a film company to provide all the technical equipment, studios and expertise to mechanically produce the programs. The group would pre-record the songs, then lip-sync with the recordings when they filmed the shows. When Hovie had tied together the loose ends, he put together a budget to present to the Nabisco brass.

"I flew to New York and met with the McCann-Erikson Advertising Agency and the man who handled the Nabisco account. Of course, I went armed with my budget: Figures on what it would cost to film these programs, how much it would cost for musicians to play, and for us to pre-record all of our music, and then lip-sync it back on camera. While I was in New York, before everything was completely settled, I was taken over to meet the president of Nabisco who had worked his way up from back in the early days of being the janitor who came in and built fires in the heaters in the office complex to being president of Nabisco. He had been there most of his life, a very fine old gentleman."

The old fellow turned to the advertising account executive, and said of Hovie, "You know, I kind of think this young man knows people, he seems to come across. Why don't we try using him as our spokesman, and let him do the commercials?" As a result, Hovie appeared in the show's Nabisco commercials, played the piano, emceed the programs and produced the TV show.

Hovie engaged the Belon King Film Com-

Hovie on the set, pitching Honey Grahams.

The Statesmen and Wade Creager's orchestra in rehearsal at the Biltmore Hotel during a late-night recording session for the Nabisco programs.

pany, located on Spring Street in Atlanta, to film the programs. He also arranged for the quartet to pre-record the soundtracks at Atlanta's Biltmore Hotel Ballroom. At that time the Biltmore was among the most prominent hotels in the South. The hotel had an incredible house band—Wade Creager and his orchestra, a nine-piece combo— that performed for ballroom dancing nightly.

"We went out and sang a few of our songs with them," Hovie remembers. "While we were rehearsing with them I felt like it was going to work, it would sound good. The Biltmore Hotel Ballroom had almost perfect acoustics. So we made arrangements to go out there at midnight when they got through with their work in the hotel. Then I would have engineers come in and set up their equipment and we would pre-record all the music, accompanied by Wade Creager's orchestra."

"The best place to record in Atlanta in those days was the Biltmore Hotel," says Jake. "They had the best sound there. People would come to the Biltmore for their big sounds."

The quartet pre-recorded enough music to fill several shows before the filming began. Hovie would then time each song and map out the song lineups for individual shows. That way he would be able to mix and match long numbers, short songs, up-tempo and slower tunes, and plan the appropriate spaces for the Nabisco commercials and song introductions. Everything was back-timed to fit into the 15-minute allotment for each program.

The group had several sets built at Belon King Studios. Each song in a show would be performed on a different set. A piano would be available on the same set for Hovie. However, no microphones were included on the sets. Hovie felt they would be distracting to viewers. In fact, the only microphones on the sets were placed out of view for Hovie's introductions of the songs and singers and to make his commercial announcements for Nabisco. After all, since the singers were lip-syncing to the pre-recorded soundtracks of the songs, they needed no microphones.

"We did it more like you would do a movie or a TV sitcom instead of the quartet standing on stage singing into mics," Hovie explains.

In fact, the Statesmen pioneered the concept of what is now known as the music video—story ideas developed visually around individual songs. In one scene, an elderly couple and a hound sat on the front porch of a little building as the quartet sang Albert Brumley's "There's a Little Pine Log Cabin." In another, the group sang "Sun-

Hovie and Wade Creager in a strategy session on the set of the Nabisco television show.

day Meetin' Time" with a painting of the exterior of an old country church as a backdrop. They were portrayed on a boat as fishers of men in "I'll Tell It Wherever I Go," a song that featured Denver Crumpler. One song featured the group sitting in a classic automobile.

"We had them to bring in that old antique automobile, jacked the thing up and had the wheels turning," Hovie says. "They got all of us in the car singing, like we were going down the road with the wind blowing our hair. For a song called 'Headin' Home' we had all the guys dressed up like hobos and some were sitting on the ground. We had a sign out there pointing various directions, different cities and things. Although it was black and white it was still very interesting to watch. They were very, very ahead of their time in production."

The first shows were filmed entirely on the sets at Belon King Studios. Later, Nabisco increased its investment in the show giving Hovie a budget that allowed the Statesmen and the production crew to film on location. Some segments were filmed at the famous Stone Mountain in Atlanta. They also filmed at Kennessaw Mountain. For some segments they filmed at a horse farm with the quartet dressed in western costumes singing cowboy songs. These included "Trails of Paradise" and Tim Spencer's "Cowboy Camp Meeting," among others.

Ozzie Nelson is often credited with pioneering the concept of the music video, developing filmed story plots around Ricky Nelson's hit songs during segments of the "Ozzie and Harriet" television show. But the efforts of Hovie Lister & The Statesmen on the Nabisco shows of the mid-1950s predated the Nelson efforts.

Statesmen Hymns

One elaborate set fashioned at Belon King was made to represent the interior of an old country church, complete with an altar, pulpit bench and an old-fashioned pump organ. Hovie wanted to include an old hymn in each show to give everyone a sense of nostalgia, since so many gospel music fans had attended an old country church in their youth. He knew the syndicated shows would reach a number of viewers who could relate to an old country church and the traditional old songs—even viewers who may have attended church in their childhood, but drifted away in later years. With all the newer gospel songs and spirituals the quartet would be singing on the programs, the hymn segment would balance the repertoire for those viewers, especially the

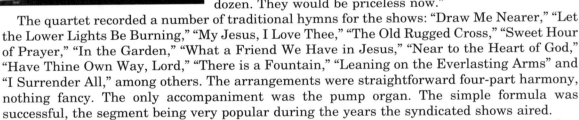

older ones, who would appreciate the traditional approach.

"I took some old Broadman hymn books out to a book-binder and had him to change it and put 'Statesmen Hymns' on it," Hovie recalls. Although the quartet members knew the hymns from memory, they would hold the "Statesmen Hymnals" during the hymn segment of the show for effect.

Hovie also wanted a traditional-sounding accompaniment for the hymns—on the soundtrack as well as on the set. "Why not an old pump organ that you had to pedal? I advertised in *The Atlanta Constitution-Journal* for someone that might have an old-fashioned pump organ that they'd like to sell to me for that use. I was given more than half-a-dozen. They would be priceless now."

The quartet recorded a number of traditional hymns for the shows: "Draw Me Nearer," "Let the Lower Lights Be Burning," "My Jesus, I Love Thee," "The Old Rugged Cross," "Sweet Hour of Prayer," "In the Garden," "What a Friend We Have in Jesus," "Near to the Heart of God," "Have Thine Own Way, Lord," "There is a Fountain," "Leaning on the Everlasting Arms" and "I Surrender All," among others. The arrangements were straightforward four-part harmony, nothing fancy. The only accompaniment was the pump organ. The simple formula was successful, the segment being very popular during the years the syndicated shows aired.

A young member of Hovie's church played a role in the Statesmen's Nabisco shows. One Sunday morning a church regular approached Hovie before the service and told the young pastor that her daughter could sing and was not bashful. She wondered if he might let her sing sometime for the little congregation.

"Why not have her sing this morning? We don't have any set order of the program here. We just let the Lord lead and do things the way we feel He wants them done," Hovie answered. Later, he was so impressed with her singing that little Joy Hood became a regular soloist at the church. When the Statesmen began producing the Nabisco shows, Hovie invited her to appear occasionally as a feature targeted for the children viewers.

"She would sing for us in church and she was a beautiful child," he recalls. "She was about 12, I guess, at the time she sang on our TV shows. She had a bright smile, a little pinafore dress, she was a beautiful little girl, so we used her several times on the Nabisco shows."

Doy Ott's daughter, Delores, appeared in at least one program. The scene opened with Delores struggling with her homework. The quartet walked in to help and ended up singing "You Can Move That Mountain."

Jake and the Hair Piece

It was after several programs had been aired during the Nabisco television series that Jake Hess changed his appearance. Jake's hair had been thinning for a few years. All of the other Statesmen had thick, dark, wavy hair. Although Jake was not completely bald, he provided a stark contrast in comparison to the appearances of his comrades.

"We were doing the Nabisco television show and a guy by the name of Bill Harrison was the director," Jake recalls with a chuckle. "One day he called me over to one side."

"Hess," said Harrison, "I need to talk to you about something."

Somehow, through his stammering and stuttering, Jake caught something about the other Statesmen all having dark, wavy hair. But Harrison, who worked for McCann-Erickson, very clearly was too embarrassed to speak his mind.

Jake saved him the effort. "In other words, you're sick of me putting dulling compound on my head under all these lights. You'd like for me to wear a hair piece."

"Well, yes!" replied the relieved director.

Jake thought for a moment, then said, "Well, Bill, you buy it and I'll wear it."

When the hairpiece arrived from Styles Unlimited in New York, Jake felt very self-conscious about wearing it at first. A few days later the quartet appeared in concert in Macon, Georgia. Jake was very timid about appearing in public with the hairpiece. He tried to be casually indifferent, hoping not to draw attention to himself. When the quartet reeled off several numbers and Jake still had not been featured in a solo, one fan, who loved Jake's unique style of singing, was beginning to get impatient and yelled down: "Hey, Hobie, let the kid with the wig sing one!"

Merchandising

Hovie served as Nabisco's pitch man on the programs, extolling the goodness of Premium Saltine Crackers, Vanilla Wafers, Sugar Honey Grahams, Oreo Cookies, and other fine Nabisco products. Often he would even take a bite of the product and follow it with a drink of milk. He put together displays of products for the commercials, including fresh banana puddings containing vanilla wafers. He believed in the product, he says, "and I still buy it!"

In their personal appearances, the Statesmen participated in a complete merchandising campaign on behalf of their sponsor, including stage displays, distributing samples, giving demonstrations and spreading the good word about Nabisco's famous products. Even the wooden boxes that the quartet's 78 rpm records were stored in to protect them on road trips were painted like boxes of Nabisco soda crackers. Hovie kept the McKann-Erikson Agency informed of the quartet's concert schedule. If the Statesmen were appearing in a city where Nabisco was sponsoring their TV show in that market, "they would have one of their distributors bring product, either saltines or whatever product we were pushing at that time. They would bring ample supplies," Hovie recalls. "They would decorate the stage with that, and then I would give that product away."

Hovie would promote the company with short sales pitches prior to giving the products away: "The Statesmen have been fortunate in being able to sing on radio and television for National Biscuit Company, because just as we try to represent the best in gospel singing, Nabisco represents the best in crackers and cookies. It's a wonderful partnership, dedicated to brightening your home with Christian songs."

Statesmen concerts throughout the South were part of a complete Nabisco merchandising campaign, including stage displays and distributing samples. Hovie kept the McKann-Erikson Agency informed of the quartet's concert schedule. If the Statesmen were appearing in a city where Nabisco was sponsoring their TV show in that market, a Nabisco distributor would decorate the stage with saltines and cookies which the quartet would give away.

Eventually, the programs were seen on about 150 television stations in markets throughout the South. Hovie recalls that stations in Texas, Louisiana, Mississippi, Alabama, Georgia, Florida, North and South Carolina, Virginia and West Virginia, along with one or two northern states aired the shows. The night on which the shows were broadcast varied from city to city.

"This gave us quite an edge, not only in publicity," Hovie observes. "We were being heard and seen in markets where we had not played. That generated more dates for us in those areas, and it gave us a little bit more prestige to have a national sponsor. It put us in a very enviable class in gospel music. God has been good through all of this. It happened through His mercy and His goodness, and through His help and motivation. I give the Lord the credit for all of it."

Controversy

When the Statesmen walked into the RCA studios in Nashville on January 18, 1955, they had no way of knowing that this recording session would trigger a wave of controversy that would be a source of both aggravation and amusement to them in the coming months. Producer Steve Sholes hired a top-notch group of session men for the four songs on the recording schedule. They included Chet "Mr. Guitar" Atkins, Harold Bradley on rhythm guitar and banjo, Ernie Newton on stand-up bass and Farris Coursey on drums to team with Hovie Lister's piano accompaniment. One other instrument, trumpet, would be required for a couple of the up-tempo songs, and to give the other two songs a New Orleans jazz flavor. Karl Garvin got the call to provide the brass part on some of the most unique recordings the Statesmen ever committed to tape.

Two of the songs the quartet recorded with their instrumental ensemble that day were "The Bible Told Me So" and "I'm Climbing Higher and Higher (And I Won't Come Down)," songs that eventually would be favorites among their fans. The other songs were "Headin' Home" and "Poor Old Adam." Both were released together on a single a few weeks later and provided one of the most interesting episodes in the quartet's career. The bluesy songs were reminiscent of Dixieland jazz—"stripping music" is what one preacher called it.

When the record was released, gospel deejays had a field day. Warren Roberts, who served as emcee and promoter of some all-night sings around Atlanta, also had a gospel music radio show in the city at the time. On one of his broadcasts he played "Headin' Home" on the air and then, with his microphone turned on, broke the record on the air to let the radio audience hear what he had done. "I'll never play that again!" he declared.

The Statesmen were appearing in Birmingham for a concert shortly after "Headin' Home" was released when a deejay on a radio station there broke his copy of the record on the air. According to Jake, the deejay then "gave a few remarks along with it that weren't too complimentary." Some of the deejays may have gone through a copycat syndrome. "We always had a record breaking going on somewhere," Jake says, laughing. He feels the controversy surrounding the record-breaking incidents actually brought a lot of attention to the Statesmen.

"My feeling is it helped," he says. "Because a lot of people would say, 'Well, those worldly characters, we want to go see if they're really all this bad, you know. What really makes them tick.' I think the curiosity after all those things happened was beneficial. We had another song called 'Poor Old Adam.' It didn't get that many plays because it wasn't really all that good a song, but it was so different that we had a few records broken on that one, too."

The Statesmen didn't go out of their way to find songs that were off the wall in Christian circles. "But anything that came our way we'd try it," Jake says. "On the Nabisco shows, we didn't show the band but we had a nine-piece band on that show. People loved it but they didn't see it. That show sounded like our records. And the people loved the sound but they didn't know what it was. We never took the band on the road with us."

Several songs they recorded over the next few years were targeted for the popular music market by RCA, songs like "Light of His Love (Gonna Open Up All of My Doors)," "I'm Going to Walk With My Friend Jesus," and "Up Above My Head."

"Steve Sholes brought us 'Gonna Open Up All of My Doors'," says Hovie. "He said he thought he could get the pop stations to play it, and they did. And it was a good recording."

Other controversy surrounded the gospel music industry. A Birmingham church columnist wrote: "They've simply jazzed up religious songs to be-bop rhythms for a fast buck."

A writer for the Moody Institute's *Moody Monthly* also got in on the act.

"*Moody Monthly* did an article on the Statesmen and really put them down pretty bad," recalls Bill Gaither. "It even called them a sideshow."

"I have nothing but great respect for the Moody Institute," says Hovie, "Somebody from that organization had been to our concerts in Chicago. I don't mean to sound egotistical or to be bragging, but Chicago was just our town. When we went there for a concert, I don't care who else was on the program, the audience was pretty much our audience. They were most receptive, a very outgoing audience, very vocal in their applause. It mattered not if we were doing something fast, they'd do that. If I wanted to get serious with them and do a little bit of exorting, they were in for that."

A short time after the article was published by the Moody Press, the Statesmen appeared in concert in the Windy City. A fan brought Hovie a copy of the article, and before the concert started he had a chance to briefly read it through. Later, during the quartet's performance, the crowd was again in the palm of Hovie's hand. The Statesmen were having a good time. Near the end of the concert, Hovie quieted the crowd and said: "You know, since the last time we were here, a certain magazine had an article that said the Statesmen Quartet were nothing but a sideshow. Let me tell you something. When Hovie Lister and the Statesmen come to town it ain't no sideshow. We're the **main attraction!**"

The thousands of gospel music supporters crowded into Medina Temple that night jumped to their feet en masse, erupting in a tremendous ovation of support. Through all of the controversy, Statesmen fans had remained Statesmen fans. They were loyal and they loved their group. Any kind of attack on the quartet was an attack on something the fans prized and held in high respect.

Amid the controversy, the quartet flew to New York to record a song for a motion picture soundtrack. On March 30, 1955, they recorded "A Man Called Peter," title song of the 20th Century Fox picture about renowned U.S. Senate chaplain Peter Marshall. Richard Todd played the title role in the picture, supported by Jean Peters playing Marshall's wife Catherine. The Statesmen returned to New York in April to sing for the film's premiere.

At the New York World Premiere of the motion picture "A Man Called Peter," the Statesmen presented the film's star, actor Richard Todd, with a copy of their RCA Victor recording of the film's title song. The Statesmen were guests of Twentieth Century Fox and sang at the Premier.

During this period, the Statesmen also became good fodder for sermon material, Jake recalls. "We've had them to use us for a text back in those days." A year later, the rock and roll phenomenon took preachers' minds off the Statesmen. A truck driver with sideburns was giving them fits down in Memphis.

On July 4, 1955, the Blackwood/Statesmen team traveled to Texas for an engagement with promoter W.B. Nowlen, a concert that would feature secular artists, including Elvis Presley, on the same program with the two quartets. By mid-1955, Elvis had become hot entertainment property on the strength of weekly appearances on the Louisiana Hayride, his unconventional stage presence, and strong record sales predominantly in the South. Several major record companies were competing in a bidding war to buy his recording contract from Sun Records in Memphis. His latest record, "Baby, Let's Play House," was about to become his first single to hit the national best-seller charts.

At this holiday appearance, Elvis knew the Texans would be expecting to hear his recent hits, such as "That's All Right, Mama," "Blue Moon of Kentucky," "Good Rockin' Tonight," "I'm Left, You're Right, She's Gone" and "Baby, Let's Play House." But, when he found out who else was on the

program, his upbringing led him to feel it wouldn't be appropriate to perform his usual show on the same bill as his old friends the Statesmen and Blackwoods. James Blackwood recalls the event:

"Nowlen every year on the Fourth of July had an annual singing out in a pasture, actually, called Hodges Park, down in DeLeon, Texas. Elvis came down there that day in a pink Cadillac. He didn't know we were going to be there and we didn't know he was going to be there. We had bought our first bus in May of 1955. Being outdoors in a park it was pretty warm. We had air-conditioning on the bus and Elvis came on the bus and stayed with us when he wasn't performing that day. I remember he said he wasn't going to sing anything but gospel songs that day."

And he kept his word.

For years after he had become a major attraction in the popular music field, Elvis and his entourage would attend the all-night sings at Ellis Auditorium in Memphis—sometimes anonymously, sometimes he would be brought onstage and introduced to the audience. Elvis & Co. always sat in the wings out of view of the crowd but in view of the singers onstage.

"One night he came in, and we were onstage," recalls Hovie. "I was sitting with the piano facing backstage, with the audience on my right. Well, I was facing Elvis, so he came in and said, 'Where No One Stands Alone.' We had about five minutes left in our time, and I was getting ready for my finale, something that would stir the crowd. Every time he would say, 'Where No One Stands Alone' and 'How Long Has It Been?' I could read his lips, but I would just shake him off—like a pitcher does a catcher—and go on. We did 'Get Away Jordan,' which was our sugarstick, and when we got through everybody onstage was taking a bow and we were just tearing that place up. We were bent over bowing, and we couldn't see what was going on, just hearing the crowd applaud. I thought, 'My word, we made a hit tonight!' All of a sudden I felt a hand on my shoulder. I turned around, and it was Elvis. He turned to me and said, 'Tell Jake to leave the stage. We are going to do "How Long Has It Been?" and "Where No One Stands Alone." ' So he sang those two songs, and it absolutely tore up the audience. It was tremendous. They were on their feet the whole time he sang both songs."

Elvis Presley singing with the Statesmen in 1956 at Ellis Auditorium in Memphis.

11

Faith Unlocks the Door

National Quartet Convention

One of the first joint business ventures undertaken by the Blackwood Brothers and Statesmen germinated in the mind of Blackwood bass singer J.D. Sumner and came to fruition in October 1957 as the National Quartet Convention. For years J.D. had dreamed of bringing all of the top gospel quartets in the nation together in one location for a series of major concerts and fellowship. He recalled the fellowship he had enjoyed in the camp meetings he had attended as a boy in Florida, where he would enjoy getting together with people he hadn't seen all year. All the great preachers and singers would be there, including some of the great quartets of the day. He envisioned the same type of gathering on a national scale for quartets and their fans.

Singing conventions had long been a mainstay in gospel music circles. Southerners for years had enjoyed county-wide singing conventions, statewide singing conventions, even tri-state singing conventions—all interdenominational in scope. There had even been some gatherings billed as national singing conventions. None of these, however, had ever brought together all of the top quartets in a single event.

To no avail, Sumner had first pitched the idea to his fellow Sunshine Boys while singing with that quartet. Promoter Wally Fowler seriously considered Sumner's idea, but apparently felt it would be too expensive a risk to take. After joining the Blackwood Brothers, J.D. found an attentive ear in James Blackwood.

The plan later was outlined by Blackwood in the book **ABOVE ALL**:

"For the people who loved gospel singing it would offer

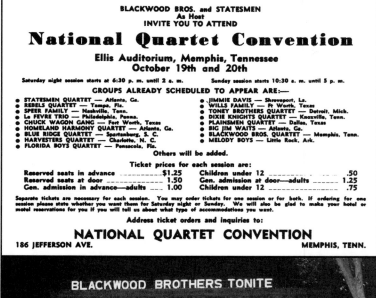

Ellis Auditorium in Memphis, site of the first National Quartet Convention, and numerous concerts hosted by the Blackwood Brothers Quartet.

the great pleasure of seeing, hearing, and meeting with their favorite quartets, as well as making the acquaintance of new quartets from all over the nation, and in a much greater number and variety than is possible on the usual concert program. To the promoters of gospel singing, throughout the nation, it would be an opportunity to make themselves acquainted with new talent, as well as getting together with all quartet managers of their choice to arrange in advance a good part of their next year's concert schedule. And, most of all, for the gospel singers it would be an inspiring time of Christian fellowship. A time for assistance. A time for exchange of ideas. A time for renewal of incentive for the year ahead."

The Blackwoods organized the first Convention, held in Memphis and attended by more than 10,000 fans. The total cost to stage the event was $15,000, including $4,000 to rent Ellis Auditorium for three days. But the Blackwoods broke even and J.D. Sumner was encouraged. As stated in the souvenir program of the 1969 National Quartet Convention, "He solicited the aid and support of James Blackwood of the Blackwood Brothers and Hovie Lister of the Statesmen Quartet to join forces with him to promote and use their influence to insure the future success of the Convention."

For years the Convention concluded with a Sunday morning service featuring Rev. Hovie Lister preaching at his Sunday best.

The first two Conventions were held in Memphis. Then, feeling that moving the event to different cities would help increase interest in gospel music, the promoters relocated the Convention to other cities. But attendance dropped off in Birmingham and Atlanta, and the Convention returned to Memphis in 1960 where it would stay for the next 11 years. By the mid-1960s, attendance was more than 25,000 and the event grew to be a week-long affair. From 1971-1993, the National Quartet Convention was held annually in Nashville, before moving to Louisville, Kentucky in 1994.

They Put Rhythm In Religion

By the mid-1950s, the national media had begun to take notice of the post-war music boom in gospel quartet circles. Appearances by the Blackwood Brothers, Statesmen and Swanee River Boys on Arthur Godfrey's Talent Scouts on nationwide CBS television had introduced millions to quartet music. Dave Garroway had featured quartet music on his NBC-TV show. The Nabisco television programs had brought the Statesmen into thousands of living rooms within signal strength of 150 television markets across the country.

As early as November 7, 1949, *Time* had already recognized this force that was moving through the South. The magazine reported the existence of a prospering "gospel Tin Pan Alley," stating that the successful Stamps-Baxter Music & Publishing Co., Inc., was publishing Christian music to the tune of $300,000 worth of business annually.

In its October 11, 1954, issue, *Time* told the nation that in the Deep South, "a profitable but unsung musical monster is flourishing." The monster, the magazine said, "takes the form of regular shows in Southern cities, featuring vocal quartets and attended by capacity crowds who come to be entertained and, occasionally, converted."

The article offered a review of a concert held a week previously in Atlanta's Municipal Auditorium. According to the magazine, all 5,200 seats of the auditorium had been sold out, and 1,300 others bought tickets to stand in the auditorium and enjoy the singing, which was described as "swinging from rowdy boogies to fervent waltzes, all in praise of the Lord."

Time stated that at the time about a dozen gospel groups were on the road full time, "roving the countryside, singing about 250 engagements a year. Top quartets get about $400 an appearance, for an annual gross of about $20,000 a man."

In a story titled "They Put Rhythm In Religion," *Saturday Evening Post* offered a four-page review of another Atlanta concert in its June 23, 1956, issue. "Where else would you find 5,000 sober people so happy on a Saturday night?" the concert promoter asked Furman Bisher, the *Post* writer. Bisher wrote that the audience responded to the quartets "in such a manner that recalled the days when the bobby-soxers of yesteryear discovered Frank Sinatra."

"Gospel-sing enthusiasts request only that their favorites gather around a piano and a microphone and fill their ears with the reassuring words and music of 'Get Away Jordan,' or 'I'm

Climbing Higher and Higher,' or 'When You Travel All Alone,' or another of the hits of the sawdust circuit."

According to Bisher, "it is perfectly proper to call this type of gospel singing a business." The article stated that gospel quartet singing drew "mingled reactions" from most churches, and that "most churchmen regard gospel singing in this commercial dress with disfavor."

In defense of gospel singing, however, Bisher offered comments by Hovie Lister: "The devil's got his kind of entertainment. We've got ours. They criticize me, say I'm too lively for religion, but I get results. That's what counts. God didn't intend for religion to wear a long face. It's supposed to make people happy. I don't think anybody ever found anything wrong with the good old hearty shouting of a man or woman filled with the spirit of the Lord at a revival meeting. That's how we sing. We give them the spirit."

Bisher referred to the Statesmen as "the hottest number in this business today," stating "the boom is on for them now. The Statesmen are typical of the prosperity that has struck the top gospel-singing groups. They travel in an air-conditioned limousine equipped with seat belts, individual radiophones and room to sleep three at a time. They say they live in the car more than they live at home and therefore it must offer all the comforts of home."

Packed houses for all-night sings were common in the 1950s. On this night, folding chairs have been placed onstage to accomodate the overflow. Doy is at the piano, while (l-r) Jake, Denver (behind Jake), Hovie and Chief deliver the crowd favorite "Get Away Jordan." Hovie always had a bad hair day after "Get Away Jordan."

Bisher closed his article thusly: "Somebody said, 'Everybody loves a quartet.' He had never been to a gospel sing. There they worship a quartet."

Collier's ran a feature on quartet music in 1955, and ran a followup photo of the Statesmen on the "Letters to the Editor" page in its November 11, 1955 issue. *Pageant*, in May, 1956, ran a feature titled "Biggest Hit in Dixie: Rock 'N' Religion." *Look* and *Life* offered similar articles about gospel music in the 1950s. When *Life* offered a feature on Hovie, it ran a photo of the Statesmen.

"Years ago," recalls Jake, "if you ever got your name in *Life* magazine, you had arrived. *Life* came down to Mount Zion Church and did an article on Hovie and they had a picture of the quartet in there. It had all the names under it, and when you got to my name it said, 'Jade Hers.' Crump never called me anything but 'Jade' the rest of his life."

Glory, Glory Clear the Road

Through the end of 1956, RCA Victor had issued eleven single releases by Hovie Lister and the Statesmen Quartet. Buoyed by the sales of these recordings, Steve Sholes began to schedule the quartet more frequently into the company's Nashville recording facilities to begin work in earnest toward building material for a long-playing album. The quartet recorded 19 songs between May 29 and September 7. Eleven of these selections were compiled for the album release. The remaining eight songs were released on singles over succeeding weeks.

On May 29, the Statesmen recorded five songs during a three hour session, accompanied by sidemen Chet Atkins on electric guitar, Ernie Newton on stand-up bass and Marvin Hughes on organ. The session concluded with "My Journey's End," a song that remains one of Jake's favorite Statesmen recordings to this day. The quartet had been singing the song for some time. It was written by Ted Brooks in the style of an old spiritual. One line in the song—"the voices keep a-hummin' to the songs of Old Black Joe"—troubled Steve Sholes and other RCA execs.

"That's when integration was coming around," Jake remembers, "and they thought we shouldn't say that. It was their idea that we sing 'the songs I used to know' instead of 'the songs of Old Black Joe.' We aim to please."

Jake recalls a slight glitch that developed when the Statesmen first began to record for RCA. The studio session men "read" the number system of music and chord notation that is standard among instrumentalists and backup vocalists that frequently work recording sessions in Nashville and other cities. "They brought us these charts with all these numbers written all over it," Jake says. "I went to Chet Atkins and I said, 'Mr. Chet, we don't know this number system.' He said, 'Just wing it!' After that we had some long rehearsals."

The quartet returned to the studio on July 7 with organist John Gordy, guitarist Atkins and bassist Newton to record four songs, three of which—"Guide My Feet," "My God Is Real," and "Hide Me, Rock of Ages"—were targeted for the album. The fourth, "How Long Has It Been," was released as a single. When writer Mosie Lister first presented "How Long Has It Been" to the Statesmen, the song received less than favorable response.

"I wrote it in probably a little more than 10 minutes," Mosie remembers, "and I showed it to the Statesmen and they really didn't like it. I think it was Jake who said, 'I think you can do better than this.' But I changed 'How Long Has It Been' very little."

Whether or not they liked it at first, the song became one of the most popular Mosie Lister tunes, for the Statesmen and numerous singers in churches all across America. In Mosie's vast songwriting experience he feels "the ideas that come very fast, that are more or less spontaneous, seem to work better. I think they flow out of the subconscious. The ones that I've labored over for weeks and weeks have a tendency to get kind of mechanical because your deliberate mind labors over it, and sometimes rather than to use your first impulse that may be the best, you keep looking at it and keep changing it and sometimes those changes are not very good."

After all these years, the Statesmen recording of "How Long Has It Been" is the one above all other songs he wrote for them of which Mosie is most proud. "They sang that so well," he says.

You can be sure the fellows are singing an up-tempo number here. The audience is likely enjoying a strong bass lead, as Chief appears to in command of the microphone.

While "How Long Has It Been" did not appear on the first Statesmen album, another Mosie Lister composition, "I Wonder What My New Address Will Be," was included. The arrangement, featuring one of the most sparkling performances of Irish tenor Denver Crumpler's brilliant career, was among six selections recorded on July 25 during a 4 1/2-hour session. Destined among these to appear on the album were "He's Everywhere," "Lord, I Want To Go To Heaven," and "Led Out of Bondage." The latter, a signature song of the Big Chief, had appeared on an earlier Capitol recording by the group. "Lord, I Want To Go To Heaven" was a 1951 collaboration of the Chief and Mosie Lister. It was the first composition by Wetherington to be recorded by the quartet. There would be many more in the years to come, as the Chief was just coming into his own as a songwriter. Harold Bradley provided the electric guitar accompaniment on this session in lieu of Atkins, while Gordy and Newton were back on organ and bass respectively.

The final session to compile songs for the album occurred on September 7, with Gordy, Newton and Atkins again providing instrumental support. Of course, all of the selections featured the piano accompaniment of the capable Hovie Lister. It was an upbeat session because the previously-recorded material which had been targeted for the album was short on fast-paced numbers. That day the group recorded "Glory, Glory, Clear the Road," which became the opening song of the album; "One of These Mornings," and "I Know It Was the Lord." All three displayed the Statesmen's trademark high-energy style of singing.

To complete the album, Sholes selected a song from one of the quartet's first sessions with RCA. Recorded on September 7, 1954, "Everybody Will Be Happy Over There" was another up-tempo number that featured bass man Wetherington on the choruses.

The album (LPM 1411), entitled "The Statesmen Quartet With Hovie Lister," was released early in 1957 to the joy of Statesmen fans everywhere. It remains a favorite of Jake's to this day.

"I guess the first one is the one that I play more than any other—the first RCA Victor album," he says.

Faith Music Company

As Big Chief, and eventually Doy Ott, became more prolific at writing songs Jake hit upon the idea of forming a music company to publish songs written by the group members, plus other unpublished material that came their way. Struggling young songwriters looking to establish themselves in the growing world of gospel music would often present their new material to the top quartets to consider for future recording projects. The Statesmen formed Faith Music Company and eventually purchased other music companies as well. These were the Lee Roy Abernathy Music Co., J.M. Henson Music Co., and Vep Ellis Music Co., and included the vast repertoire of compositions by the namesakes of those music companies. Whenever groups or other singers recorded the music of these companies, the Statesmen earned royalties as well as the songwriters.

Eventually most of the Statesmen would write songs for Faith Music Company. Chief was the most prolific writer in the quartet, although Doy and Hovie contributed some excellent material through the years. In fact, the Statesmen recorded two of Doy's songs in 1957, "Stop, Look and Listen for the Lord" and "When My Master Walks With Me."

Among other writers published by Faith Music Company were Henkle Little, who wrote "Sorry, I Never Knew You" and "Closer To Thee," among others; "Smiling" Joe Roper, original pianist for the Blackwood Brothers who later tickled the ivories for the Stamps and Prophets quartets, wrote "What A Happy Day," "I Like The Old Time Way," "Love So Divine," "Glory, Glory, Amen" and several other big songs for the company; Wally Varner, former Melody Masters cohort of Jake and Big Chief, who

contributed "Until Tomorrow" and "I've Got That Feeling"; Bob Prather, who wrote "Get Thee Behind Me, Satan"; Eldridge Fox, writer of "What Love"; and Don Butler, who contributed "This Great Love of Jesus," "You'd Better Run" and others. Even Warren Roberts, the Atlanta disc jockey who had broken the "Headin' Home" record on his radio show, wrote "God Bless You, Go With God" for Faith Music Co.

In time, managing the music companies became too much for the group members who hired Eldridge Fox to operate them. Fox later purchased the Kingsmen Quartet and continues to travel with them to this day. When Foxy left the Statesmen operation in the 1960s, the quartet hired Don Butler, formerly of the Sons of Song, as their office manager to direct the operation of their publishing interests.

Faith Unlocks the Door

The Statesmen went into the RCA recording facilities in Nashville on October 10, 1956, with Chet Atkins as producer and recorded two songs that were released together on a single shortly thereafter. "Prayer Is the Key to Heaven but Faith Unlocks the Door" was released as the "A" side of the record, backed by "My Heart Is A Chapel." "Faith Unlocks the Door" immediately became a hit on the strength of Jake's soulful delivery and a recitation by Big Chief in his inimitable style. The song has appeared on numerous records in the years since, including releases by later groups in which Jake sang: the Imperials, Masters V and in later appearances with a new version of the Statesmen. Hovie explains that every major star has at least one song with which he or she has become synonymous. "Faith Unlocks the Door," says Hovie, is Jake's "signature song."

"My Heart Is A Chapel" is also significant apart from its clever, upbeat arrangement which featured Denver Crumpler at his clear, ringing-tenor best with his three sidemen tossing in such backup vocals as "doo-pah, doo-pah-oh-wah-wah, doo-pah"; and "rat-tat-tat-tat-tat-tatta" in support.

"I think the word the Chief used once was 'raucous'," says Mosie Lister in describing the unusual style of singing and arranging the Statesmen used on songs such as "My Heart Is A Chapel." "They sounded as if it was sort of every man for himself but it was actually very, very controlled. They always knew exactly what they were doing but it had an almost rough and tumble sound on some of the songs that they did." Mosie should know. As arranger during many of those early years, he helped develop the classic Statesmen style. "We spent a lot of hours in a room, just me and them, experimenting with sounds and all kinds of gimics to find out what would work with their voices."

The recording was such a great up-tempo number that it served as the opening tune on the quartet's third album, released more than a year later. Perhaps it is fitting that "My Heart Is A Chapel" featuring Denver Crumpler was the song with which the Statesmen chose to conclude their session that afternoon. Although the Statesmen had no way of knowing, that October recording session proved to be last opportunity for the magic blend of the voices of Denver, Jake, Doy and Chief to be committed to vinyl. The four voices considered by many to be gospel quartet music's "perfect quartet" would never again be captured in a professional recording for posterity.

12

I Wonder What My New Address Will Be

Two significant developments in the lives of The Statesmen occurred in the closing days of 1956—group founder Hovie Lister took the matrimonial plunge on December 20, marrying a well-known Atlanta basketball and softball athlete, Ethel Abbott; and Jake Hess announced that he was leaving the Statesmen at the end of the year. Jake said at the time "he had felt for some time that he would be happier and could serve better if he could have more time at home with his family than is possible with a traveling quartet," wrote E.O. Batson in his periodical *Gospel Singing World*. Jake at the same time announced plans to open a piano store in Avondale Estates, Georgia. He planned to continue singing, making appearances as a soloist in churches and revivals.

To replace Jake, the Statesmen called a young man by the name of Les Roberson to handle the lead vocals. He had been singing baritone with the Oak Ridge Quartet for much of 1956. Cat Freeman, who had been singing tenor with the Oak Ridge, had recommended Roberson when he heard of Jake's plans to leave the road. Roberson had previously worked with the Weatherford Quartet, singing with George Younce, later of the Cathedral Quartet.

Despite leaving the Statesmen, Jake remained quite busy in quartet circles. He recorded a single featuring two Mosie Lister songs—"Then I Met the Master" and "Walk on the Water, Peter." He made a number of appearances in Alabama, Tennessee and Kentucky, backed by Connor Hall and the Homeland Harmony Quartet. Members of Homeland Harmony at the time included Hall, Tommy Rainer, James McCoy, Rex Nelon and pianist Liverly Freeman. Jake also made the rounds of several Wally Fowler concerts in the South, including Wally's monthly stops at the Ryman Auditorium in Nashville. At several of these appearances the Sunshine Boys—Ace Richmond, Eddie Wallace, Fred Daniel and Burl Strebel provided backup vocals. The Sunshine Boys had worked with Louisiana Governor Jimmie Davis and country legend Red Foley on numerous occasions previously.

The Jake Hess Piano House opened with a fanfare on Saturday, January 5, 1957. A number of quartets were in town to appear that night in a concert at the Atlanta Municipal Auditorium. Decatur broadcaster Warren Roberts, of WEAS radio, gave Jake's grand opening a big boost by broadcasting his regular Saturday afternoon show, "Gospel Homecoming," from the porch of the Piano House. Among the groups appearing at the Piano House that Saturday were the Blackwood Brothers, Homeland Harmony, the Sunshine Boys, the Songmasters, the Harmoneers, and even the Statesmen—all of whom sang on the live broadcast. Fans came from all over the Atlanta area, crowding every room of the store and filling every available parking space in the neighborhood.

The Statesmen released a couple of singles early in 1957, which ultimately would be their only commercial recordings with Les Roberson in the lineup. On one record were the songs "Living With Jesus" and "These Are the Things That Matter." The other featured Big Chief on the rhythmic "I Wanna Know," backed with one of Denver Crumpler's signature songs "My Heavenly Father Watches Over Me."

A Voice As Big As Stone Mountain

The Statesmen, like many other great quartets of the 1950s, were frequent attractions at Wally Fowler's popular all-night sings at Nashville's Ryman Auditorium, home of the Grand Ole Opry. By early 1949—soon after his successful all-night sing debut of November 5, 1948—Wally had begun promoting gospel concerts at the Ryman on a monthly basis. Quartet fans could count on an all-night sing to be held the first Friday of every month at the Ryman. And if they were unable to attend in person, not to worry. An hour of the concert, from 11 p.m. to midnight, was broadcast live on powerful WSM radio.

Hovie recalls that, on the weekends when the Statesmen were scheduled for Fowler's concerts at the Ryman, the quartet would usually schedule a concert on Thursday night in Alabama. "Then we would drive on in to Nashville. We'd get there about 2 o'clock in the morning." There was an all-night cafeteria across the street from the hotel where the Statesmen stayed. Often, after they had checked into their rooms, the guys would slip over to the cafeteria for a snack before turning in. Early on one of those Friday mornings in 1956, the quartet had a real scare.

"It was the beginning of strawberry season," Hovie recalls. "Denver ate a big bowl of strawberries and went to bed. Something didn't sit well. He had a real bout with vomiting and almost went into a coma" there in the hotel. "We took him to the hospital in Nashville and they said he didn't ever need to go through a lot of vomiting because it was bad on his blood veins." A diabetic, Hovie explains, Denver had taken insulin since the age of nine. The strain on his heart and blood vessels caused by prolonged vomiting could be dangerous.

It had not been Crump's first scare of this nature. Mrs. Vernon Hyles recalled another incident which occurred while Denver and the Rangers Quartet were working in Charlotte, North Carolina. "In 1943, Vernon and Denver were called up for examination for the Army. Both were put in 4F—Vernon because of his eyesight, and Denver because of diabetes... Just a few months later Denver was rushed to the hospital in a diabetic coma from which we all feared he would never revive. It was then that we all learned how much that this group of men meant to each other. The other three stood by every minute and did everything they could to help."

Gospel quartet fans who tuned in the WSM broadcast segment of Wally Fowler's All-Night Sing from Nashville's Ryman Auditorium on March 1, 1957 were treated to the crystal clear tones of Denver's inimitable Irish tenor as the Statesmen featured their elder "statesman" on one of his signature songs, "My Heavenly Father Watches Over Me." No one could have guessed it would be Crump's final national broadcast.

In mid-March of 1957, the Statesmen worked a weeklong revival at the large Baptist Temple in Detroit, taking leave of the meeting for appearances in Evansville and Indianapolis, Indiana on March 15 and 16. They returned to Detroit for the conclusion of the Baptist Temple revival on Sunday, March 17—one of the rare occasions that Pastor Hovie missed services at Mount Zion Baptist Church in Georgia. Driving through the night, the Statesmen returned home to Atlanta early on Monday, March 18. They were looking forward to a few days of relaxation with their families. Denver was anxious to get home to Decatur where his home church, Glenwood Hills Baptist, was beginning a week of revival services. He was very active in his home church, serving as Chairman of the Board of Trustees. The church had just completed an expansion project, having built a new auditorium.

"By the way, guys," Denver said as the quartet motored south to Atlanta, "we're having revival at my church and since we have to go back out on the road Thursday night of this week, would you guys be willing to come out to my church Wednesday night and sing?"

"Of course," Hovie said, "we'll be glad to." Chief, Doy and Les cheerily agreed. They knew Denver was proud of his church and his new home and wanted to show them off to the quartet. He was also proud of the Statesmen and was anxious to share their ministry with the congregation that had become like family in the four years the Crumplers had been in Decatur.

"Denver had just moved into a new home, a new house," says Hovie, "and I think it was the first house he had ever owned. So we went to his church that Wednesday night and sang. He seemed to be in perfect condition and sang beautifully."

The quartet was due to leave at 11 o'clock the next morning, Thursday, March 21, for an evening concert in Columbus, Mississippi.

"At about nine o'clock," Hovie recalls, "I had a call from Frankie, Denver's wife, stating that he had been ill the night before and had been vomiting. That was something that Denver had been warned against by the doctors. They said he should seek immediate help if he began to vomit on a regular basis, because of the fact that he had taken insulin for so long that his blood veins were so thin. They were afraid of that sort of thing."

"I'm afraid Denver's not going to be able to leave at 11 o'clock," Frankie said, unable to mask the fear in her voice.

"What's the matter?"

"Well, he was up all night vomiting. I can't get him to speak to me, I think he's in a coma."

"Have you called a doctor?"

"No," she said.

"Well, I'll call the ambulance to come and get him and bring him to Emory University Hospital," Hovie told his friend's distraught wife. "I'll meet you at the hospital."

Hovie and his wife, Ethel, got in the car and rushed over to the hospital, located in downtown Atlanta. The ambulance carrying Denver, his wife, and the paramedics arrived shortly.

"I was standing there when the ambulance pulled up," says Hovie. "They took him out of the ambulance to take him in the clinic. I knew that he was either in a coma or he was already dead."

As the Listers gathered Frankie in their arms, the paramedics rushed past, wheeling Denver to a trauma room.

"They worked with him about 30 to 45 minutes," Hovie remembers, "and came out and said he was dead."

Husband, father of three, and a great Christian man loved by millions of gospel music fans nationwide, Denver Crumpler was only 44. Pathologists performed an autopsy and determined he had died of a massive heart attack. "They said his heart was just like it had exploded," Hovie recalls.

The Listers spent the next several minutes consoling the widow, calling her pastor and helping with the pre-planning for funeral arrangements. Hovie then made a series of phone calls with the news that would send a shock wave throughout the gospel quartet world. First, he notified Chief, Doy and Les of the tragic news and informed them that their schedule was suspended for a few days. Next, he called pastors and promoters to cancel or postpone the engagements for which they had been scheduled that weekend. He called Jake, then attempted to track down his friends the Blackwood Brothers, who were preparing for a concert that evening in Decatur, Illinois.

The news was a severe blow to Jake. Although he was no longer traveling with the Statesmen in the weeks preceding Denver's death, he and Crump had managed to get together for a round of golf on several mornings when the Statesmen had been in town. "I got a call early that morning," Jake says. "In fact, Denver and I were supposed to play golf that week sometime. I didn't know they were leaving that early that day. We'd get up early a lot of mornings, the phone would ring and it would be Denver ready to go play golf."

When the news of Denver's untimely passing reached James Blackwood he immediately recalled how supportive his friends the Statesmen had been in the Blackwoods' airplane tragedy in 1954. It was time to return the debt of kindness. The Statesmen and Denver's family were now in need of the Blackwood Brothers' strength and friendship.

"When Denver Crumpler died," he recalls, "Hovie called our office in Memphis and found out where we were and called up there and got ahold of us. We gave the concert that night and then I remember J.D. drove all the way from Decatur, Illinois to Memphis, and drove at a breakneck speed, actually. I remember how fast he drove all the way in order for us to get back to Memphis in time to catch a plane and fly to Atlanta. So we flew to Atlanta and were at Denver's funeral service there. Then Denver was buried out in Magnolia, Arkansas, and my wife and I drove from Memphis out there for the burial ceremony."

"We, of course, didn't sing until after his funeral," Hovie says. "We called Cat Freeman again.

Cat Freeman came back with the group and we went to Denver's funeral. They had a big funeral in Denver's church in Decatur, Georgia. That was a very unusual funeral. Everybody that was anybody in gospel music east of the Mississippi, I think, was there. Rev. Vep Ellis, the great songwriter and singer, sang and several groups sang. The church was overflowing. Then, of course, we took his body out to his hometown of Magnolia, Arkansas, and his home church he grew up in out there in Arkansas. There was another huge crowd, and everybody west of the Mississippi in gospel music was there."

Services were held at the Village Methodist Church, in Village, Arkansas, a few miles from Magnolia. Denver's earthly remains were laid to rest in the Crumpler family plot in the Village cemetery. Those who knew him best know his spirit is rejoicing in the presence of the Almighty. He lives on in the hearts of those heard him sing, and especially those who lived and worked with him. Sound recordings preserve his life's work as priceless treasures to enjoy again and again.

"In his chosen field there were two important things that made him stand out from so many of the rest," wrote E.O. Batson, Jr., in the April, 1957 issue of *Gospel Singing World*. "First there was his exceptional voice, a God given talent which he enriched with the sincerity that can only come from the heart. During the last few years that I knew him best, just to hear this man sing the words of the gospel story made you know that here was a man who knew his God and His promise of an everlasting life to those who believe in Him.

"There was another thing equally as important which Denver had," continued Batson. "This was his sincere love of his fellow man. His very closest friends can never remember a harsh word or a spiteful expression toward another. This quality so rare among all of us today made all who knew him call him their friend. The people who attended the concerts and heard him and all the singers he worked with felt the warm, understanding friendliness of this man."

"You'll never work with a more professional guy than Denver Crumpler," says Jake. "I've heard tenors say to Hovie, 'Don't feature me until we sing four or five songs to give me a chance to get warmed up,' but not Crump. You could sing anything, anytime, anywhere, and that would suit him just fine. He never complained about a key or singing a bunch of high songs one after another and he was never hoarse. It's hard to describe Crump. He stayed around backstage a lot of times, just talking to people, talking to stage hands or other groups. And when it came time for us to go on, he was always there."

"Each Statesmen tenor had a different delivery," observed the late Lee Roy Abernathy, who worked with scores of gospel music standouts as a vocal coach. "Crump didn't put the feeling in it; he had the ability. He sold ability like no one I ever saw. Denver could command respect because he had a voice as big as Stone Mountain." Most tenors, Abernathy added, dreaded following Denver after the Statesmen had been on stage, he had such an intimidating voice.

"Some people said he didn't blend, that his voice stood out," Hovie once told a writer for *The Singing News*, "but, boy, as far as I was concerned, his voice could stand out. What a great voice! He was one of the greatest tenors I've ever listened to. He was a trouper. He never complained. Denver Crumpler was a beautiful person who would do anything in the world for anybody! He was one of the most professional men who ever worked in gospel music."

When he was voted to the Gospel Music Association's Hall of Fame years later, his GMA biographical data stated: "Denver gave to gospel music dignity, the performance of a true professional, and one of the highest lyric tenor voices we have ever known. Among his greatest pleasures and contributions was encouraging and advising young people in the business. He was never too busy to visit with a youngster. He gave to gospel music all any man can give—his entire life."

Denver's passing wrote the end of an era for the Statesmen. Hovie's great dream from the beginning had been to have Denver Crumpler as tenor singer for the Statesmen. The superlative combination of Denver Crumpler, Jake Hess, Doy Ott and Big Chief, accompanied by Hovie Lister may well have been the best ever to proclaim the gospel, or any form of music for that matter, in song.

"This was, by all means, gospel music's greatest group of all time. No doubt about it," song evangelist Roy Pauley has written. Pauley, whose "In My Opinion" column is a regular feature in *The Singing News*, added: "And also one of our most unique groups in that they had every

single element or quality that you would want in a Gospel Quartet—rhythm, harmony, smoothness, and Hovie Lister at the piano who was magic at setting up their songs with his unorthodox MC work and his ability to keep a crowd on the edge of their seats. Their real uniqueness is attributed to their unbelievable arrangements which consisted of numerous key changes and modern harmony... There's never been a group like them, and there never will be."

"As far as I'm concerned," Brock Speer has said, "that was the best quartet that gospel quartet music has ever had, and I've heard them all since then. Now I didn't hear them all back before the Statesmen organized. There were a few then, some Vaughan quartets and some Stamps quartets, and some of them were very good. But since then I don't think any quartet has ever achieved the precision of singing that the Statesmen had. They had voices that fit together because they **made** them fit together. They rehearsed. They rehearsed—work, work, work— so all the words were spoken at the same time, so the blend was right, and I don't think there has ever been a quartet since then that sang as good."

Bob Terrell, in his celebrated book **The Music Men**, wrote: "There was nothing this quartet could not sing, no crowd it could not entertain. There was nothing it couldn't achieve.

"You see, when Hovie added Denver Crumpler to the Statesmen Quartet, he completed the first and only perfect quartet. There had never been one before; there has not been one since.

"The Statesmen had it all!"

When My Master Walks With Me

Since leaving the Statesmen in 1953, Cat Freeman had worked with several groups, most notably the Oak Ridge Quartet. He pulled two hitches with the Oak Ridge, singing with them briefly in late 1953-'54 and returning in 1956. The later version of that quartet featured Cat on tenor; Calvin Newton, lead; Les Roberson, baritone; Ron Page, bass; and Bobby Whitfield on piano. The quartet disbanded at the end of 1956, shortly before Roberson went to the Statesmen to sub for Jake Hess. Ron Page and Smitty Gatlin reorganized the Oak Ridge shortly thereafter.

He had also worked with Aycel Soward in the Church of God Quartet in Greenville, South Carolina; and teamed up with Jimmy and Brownie Jones, Bob Crews and former Melody Masters cohort Wally Varner in the Deep South Quartet for a while.

"Cat was just always moving. He was never content," remembers Vestal Goodman, Cat's younger sister. "If he found a group that was struggling and they didn't know their parts good, he'd want to go to that group and help them and teach them their parts, teach them music. He was a great teacher."

He also was still a clown. As the Statesmen were working most of their concerts with the

Blackwood Brothers, Cat and J.D. Sumner enjoyed bantering and pulling practical jokes on each other. One night the two groups were appearing in an old auditorium in south Georgia. Because of the lighting and the way the building was constructed, the singers on stage could only see that part of the audience which was seated directly in front of them. J.D. was in the middle of a comedy routine during the Blackwoods' set. When he would come to a part of the routine that was serious, someone under the balcony would fall out of his seat laughing. As this continued, the spectator was more the center of attraction than Sumner who was beginning to sweat on stage. The audience was laughing at the clown in the back of the auditorium more than it was the entertainer on stage. When Sumner reached a line in his routine that should have been funny, the prankster in the audience wouldn't crack a grin. The crowd began watching him as much as J.D. and if Sumner told a funny line and the clown in the back didn't laugh, the audience wouldn't either. When J.D. was serious, the prankster would break into a belly laugh, get out of his seat and walk around holding his stomach, haw-hawing all the while. The showoff was just out of J.D.'s line of vision thus far, but, finally, near the end of the skit, J.D recognized who it was that was stealing his thunder—Cat Freeman!

Later the two quartets were appearing in Oklahoma City. The Blackwoods began their stand in front of a big crowd. Midway through the first song someone in the back of the crowd yelled, "Cut down the bass mic!" James Blackwood turned to J.D., who always operated the P.A. set. "You'd better cut your mic down some," he said. After the second song the voice yelled again that the bass was still too loud. At this the quartet took some more volume off the bass end. After the third song the spectator yelled, "The bass is drowning everybody else!" Again James turned to Sumner: "Cut your mike down, J.D., you're too loud!" Again, the volume on J.D.'s mike went down. After four songs the voice yelled, "I can still hear the bass!" This time there was no mistaking the voice from the crowd—Cat Freeman strikes again!

Cat Freeman

"I left the dad-blamed stage and chased him all over that auditorium trying to catch him," J.D. recalls with a chuckle. "He was quite somebody! He would come down to the coffee shop at the Texas Hotel in Fort Worth and eat out of my plate. They had some good chipped beef and gravy on toast there and he would come down and just start eating out of my plate. I caught him eating breakfast one morning and I was gonna pay him back and eat out of his plate. Well, he spit in his plate, and I wasn't about to eat that. In Oklahoma City we were staying at the Skirvin Hotel. They had Bishop's Cafe across the street. I love fresh strawberries and cream and sugar. So I had a big bowl of strawberries, cream and sugar. Here he came. When he started eating my strawberries, I went ahead and spit in my strawberries like he had done. Well, that fool, he ate 'em anyway. He didn't stop!"

By this time Wally Varner had replaced Jackie Marshall as pianist for the Blackwood Brothers. He recalls a funny episode that occurred shortly after he joined the Blackwoods:

"One time we were down in Waycross, Georgia. We always played a ball field down there. Hovie was up doing his big thing with the Statesmen and he had one of these tear-jerking things going. Somebody dared J.D. to put on a ball cap backwards and roll his britches legs up and run all the bases on the ball field. Well, not only did he take the dare, not only did he roll his britches legs up and put his cap on backwards and run the bases, but people were eating it up, laughing and clapping. Cat used to do an act where he would run and just fall all to pieces. I don't know how to describe it. It was about the funniest thing you could ever look at. Well, about that time old Cat came out and started chasing J.D. around third base! I'm here to tell you, brother, he was a clown!"

"He was a very big clown," Vestal Goodman says. "He was a wonderful all-around guy!"

Not long after Denver's death, Les Roberson, a natural baritone, began to experience problems with his voice. According to Sumner, Roberson, in trying to cover the lead role for the Statesmen, was simply singing out of his range. And with the high-energy style of belting out their songs that the Statesmen were known for, Les eventually lost his voice. Soon after leaving the Statesmen in the spring of 1957, Roberson's gospel singing career essentially was over.

The Statesmen's syndicated television programs for Nabisco also ceased production following Denver's demise. The shows that had already been filmed continued to air for awhile. But Nabisco executives decided to conclude their sponsorship arrangement with the quartet. The reason, Jake believes, "was that we had become a different type quartet. We were no longer the Statesmen they had bought."

By June, the Statesmen were back in the groove. Jake returned, the quartet's sound was again beginning to gel, and RCA's Steve Sholes resumed scheduling them in the recording studio on a regular basis. Between June and the end of the year the Statesmen recorded 22 songs in six sessions. Several of these appeared on singles during the year. One of the singles was the title song of the motion picture "God Is My Partner" which they also sang at the film's premiere in New York.

After recording six more songs on January 8, 1958, Sholes selected 12 songs to appear on the quartet's second long-play album. These included "Wonderful is the Lord," written by Jay Greene; "It's a Wonderful Feeling," composed by Charles Matthews; "I Know He Heard My Prayer," a Vep Ellis composition; "The Gentle Stranger" and "If to Gain the World," more fine products of Mosie Lister. Mosie also arranged an old spiritual for the album—"Stand By Me," which, he says, "had a special line in it for Hovie with the other four voices singing behind him." Also included on the album were "Nicodemus," a spiritual-type song by Berni Barbour; "Ransomed Millions," written by singing funnyman Wendy Bagwell; Country Earl's "God Is My Shepherd," one of the first songs published by the Statesmen's Faith Music Company; "The Sea Walker," from the pen of Tim Spencer, who was one of the original Sons of the Pioneers; and "When My Master Walks With Me," by Doy Ott.

The Statesmen lineup following Denver's death (clockwise from top left): Cat Freeman, Les Roberson, Doy, Hovie and Big Chief.

The latter featured one of the finest examples of modern harmony of any arrangement the Statesmen, or any other quartet for that matter, ever sang. They performed it flawlessly. The song is arguably the best recording the Statesmen ever made. It is certainly one of Doy's best songwriting efforts.

Although the Melody Masters were singing modern harmony as early as the mid-1940s, the Statesmen became the quartet most identified with it.

In straightforward, four-part harmony, there are three notes in the triad chord, the "one," "three" and the "five." To add the fourth part, the quartet has to double one of the notes. Therefore, the bass singer doubles a "one."

In modern harmony, explains Hovie, "you're more or less inverting the parts. You're bringing the bass up and giving him a fourth part. It gives you a modern sound, so to speak, like the Manhattan Transfer. It gives the song a flair. It's so much different than do-mi-sol-do, or regular straightforward harmony."

"In the pop field," says Bill Gaither, "there were the Modernaires who, every time they started a song, if they had a one in the chord and the three and the five, they would put in the sixth, if you were just singing it straight. If they were moving to another chord, they might put in a diminished chord, which would mean that you would have a five and a three, but in the middle you would have a one sharp and a sixth sharp or a seventh flat. That meant nobody was doubling anybody's part."

Gaither says there are times when doubling the part gives the chord more muscle. When a vocal group adds that other part without doubling notes, it gives chords a more "hip," modern or contemporary feel.

"That kind of chord structure in the church probably would have sounded very worldly at the time. But it would just give the lyric more punch. And it set the Statesmen apart musically from other groups whose bass singers couldn't hear parts up that high. They could hear the low stuff but they couldn't hear a higher part and actually sing it. It was a matter of a good ear and the Big Chief had a wonderful ear that was far ahead of his time. He could hear those kind of things. That made their harmonics different."

There was a time when quartet people would be talking about a bass singer, one might ask, "Can he sing modern harmony?"

"What they meant was, 'Can he get up out of the bass range and put in the extra part?'," says Gaither, "and probably do it with more breath and airy tones than what we normally think typical of a bass singer—the big bullfrog bass voice, you know. Can he make it blend where you don't pick out his voice? Is it so good that he can sing it up that high and you don't hear the voice? Then he would be called a modern harmony bass singer."

Released by RCA Victor early in 1958, "The Statesmen Quartet Sings With Hovie Lister" (LPM-1605) is the only Statesmen album on which Cat Freeman appears on every song. There were, however, later RCA Camden albums which included a few selections featuring Cat. "The Statesmen Sings" album is a fine example of his ability to blend.

"Listen, when Cat Freeman wanted to sing you couldn't beat him," says Jake. "You never did know what day to book, because you never did know what day he wanted to sing. But when Cat settled down to sing he'd sing some of the prettiest, smooth harmony you'd ever heard. And then on the next song, he'd tear an audience apart just doing nothing but his funny business."

The Bible Told Me So

A short while after the release of the Statesmen's second album, RCA Victor issued a third album that proved very popular among fans of the late Denver Crumpler. The studio had a number of songs in its vault that had been released as singles during Denver's lifetime. Of these, Steve Sholes assembled the following for "The Bible Told Me So" (LPM- 1683): "Move That Mountain" and "If God Didn't Care," from the very first Statesmen recording session with RCA back in August, 1954; "Taller Than Trees," "In the Beginning" and "My Brother's Keeper," all recorded in January, 1955; "The Bible Told Me So" and "I'm Climbing Higher and Higher (and I Won't Come Down)," featuring the trumpet work of Karl Garvin from the same session that produced the controversial "Headin' Home"; from a May 1956 session came "Brand New Star," Stuart Hamblen's "Your First Day In Heaven," and a song written by Henry Slaughter, "No One But Jesus Knows"; and "My Heart Is A Chapel," from Denver's last recording session. Since all but one song on the album had been released previously on RCA singles, the album could easily be perceived as "Denver Crumpler and the Statesmen Quartet's Greatest Hits." The only exception was an August 1954 recording of Stuart Hamblen's "Known Only to Him" which had never been released, although the Statesmen had released an earlier recording of the song on their own custom label.

"Few singers are better qualified to re-create the words and spirit of the Good Book than are the Statesmen," stated the album's jacket notes. "Their zeal and inspiration are everywhere in evidence and it's truly inspiring to hear them... And when the Statesmen sing the title selection, 'The Bible Told Me So,' are there any among us who do not feel impelled to say 'Amen'?"

13

Rosie Rozell

Touring by Bus

The Statesmen limousine was flying down the paved country road in South Georgia at 75 miles per hour. James "Big Chief" Wetherington, slouching comfortably in the driver's seat with both hands resting on the lower half of the wheel, believed in wasting no time getting to his destination. Trailing the Statesmen limousine in a rented sedan were the Blackwood Brothers, aggravated with yet another breakdown of their old Aerocoach bus. Wally Varner, who had replaced Jack Marshall as pianist for the Blackwoods, was at the wheel of the Blackwood car. "Back in those years we traveled together," Varner recalls.

Suddenly, the speeding limousines popped over a small hill and the drivers found themselves rapidly bearing down upon a fork in the road. Chief, confused by the road signs, had split-seconds to determine which direction to take. Before he could make a decision the Statesmen limousine sped into a patch of loose gravel between the forks in the road. Chief slammed on the brakes sending the sedan spinning dizzily out of control. The limousine spun wildy, sending rocks flying in every direction. Before Chief could get it straightened out the car made several complete circles, then skidded into the lot of a gas station at the side of the road. The car finally screeched to a halt against the gas pumps. A startled service station attendant, stood transfixed in trembling terror scant inches from where the limousine stopped. Big Chief, unruffled, calmly climbed out of the car—not a hair out of place—and said casually to the attendant: "Fill 'er up, please!"

"Chief was a very cool, calm, laid-back guy," says Varner, laughing.

The Blackwood Brothers had resumed traveling by automobile after their tragic airplane crash in 1954. But in May of 1955, J.D. Sumner talked James into purchasing a bus. For a while, they were the laughingstock of the industry. At first, upkeep was expensive. Eventually, the quartet hired Bundy Brewster as driver. His first trip with the group was from Memphis to Tupelo, Mississippi. The Statesmen were working the same date and arrived at the auditorium ahead of the Blackwoods.

Hovie was standing in front of the auditorium when the Blackwood bus arrived. Sumner told the new driver to pull in front of the auditorium where it would be convenient for the quartet to unload equipment and records. The auditorium was equipped with a large canopy over the front of the building to protect concertgoers from the weather. Taxicab drivers could pull right up under the canopy and unload their passengers who could then enter the auditorium without getting wet.

But no one told Bundy Brewster there wasn't room to drive a bus under the awning.

Hovie saw what was about to unfold and ran wild-eyed to get away from the oncoming catastrophe. The bus slammed into the canopy, nearly rocking it from the facade of the building. The members of the quartet and Brewster, numb with embarrassment, filed in silence from the motorcoach. Sumner was the last to depart. He had to walk past Hovie Lister who was surveying the damage and "grinning like the cat who swallowed the canary," according to Sumner.

"Terrific bus driver you got there, John. Terrific!"

While the Blackwoods settled into the new routine of criss-crossing the country by bus, the Statesmen continued to drive their comfortable Cadillac limousine while pulling "Elmer" the trailer loaded with records, photos, songbooks, clothing and sound equipment. The cumbersome old bus didn't make good time in comparison to the Cadillac. Following concerts the two quartets would load up their respective vehicles and pull out for the next destination. By the time the Blackwoods would get the lumbering old bus out of town and get it wound up on the open highway, the Statesmen would be long gone. In a trip of 300-400 miles, the Statesmen would arrive about 45 minutes ahead of the Blackwoods. According to Sumner, Jake would check into the hotel, then stay up to wait for the Blackwoods to arrive.

"He'd put on a big show about how long they'd been there and how rested he was," Sumner told biographer Bob Terrell later. "When I came in, he'd be waving at me like he'd been there a day and a half."

J.D. frequently tried to convince the Statesmen they, too, needed a bus. But every conversation lapsed into jokes and ridicule. One night, after the Statesmen and Blackwoods had appeared at a concert in Little Rock, Arkansas, J.D. concocted an idea. He invited Jake to ride with the Blackwoods on their bus to the two groups' next engagement in Fort Worth, Texas. Jake protested. He didn't want to ride that contraption.

"I had been giving him a bad time about that bus and told him it wasn't practical," Jake recalls, "which I didn't think it was at that time."

But Sumner persisted. "I want to talk some business with you," he said.

"Man, I need to get some sleep," Jake protested. "We can talk tomorrow."

"No, I really need to talk some business with you," Sumner urged. "I want you to go on the bus and let's talk tonight."

Jake relented and soon the bus was lumbering out of Little Rock, headed for Fort Worth some 350 miles distant.

"When we got on the bus I put him in my big chair which was a recliner that made into a bed," says Sumner.

"Now go to sleep," he said to Jake, "I ain't got nothing to talk to you about. I just want you to see what a bus ride is."

There was little for Jake to do but sit back and enjoy the ride, for the Statesmen and their Cadillac were long gone. Jake quickly nodded off.

"He had me to ride from Little Rock in to Fort Worth and I slept all the way," says Jake. "I thought, 'Man! This is the life!' "

J.D. roused him when the bus pulled up in front of the Texas Hotel in downtown Fort Worth, incidentally, the same hotel where six years later John F. Kennedy would spend his last night before a tragic appointment with history in Dallas.

"I tried to get Hovie and the boys just as soon as we could to get a bus," Jake recalls. He found Hovie eating breakfast at a nearby grill. The two had a lengthy discussion, then found Sumner in the hotel lobby. Hovie came right to the point.

"Where can we get a bus?"

J.D. called the Greyhound office in Dallas. Company representatives quoted him a price of $5,000 each for a pair of used Greyhound Silversides coaches. The Statesmen and Blackwoods bought the two 37-passenger, diesel buses.

Back in Memphis, Sumner was assigned to customize the buses to provide traveling comfort for each group. Sumner was experienced in such matters, as he had refitted the Blackwoods' original Aerocoach. "I put springs and mattresses in there, not realizing that wouldn't work," he says. "We couldn't sleep on them because they'd bounce you all the way to the ceiling. So when we bought our Silversides, we had no time to fix it up" while in the process of a tour, "so I just took those four mattresses out of the Aerocoach and laid 'em on the floor in the Silversides— because we just had to ride in the bus empty—and they slept like a lamb! So I found out that you couldn't have spring mattresses in a bus, it had to be on a solid floor. And they slept just as good or better, you know."

Back in Memphis, J.D. began refitting the interiors of the two buses. The entire interior of each bus was removed. He ordered reclining chairs built to match the height of each man in the two quartets. These were installed in the forward section of each vehicle. A wall was installed to partition the forward seating area from the next compartment, which was the sleeping area.

Bunks with three-quarter inch plywood bottoms were added and fitted with six-inch airfoam mattresses. Elizabeth Wetherington made curtains which were fitted to each bunk to give its occupant privacy. The beds were similar to Pullman berths on a train. A wardrobe department to accomodate their many changes of clothing, a restroom and make-up department were installed on each bus. The two coaches were painted alike in bright gold with white tops and the appropriate group name painted in black on a gold banner across the silver side panels.

"I'll never forget, the buses cost $5,000 each to customize," recalls Sumner, "and man! To customize one today is $200,000!"

Even bus travel can wear on a person, especially during long trips. Traveling as the quartets do is not an easy life, although touring by bus provides many more comforts of home than the confines of an automobile, even a limousine. On harried trips the Statesmen would often miss meals, sometimes grabbing a sandwich on the run, whenever they could. Occasionally, they would miss sleep. Even today a quartet's schedule on the road is not one on which a nine-to-five working man could survive comfortably. Concerts often end long after midnight. Then comes packing the bus, and maybe catching a quick bite at a local restaurant (if there is time) before traveling to the city of the next appointed engagement. The quartet might arrive at their hotel by three or four in the morning, check in and sleep until late morning or noon before getting to the auditorium to set up equipment for the evening gig. Of necessity, quartet folks are night people. But, despite their marathon sessions of kidding the Blackwoods and their reluctance to make the step from limousines to buses, the Statesmen realized very quickly they had made the right move.

Being a quartet man meant not only working with the same people every day, but often living with them day and night. Where nine-to-five employment offered the opportunity for a person to walk away from his friends at work to spend several hours of relaxation and fellowship with his family at home, quartet work meant spending days, even weeks, on end with the same four people during a long tour. But, as Jake recalls, even in the years of cramped discomfort when

the group traveled by car, seldom did the members of the Statesmen let the long trips of seemingly endless miles wear their nerves to the breaking point.

"I guess it depends on what day you're talking about," says Jake. "Sometimes long trips would get on some of the guys' nerves more than they did others, but we didn't had too many bad experiences in the Statesmen. When buses came along you felt like you had died and gone to Heaven. It's hard to come home and complain about how rough a trip was. You just live like it's home away from home!"

O'Neill Terry

By 1958, the Statesmen were traveling more than 100,000 miles a year to meet 250 engagements. Their travels were taking them all over the country, including occasional extended journeys to California, on to the Northwest and into Canada. Although they were appearing regularly in large concert halls in cities and towns across America, they continued to work in small churches, often earning enough money to cover the fuel expense for the trip between two major concerts. And wherever they appeared, whether it was before 10,000 fans at the National Quartet Convention, or for an appreciative audience of 75 at a little rural church, the Statesmen always gave their best.

For the first year or so after they began traveling by bus, the Statesmen took turn about handling the driving chores. By 1959, they decided to sit back and leave the driving to someone else. O'Neill Terry was the professional driver with whom they entrusted their lives for many years and millions of miles across the roadways of this great land.

Cat Freeman

By late 1958, Cat Freeman was ready to move on. Although he was enjoyable to work with, the other Statesmen found his clowning sometimes excessive for their style. By the same token, Cat felt the Statesmen rehearsed excessively. As energetic as they were about singing and entertaining, the Statesmen may have been too serious for Cat Freeman. According to family and friends, divorce played a big role in him leaving the Statesmen for good in the fall of 1958.

"He had family problems," recalls his sister, Vestal Goodman. "His home broke up and he was ready to leave Atlanta."

"We had hoped that he would work out," Jake

Cat Freeman, far left, cracks up the gang during a 1958 appearance in Alabama.

says, "but he just didn't, and he didn't care. See, Cat was so well in demand back in those days. He was so funny, and he didn't particularly spend much time on improving his skills, you know. He didn't like to rehearse. He liked to have a good time. He was quite a guy!"

"Cat was not difficult in the sense of getting along with him," recalls Hovie. "He was one of the easiest guys to get along with there ever was. Lots of fun, loads of fun. A little negligent, irresponsible to a certain extent, but nothing serious. He was one of the funniest guys. Cat had figured a way to be so entertaining on the stage that, if it was a hard note to hit or it was a difficult song, he clowned his way through it. That was not what I wanted. I wanted singing. I didn't mind the clowning at the right time. But when you've got inverted harmony, and you've got some men up here on the other three high parts—maybe Cat was on the melody, although he was a tenor, and the other parts were under him and they're singing at their peak. If Cat didn't put his part in there, as Jake would say, it would just about choke you to death. So we had no real problems with Cat in any way whatsoever. He was one of the nicest guys to get along with, except for the fact that he would find a way to clown when it was a very extremely timely thing for him to just sing. And, of course, we discussed that several times. I think that by this time he was more or less ready to get off the road and he left very amiably."

Although no longer a fixture on the national quartet scene, Cat remained active in gospel music throughout the South in the years to follow. The Statesmen had contact with him from time to time. "Cat was one of my dearest friends. I dearly loved him," says Jake. "We remained friends until he died."

"I really don't know that he ever after that sang full-time," says Hovie. "He sang with the Revelaires for a while. But the Statesmen were first in everybody's lives, especially Jake's, mine, Chief, Doy, and so we were getting on with what we needed to do."

Says Vestal Goodman, "He was always singing with little groups, down in Gadsden, Birmingham, Chattanooga, Fort Payne—groups that were just getting started that were struggling. He had a television program out of a little station there in Fort Payne where the country group Alabama is from. He was always around where music was."

The late Lee Roy Abernathy once called Freeman "the most congenial gentleman to ever come from Alabama." Abernathy chuckled as he recalled that Freeman "talked in that upper tone all the time. When you think of Cat you don't think of anything negative."

Occasionally, Freeman would telephone his successor, Rosie Rozell, and without identifying himself would ask, "Who's the greatest tenor singer in the world?"

Rozell, recognizing the put-on voice, would answer. "I reckon that'd have to be Cat Freeman."

"Hi, Rosie," Cat would say, "this is Puss, your favorite tenor. How are you?"

Cat eventually retired to the Sand Mountain area on the family homestead in Fyffe, Alabama, where he died quietly at home in 1989 at the age of 68. In recent years a scholarship has been named in his memory by the June Jam Gospel Jubilee, held each June at the VFW Fairgrounds in Fort Payne, Alabama. Recipients of the Cat Freeman Memorial Scholarship have their choice of three schools to attend: the Alabama School of Gospel Music, the Stamps-Baxter School of Music or the Steve Hurst School of Vocal Ministry and Performance.

Roland Dwayne Rozell

To replace Cat the Statesmen called Roland "Rosie" Rozell, a man who Jake says had caught their attention sometime earlier when they were on tour in Oklahoma.

"We had heard him sing with the Tulsa Trumpeteers. Rosie Rozell was great and we had known that he might be available. He was on the Tulsa police force at that time and still singing with the Tulsa Trumpeteers. Rosie Rozell was quite a man."

Rosell was born to Loy Rozell and Gladys Martin Rozell in Hardy, Oklahoma on August 29, 1928, but grew up in Skiatook, Oklahoma, which is a suburb of Tulsa. His mother, a preacher, died in the late 1940s. When Rosie was in his late teens he began singing with the Tulsa Trumpeteers, a part-time group in the Tulsa area. Later, he also sang on occasion with the Foggy Rivers Boys, based in Springfield, Missouri; while still working with the Tulsa Trumpeteers.

"When we called Rosie to come and join the Statesmen," recalls Hovie, "he rode the train from Tulsa to Atlanta. They had a plane strike so he had to ride a train. When he got off

Rosie Rozell

the train in Atlanta, he turned his foot and broke his ankle. When I first saw him he was hobbling around with a foot as big as my head. I thought, 'Have we done the right thing or not? I don't know if the boy's alright or not.' But I want you to know it didn't take long to know that we had made the right choice. Rosie Rozell was a great tenor!"

Rozell's singing delivery was quite different than Bobby Strickland, Cat Freeman and Denver Crumpler before him. Song evangelist Roy Pauley, long an observer of the gospel quartet field, calls Rosie "the standard by which all other tenors, before and after, were and are to be judged." Although the quartet retained its basic sound, the harmony featured a slightly different edge. While Denver had been a great lyric tenor, Hovie opines, "I think Rosie might have sung with more soul."

"Rosie was the type that brought a lot of emotion to the group," says Jake. "You can't compare Rosie and Crump. It's like comparing apples and oranges, of course. Rosie was one great tenor."

"When you lose a singer and you replace him with another singer, you always lose something and you gain something else," observes Bill Gaither. "I think they gained some things with Rosie they didn't have with Denver. I think anybody who's followed music for a long time would say Denver had to be one of the greatest first tenors that ever sung in our field. But when Rosie came along, he not only was a great first tenor, he also brought some heart and soul to it that maybe even Denver didn't have, as great as Denver was. So there was another little extra edge that Rosie brought to the whole thing."

That edge was exhibited early in Rosie's career with the Statesmen on such songs as "Hide, Thou, Me," "Room at the Cross" and "Surely I Will, Lord." Desirous of having a record available with their new tenor, the Statesmen booked time in a recording facility in Nashville and recorded an album of songs with Rosie, including "Hide, Thou, Me," which they released on their own custom label. Although they had produced many 45 rpm and 78 rpm records on their own label through the years, this was the first time they had self-produced a long-playing album of 12 songs. When it was released the album was packaged simply in a sleeve without a jacket. A few months later it was re-issued as one of the first releases on the Skylite label when the Blackwoods and Statesmen formed a joint recording company in 1959.

The quartet recorded Ira Stanphill's "Room at the Cross" in February 1959. RCA released the song on a single backed with "Something Lifted Off of Me" shortly thereafter. "Room at the Cross" became one of Rosie's trademark songs during the next few years.

I'll Meet You By The River

On March 3, 1959, the quartet went into the studio with producer Chet Atkins to begin recording an album of songs written by Albert E. Brumley. Since Brumley's songs had long formed a staple part of the Statesmen's repertoire, it seemed fitting that the quartet should record an album devoted exclusively to his music.

Brumley was born in 1905 in Spiro, Indian Territory, in what is now the state of Oklahoma. He attended the Hartford Musical Institute at Hartford, Arkansas, later singing with one of the early Hartford quartets. Brumley's success as a songwriter blossomed when "I'll Fly Away" was published by the Hartford Music Company in 1931. He later wrote songs for publication by Stamps-Baxter, and the Stamps Quartet Music Company as well as Hartford. His music found widespread popularity. In addition to their melodic beauty, Brumley's songs are marked by lyrics of sincerity and rich imagination.

Albert E. Brumley

On the first night of the session the Statesmen recorded "If We Never Meet Again," the classic "I'll Fly Away," "Surely I Will, Lord," "I'll Meet You in the Morning," "Jesus, Hold My Hand" and "I'll Meet You By the River," which was destined to become the title song of the album.

Normally, the quartet and their complement of backup musicians—Bob Moore on standup bass, Marvin Hughes on the organ and Atkins on guitar—would record just a few takes of a song before they were satisfied with the end result and then move on to the next song. "The most takes we ever had on any song was on 'Surely I Will, Lord' and we recorded 27 takes of that," Jake remembers. "And then we ended up going back and taking, I think, the second one after singing ourselves hoarse."

"Rosie didn't want to sing that song," explains Hovie. "He did not care for it. He thought it was bragging—'if anyone makes it surely I will, Lord.' Rosie was a great guy, one of the greatest tenors in his style as Denver was in his style. If he liked a song, fine. If it was work, then it was a poor song. But if he was getting some kind of response, feedback from the audience, the sky was the limit, encores didn't matter. Eventually, rather than to hassle with him, we just quit singing it onstage."

But one night some years later the R.J. Reynolds Auditorium in Winston-Salem, North Carolina, was jam-packed. That night the Speer Family sang on the program just ahead of the Statesmen. As Hovie recalls, "Mom and Dad were still with them in their last years. They were very effective, emotionally, with a crowd, especially if that crowd was the kind of crowd that gave you feedback. The Speers were having a great stand. Everything they did was being received wonderfully. When they came off they left that stage hot as a pistol."

Hovie had been in the wings watching. As it came time for the Statesmen to be introduced, he told the quartet, "Just nobody come on the stage until you hear me play."

The promoter was a boisterous emcee. "And now, ladies and gentlemen," he blustered, "from Atlanta, Georgia, the famous, the most sensational gospel group of the century, Brother Hovie Lister and the Statesmen Quartet!"

Hovie casually walked onstage, pulled back the piano bench, sat down and got himself settled.

"People were still shouting from the Speers being on. All this time I was just letting the crowd get settled down. They were all watching me and wondering 'Well, where's the quartet?'. I was giving them time to come off of that high. Then I started in on the introduction of 'Surely I Will,' Lord.' While I was doing that the men began strolling out on stage. I could just feel daggers from Rosie behind my back. But what could he do except walk off stage or sing it? He hit that thing and by the second phrase or two somebody started shouting, 'Praise the Lord!'. And that's all it took to set him on fire. I know he hit pitches that night he ain't never hit before. And we must've encored the thing three or four times."

Because of the 27 takes required to record that one song, that Tuesday night recording session in 1959 stretched from a scheduled three hours to 4 1/2 hours. It was after midnight when the session concluded. The following night the quartet recorded "There's a Little Pine Log Cabin," "Did You Ever Go Sailin'," "Turn Your Radio On," "He Set Me Free," "Her Mansion Is Higher Than Mine" and "I've Found a Hiding Place" in a little more than three hours. The entire album had been recorded in about eight hours over two nights. Released in the summer of 1959, it remains one of Hovie's favorites of all the albums by the Statesmen to this day.

Mansion Over the Hilltop

The quartet's fifth long-playing album for RCA Victor featured a fresh approach. Three soft, harmonious ladies' voices were added to complement the manly timbres of the Statesmen. The clever arrangements, combined with the vocal accompaniment of the Anita Kerr Singers, resulted in an appealing blend of harmonies and contrasts. The album included five songs published by the quartet's Faith Music Company: "I've Got That Feeling," written by Wally Varner; "Tenderly," written by Big Chief; "He Will Show You the Way," written by Jake Hess; "No Greater Love" and "Provided by His Love." "He Will Show You the Way" was the first of Jake's compositions to be recorded by the Statesmen. By 1959, Big Chief was making a substantial contribution as a songwriter. "Tenderly" was a successful song for him as several quartets added it to their performance lists.

Also appearing on the album were Ira Stanphill's "Mansion Over the Hilltop," "Go Down to the Jordan," Brock Speer's "I Can Call Jesus Anytime," a Cleavant Derricks composition— "God's Got His Eyes on You," Mosie Lister's "He Knows Just What I Need," "The Love of God," and Rev. Vep Ellis' "Heaven's Joy Awaits." The latter was among the first songs the original Statesmen had learned and recorded with Capitol a decade earlier.

Produced by Chet Atkins, the album "Mansion Over the Hilltop" was recorded in eight-and-a-half hours over two days in May, 1959. However, it was held for release until January, 1960.

On Stage at the Ryman

The final Statesmen recording project of 1959 occurred on the evening of November 6, during one of Wally Fowler's all-night sings at the famous Ryman Auditorium in Nashville. The Statesmen had been thrilling audiences with their exciting concert presentations for many years. RCA Victor wanted to try to capture on record the onstage spirit and enthusiasm of the quartet as heightened by tremendous audience reaction. If they were successful, the record-buying public could enjoy it in their homes again and again.

It was fitting that gospel singing had become such a popular attraction at the Ryman Auditorium in the 1950s. The old building had been built as a religious tabernacle in 1891 by riverboat captain Tom Ryman. Earlier Ryman had attended a tent revival with the intention of heckling the preacher. He didn't count on the power of the Word of God. During the service, Ryman's attention was diverted from his mission of malice to the message being delivered by the preacher he had been bent on troubling. He fell under the power of conviction. When the invitation was given Ryman was on his knees before God and prayed through to his conversion. He built the tabernacle that bears his name for the Rev. Sam Jones.

In 1943, the facility became the home of WSM's world-famous Grand Ole Opry. Statesmen producer Chet Atkins was a major part of the Opry scene for several years as a sideman for such country music acts as the Carter Family and Wally Fowler's Georgia Clodhoppers before picking his Gretsch guitar to a lucrative recording deal with RCA Victor. The Ryman was like home to him. He knew of no better place to record the Statesmen in a live concert setting.

The Statesmen, with Brock and Ben Speer providing support on guitar and bass guitar, sang 16 songs that Friday evening, including both new songs and old. "I Wanna Know" had been a Statesmen standard for several years. Several other songs had appeared on single releases previously, including "Something Lifted Off of Me," "Room at the Cross," "He Set Me Free," "He's Already Done What He Said He Would Do" and "Gonna Open Up All of My Doors (Light of His Love)." Among the newer songs were "I'm Fine Thanks to Calvary" and "The Amen Corner," both written by Vep Ellis; Mosie Lister's "Wade On Out;" and "It's Worth More," a Henry Slaughter song that featured Jake. They also introduced a hymn medley that was to become a big hit for them over the next few years.

"Neighbors, at this time I want your attention, please," Hovie said to the audience as the concert drew to a close. "You know, tonight we've sung many fast songs that you've enjoyed, we hope. If you haven't enjoyed it you're the biggest bunch of hypocrites I ever saw because you really have made out like you have. But right now, would it please you, please, if we had the Statesmen, each man, to sing his favorite hymn for you. Would you like that?"

This question was met with enthusiastic applause.

"You know," he continued, "I like all of these fast songs. I get a blessing, emotional blessing, from all of these. But to me there will never be a replacement for the old hymns. So tonight, in all reverence, if you'll be just as quiet as you possibly can until we have finished the last song. Then if you want to show your appreciation with your applause it will please us so very much. But I'm going to ask each individual member of the Statesmen now to sing his favorite song about the Master, the Lord Jesus Christ. Will you listen?"

The medley

Nashville's Ryman Auditorium, home of Wally Fowler's All-Night Sings opened with

Big Chief singing alone the verse and chorus of "Oh, How Much He Cares for Me." Hovie modulated to the correct key for "Jesus Is All the World to Me (He's My Friend)," sung by Doy Ott. The quartet joined him in harmony midway through the selection. Jake Hess stepped forward to deliver "Jesus is the Sweetest Name I Know," again joined by his fellows harmonizing to bring this hymn to its conclusion. Rosie Rozell stepped into the spotlight for "Standing Somewhere In the Shadows." The arrangement changed keys with each new hymn. Hovie put forth a spirited rendering of "Jesus is the One" to conclude the medley. The audience reaction demanded an encore and the Statesmen hastily obliged. They followed the encore and concluded the concert with "Get Away Jordan." The spiritual had long been the quartet's sugar stick.

Some years before, Hovie recalls, "We did a live radio program in Savannah, Georgia. The Gospel Harmonettes, a women's group, were doing a live radio program. We were going to follow them with a live radio program. All five of them were schoolteachers in Birmingham, Alabama. They loved to sing and they were singing 'Get Away Jordan.' We just about had a fit. They weren't just putting on a show, they were being annointed right there on the radio. There wasn't any audience there in the studio except us, and they didn't care whether we were watching or not. They were having so much spiritual enjoyment out of that song. That thing just got ahold of us. We said, 'Man, we've got to have that!' So we got them to teach it to us. They sang it until we learned it right there in the studio."

"Get Away Jordan" featured vigorous solo deliveries by both Jake and Hovie and became synonymous with the Statesmen in the 1950s, even into the early 1960s. Midway through the song, Doy Ott would slide in at the keyboard to supplant Hovie who would take the solo mic, and with a burst of high-energy, bring the song to its conclusion. Often, Hovie would encore the song time and again until he had shaken down his hair to the great delight of the quartet public.

"The Statesmen On Stage" was released early in 1960 on the heels of "Mansion Over the Hilltop" and proved to be quite successful for the quartet and RCA Victor.

14
Skylite Recording Company

Blackwood-Statesmen Enterprises

Few professional gospel quartets in the late 1950s were in the enviable position of having a recording contract with a major record company. The Blackwood Brothers, Statesmen and Speer Family were members of the RCA Victor roster. For years the Chuck Wagon Gang had been recording for Columbia. Most major record labels had religious artists in their stables of talent, but quartets were seldom among them. Decca, once the home of such groups as the Sunshine Boys and Blue Ridge Quartet, was recording religious albums for Gov. Jimmy Davis and country star Red Foley. In its infancy Capitol Records had released several recordings by Wally Fowler and his Oak Ridge Quartet in 1947. By the end of the 1950s, Capitol on the strength of one artist was competitive with all religious product distributed by most other record labels. Although that one artist, Tennessee Ernie Ford, was recording secular product as well as gospel albums, his hymn albums were extremely successful. By 1962, five of his sacred albums had earned gold record awards which signified sales of $1million each.

Prior to signing with RCA in 1954, the Statesmen had recorded for Capitol. Several years after the Statesmen had left Capitol, the company decided in 1960 to cash in on the quartet's popularity by releasing an album of songs from the old master recordings made by the Statesmen in the late 1940s and early '50s. "Something to Shout About" (Capitol T-1508) was the group's first Capitol LP release. All of their previous Capitol product had appeared on 45 and 78 rpm singles. Capitol would issue another Statesmen album—"Happy Land" (Capitol DT-2539)—in 1968, featuring a number of recordings that were nearly 20 years old.

Since so few quartets were able to secure a contract with a major secular record label, there was certainly a need for a recording firm which was dedicated to not only recording these groups, but developing a distribution system to get the records out to the record-buying public. Several quartets had recorded custom albums on independent labels, but distribution was a problem. Their only method of selling the product was at the record tables during concert appearances. There were a few small companies dedicated to religious recordings, Word Records of Waco, Texas, among them. But in 1959, Word was principally recording soloists and speakers, such as actor Burl Ives, Frank Boggs and Jim Roberts.

Jake Hess, as he talked with friends from other quartets around the country, not only recognized the need for a major recording label for quartets but he wanted to do something about it. Why couldn't the Statesmen and Blackwoods as business partners form a recording com-

The Blackwood Brothers Quartet in the late-1950s (from left): Wally Varner, pianist; Cecil Blackwood, baritone; J.D. Sumner, bass; Bill Shaw, tenor; and James Blackwood, lead.

pany of their own? He posed the question to Hovie, and they approached James Blackwood and J.D. Sumner with the plan. After much discussion, the two quartets formed the company in 1959 as a subsidiary of their joint business venture Blackwood-Statesmen Enterprises.

"Jake and I first started publishing companies," explains J.D. Sumner. "Jake started Faith Music Company, and I started Gospel Quartet Music Company, and we had a bunch of songs. So we came up with the idea of having our own record company, and then we would get other quartets to record our songs on our label. So it got to be a pretty prosperous venture there."

Jake and J.D. were assigned the responsibility of managing the new Skylite Recording Company, the name suggested by Blackwood pianist Wally Varner.

RCA had a custom recording division which pressed and packaged records for independent recording companies. RCA subcontracted the work of printing and manufacturing album jackets to Crown Album Corporation in Philadelphia, Pennsylvania. Since both the Blackwoods and Statesmen were under contract to RCA Victor, Blackwood and Sumner approached the company about a business arrangement between Skylite and RCA's custom division. Skylite would book its sessions at one of RCA's Nashville studios. The Skylite sessions would be booked at times that wouldn't interfere with the session schedule of RCA Victor's stable of artists. A fair financial arrangement was agreed to by the parties involved. Skylite was ready to do business and would feature the finest technical quality available in terms of studio and packaging expertise.

Distribution would be no problem because James Blackwood previously had been made a distributor of RCA religious products. James was the first distributor of exclusively-religious record products in the country. Since RCA had placed no restrictions on his territory, James had been shipping RCA records all over the United States for some time. Skylite product would be distributed through the same network of stores and outlets that James had established with his RCA-related connections.

Enter Brock Speer, Producer

The first group to sign with the new label was the Speer Family, who, like the Blackwoods and Statesmen, were not getting enough product from RCA each year to meet the demand of their audiences. In fact, the first two releases on the new Skylite label were Speer Family albums. The label's first release was LP-701 "Dad Speer's Golden Anniversary In Gospel Music," featuring a collection of 12 of G.T. Speer's best-loved compositions. On the heels of that popular album came LP-702 "Songs You've Requested." Among the songs on this album was "I'm Bound for That City," featuring Dad Speer.

Brock Speer served as producer for the two projects. His efforts impressed James Blackwood and J.D. Sumner to the extent that they offered him the role of serving as producer in future Skylite projects for other artists.

Brock Speer

"Back in those days," Brock explained years later, "I had a deal with the owners of the Skylite Record Company, which was the Blackwood Brothers and the Statesmen Quartet. They lived in Atlanta and Memphis—the Statesmen in Atlanta, and the Blackwoods in Memphis. The big studios, even at that time back in the 1950s, were in Nashville."

Since the Speer Family lived in Nashville, it was more convenient for Brock to serve as producer than for any member of the Blackwoods or Statesmen.

As producer, Brock would be responsible for booking recording sessions with the studios, scheduling the necessary engineers, technical personnel and backup musicians; and directing the recording sessions. He would secure permission to record selections from the proper performance rights organizations, and coordinate with the recording artists the order in which the songs would appear on the records, what cover art and jacket design would be used, and write the jacket backliner notes. He directed Skylite employees in the process of forwarding jacket information, artwork and photos to the jacket printer in Philadelphia to be processed.

Hymns By The Statesmen

Not only was Skylite to be a major record label for other gospel quartets, but the Blackwoods and Statesmen sought an option from RCA to record a limited amount of product on their new company label.

According to James Blackwood, both quartets secured "permission from RCA to re-record on Skylite albums any of the singles that we had previously recorded on our own labels—both Blackwoods and Statesmen, and we did that. We recorded several albums, each group, on the Skylite label."

"RCA knew what we were doing," notes Jake Hess. "That was an understanding that we had. We needed more albums a year than the two that we were getting from RCA."

In fact, the Statesmen released two albums for the company in each of the first two years Skylite was in business, in addition to the product released by RCA Victor in those years.

Skylite's first Statesmen release, LP-1198 "Hymns By The Statesmen," followed the two Speer albums. The "Hymns" album was less expensive to produce than most of the company's projects because no recording sessions were required. The Statesmen still owned the soundtracks from the discontinued Nabisco television shows. Twelve hymns were transferred from these soundtracks directly to the album master for production into records. These were the recordings made in the Biltmore Hotel ballroom featuring the voices of Denver Crumpler, Jake, Doy and Big Chief, accompanied by Hovie on an old pump organ. The songs had been used in the chapel scene during a hymn segment of the Nabisco programs. The album jacket featured a photograph of the TV studio's chapel set.

This album was released at the time their hymn medley, featured on the RCA Victor "Statesmen On Stage" live album, was blessing audiences all over the country.

Get Away Jordan

The next Statesmen release on Skylite was SRLP-5965 "Get Away Jordan," a re-issue of an album the Statesmen had recently produced on their self-named "Statesmen" label. Previously, the album had been titled simply "The Statesmen Quartet." All new pressings of the disc featured the black Skylite label on the record. For jacket art, Skylite cropped the photograph that had appeared on the back of the RCA Victor "I'll Meet You By The River" album, and printed it in sepia tone against a blue background. As the company's logo had not yet been designed, the name Skylite appeared in simple block letters in a small box on the jacket cover.

In compliance with the agreement between the quartet and RCA, all of the songs on the album were new recordings of titles that had been previously re-leased on either the Capitol or "Statesmen" record labels. Spirituals on the album in-cluded the title song and "Sho' Do Need Him Now." Also in-cluded were "Hide Thou Me," "On Revival Day," "I Bowed On My Knees and Cried Holy," "In the Sweet Forever," and "Jesus Fills My Every Need," the latter featuring a vocal solo by Hovie. Among the newer songs was "What A Day That Will Be," written by Jim Hill who was destined to sing with the Statesmen a decade later. The quartet included three compositions by Mosie Lister: "When You Travel All

Cover photograph from the "Get Away Jordan" album

The logo at left appeared on most of Skylite's record jackets. The stylish logo at right first appeared on Skylite product in 1962.

Alone," "Happy Rhythm" and "Where No One Stands Alone."

Mosie recalls how the chorus to "Where No One Stands Alone" came to him spontaneously: "I went to a gospel concert at Macon, Georgia, about 90 miles south of Atlanta. A lot of the groups that I knew were there. I left there at about 10 or 10:30 and drove to Atlanta by myself. I was driving alone in the car not thinking about anything when all of a sudden I started singing the chorus to 'Where No One Stands Alone.' I started at the beginning and went to the end.

"Hold my hand all the way, every hour, every day from here to the great unknown. Take my hand, let me stand where no one stands alone.

"In my mind I could hear the entire sound of that. I could hear the voices, orchestra, the whole thing. Then it just dawned on me what was happening. I sang it again, and I sang it again, and I sang it again. And it never did seem to change. It was always exactly the same way."

More than a year passed before Mosie added verses to this refrain. His inspiration came from the book of Psalms "where David, and I just quote roughly, where he said, 'Lord, cause Your face to shine upon me.' It was coming from a very bad time in his life. I began to think of David as a king living in a palace but being alone from God. I began to imagine what a terrible thing it is to be alone, but to be alone from God is even worse. And I could sense that something was going to start. I told my wife that I'd be back in a few minutes and I walked around the block. When I came back to the house I had both verses in my mind. I don't guess anyone would ever imagine it, but the verses really kind of picture David being alone from God and crying out to God. And that line that says, 'Don't hide your face from me,' kind of comes out of David's heart."

Statesmen Encores

Following the release of two albums by the Blackwood Brothers, "Give the World a Smile" and "Sunday Meetin' Time," the Statesmen readied their third album for Skylite. Released early in 1960, SRLP/SSLP-5968 "Statesmen Encores" again featured new recordings of a number of songs that had appeared on earlier custom records and Capitol releases. The earlier versions had been recorded when Denver Crumpler or Cat Freeman had been singing tenor with the quartet. The new recordings offered the opportunity for the public to hear new tenor Rosie Rozell singing with the group in a collection of frequently requested selections.

The collection included "I'm Gonna Walk Dem Golden Stairs," "In My Father's House Are Many Mansions," "A Newborn Feeling," "Everybody Ought To Know," "I'll Leave It All Behind" and "Oh, My Lord, What A Time" on side one. The second side consisted of "Something To Shout About," Mosie Lister's classic "His Hand In Mine," "Heavenly Love," "I Have A Desire," "I Just Can't Make It By Myself" and "Jubilee's A-Comin'."

Following the release of "Statesmen Encores," Skylite concentrated in 1960 on signing artists and recording the company's growing stable of talent. It was to be a very busy year. First came the third release by the Speer Family, "Because of Him," then the Weatherford Quartet recorded an album entitled "I'll Follow Jesus," the Florida Boys were recorded for a release entitled "God

Will Bless You All," followed by the Harmoneers with "It's the Harmoneers Again." Also recording projects with Skylite that year were the Harvesters Quartet, "God Is My Shepherd;" Oak Ridge Quartet, "Sing And Shout;" Blue Ridge Quartet, "He Bought My Soul;" Stamps Quartet, "What A Savior;" Rebels Quartet, "When I Stand With God;" and Wendy Bagwell and the Sunliters, "Old-Time Religion." The Speers recorded "The Singing Speers," their second Skylite release of the year.

To close the year, the Blackwood Brothers and Statesmen recorded an album together. This release, entitled "Statesmen-Blackwood Favorites" (SRLP/SSLP-5980), featured five songs by each quartet and two songs with the quartets combined.

Brock Speer, in addition to his duties as producer, served as a studio musician on several sessions as well. "I played sessions on guitar. Ben, my brother, played bass. That was before he became the pianist he is now. We would play on all of those recording sessions." The two also played on several Blackwood and Statesmen sessions for RCA Victor.

With the exception of the first two Speer Family albums and "Statesmen Hymns" album—all of which appeared only in high fidelity format—the Skylite albums were available in either high fidelity (for those buyers who did not own one of the newer stereo-compatible phonographs) or in stereo.

"One track monaural recording was the way it started out," recalled Brock Speer. "Then they went to stereo."

Almost all of the albums were also released in abbreviated form on 45 rpm EPs, or extended play records. The long-playing, 33 1/3 rpm albums featured twelve songs on 12-inch records. Four of these would be selected to appear on the smaller, 45 rpm EP version of the album. The extended play, 7-inch disks were packaged in a smaller jacket with the same jacket art and backliner notes as the 33 1/3 LP version. The quartets sold the high fidelity albums for four dollars, stereo albums for five dollars, and the 45 rpm EP albums for two dollars. The records of each album were packaged in paper sleeves containing photos and information about other Skylite releases before being inserted within the cardboard jacket. In this fashion Skylite advertised all of its stable of artists and the products that were available from each. Most backliner notes on the jackets of both albums and EPs also included information about other releases by the company.

Blackwood-Statesmen Enterprises then formed another company, called StatesWood Records, as a subsidiary of Skylite Recording Company. StatesWood Records produced an economy line of two dollar albums for groups or individuals who were interested. Several quartets recorded product for StatesWood to enable them to provide an economically priced product for some of the fans who lived on a tighter budget.

James Blackwood recalls that the name StatesWood had been used previously by another record company. "There was a guy that was selling records from Greenville, South Carolina. He was traveling around selling records and he came up with the name StatesWood. When we started Skylite, we made a deal with this guy and, of course, told him that he knowingly named his company StatesWood to cash in on the Blackwoods' and Statesmen's popularity. Then we took over the name StatesWood."

Among the albums released on the StatesWood label were recordings of Hovie Lister's sermons which he delivered in the closing service of the National Quartet Convention each year.

In 1961, Skylite continued producing new albums for the quartets already signed to the label, and added new talent to the roster. Among the releases that year were: "Hide Me, Rock of Ages," the Blue Ridge Quartet; "What Then," the Rebels; "Go Out To The Program" and "You'll Never Walk Alone" by the Oak Ridge Quartet; "The Ninety and Nine," by Jim Hill and the Golden Keys; "Glory, Glory, Amen," the Prophets Quartet with "Smiling" Joe Roper; "All-Night Singing" and "Family Favorites" by the Speer Family; a self-titled album by the Lee College Touring Choir; "I'll Praise His Name," the Weatherford Quartet; "Keep Walking," Wendy Bagwell and the Sunliters; and "I Believe," by the Rangers Trio.

The Oak Ridge Quartet's "Go Out To The Program" album featured a friendly imitation of some of the best known gospel quartets—the Blackwood Brothers, Speer Family, Chuck Wagon Gang and the Statesmen. The Prophets album featured two compositions by pianist and manager Joe Roper, both published by the Statesmen's Faith Music Company. The Golden Keys album featured the first song by an up-and-coming songwriter from Alexandria, Indiana, to be recorded on a major label. The song was "I've Been To Calvary" by young Bill Gaither.

Among the Skylite releases was an album (SRLP-5998) featuring the Golden Stairs Choir from Big Chief Jim Wetherington's home church, the Assembly of God Tabernacle in Atlanta. Wetherington served as choir director at the church and had formed the Golden Stairs Choir from among the wealth of talent available in the large church.

With the volume of releases coming out of Skylite, Brock Speer was kept quite busy when the Speer Family was not on the road. "I just kind of had a corner on that back then," he says. "But it kind of got tiresome, you know, doing that and having to travel, too."

Singing Time In Dixie

The next Statesmen album for Skylite was released in 1962. Producer Speer describes how that project differs from the art of recording today: "We did live sessions back then. You did the singing and the playing of the musicians all at the same time. And if somebody missed a word over in the end of the song you had to back up and just do it all over again. Nowadays, you can patch those in and it's so much quicker and easier to do. But I think we kind of lost something when we quit doing that. We make tracks now. We make the instrumental tracks and we go in later and dub in the voices."

Brock says the session musicians he has worked with through his years of recording with the Speer Family were so great "that they just thrill me to death singing with them. It gives me, I think, a better spirit to sing than having to go in and just overdub the vocals later on. We have electronic instruments now that can give you a lot of effects that we didn't have back then which is another improvement. Some people think it's a detriment instead, that you've got too much instrumentation."

For the "Singing Time In Dixie" album (SRLP/SSLP-6000), the Statesmen selected four songs written by Mosie Lister: "Nothing Can Compare;" "All Alone," a song about the crucifixion of Christ; "Sunday Meeting Time" and "Mother's Prayers Have Followed Me," both featuring recitations by the Big Chief. Also included were "Church Twice On Sunday," "I Saw A Man," "When I Move" and "These Are The Things That Matter." Others were "Living With Jesus," "The Old Landmark," featuring a solo by Hovie Lister, and Lee Roy Abernathy's "I've Got News." Doy Ott was featured on "Someone To Care," written by Gov. Jimmie Davis. Some of the arrangements dated back to the Nabisco years as the Statesmen had performed them on the syndicated

RCA Victor's Studio B in Nashville, for many years a hit factory for the likes of Elvis Presley, Jim Reeves, Chet Atkins and many others. Many Statesmen Quartet albums on both the RCA Victor and Skylite labels were recorded at this facility. The studio is now operated as a museum by the Country Music Hall of Fame.

television program and in their concerts during the early- to mid-1950s.

Brock says almost all of the Skylite albums were recorded in three sessions of three hours each. "I guess we accepted some stuff that we wouldn't take now. But three sessions was the limit and if you went over that you had to pay the musicians time-and-a-half for their work. So the producer tried his best not to go over."

It was important to bring the "Singing Time In Dixie" album in under budget on the recording end, because the album jacket would be more expensive than usual. But Brock needn't have worried about this album. In every take he accepted for the finished product, the quartet's singing and the musical accompaniment was superb.

The jacket, produced by the Benson Company, was more elaborate for this album than for any record previously released by the Statesmen. Color photos of the quartet used on the front and back covers of the jacket were taken at the Tennessee Botanical Gardens and Fine Arts Center in Nashville. The jacket, which opened like a book, featured photos inside of each individual member of the Statesmen with his family, a photo of bus driver O'Neill Terry, photos of the Statesmen with Tennessee Ernie Ford during preparations for their October 1962 appearance on his ABC television show, and photos of the quartet in concert. Brock Speer, in the album's jacket notes, recalled that the Statesmen's radio show over WSB and other radio stations across the country was called "Singing Time In Dixie." Hence the album's name.

"The recordings then were pretty much as good as they are now," said Brock, 30 years later. "We have improved in high-tech recording equipment, and so on. We sound maybe a little better now. And, of course, getting rid of the old plastic records and getting tape and, currently, CDs give us much, much better sound quality."

Skylite Recording Company opened the door to a new world of recording and nationwide distribution opportunities for most of the nation's top gospel quartets. Soon, the LeFevres opened Sing Recording Company in Atlanta to complement their music publishing business of the same name. Sing produced, in addition to recordings by the LeFevres, records for such groups as the Prophets Quartet, Blue Ridge Quartet, Rebels Quartet and Johnson Sisters, among others. Word Records continued to grow and eventually opened a subsidiary label for gospel quartets called Canaan Records. The Benson Company, long a renowned publisher of religious music, formed HeartWarming Records. Among others were Sword and Shield, Zondervan and Songs of Faith. Almost all of these record companies jumped on the gospel quartet bandwagon after evaluating the success of Skylite.

15
Through the States with The Statesmen

Peace, O Lord

In 1960, fans of Hovie Lister and the Statesmen Quartet found a wealth of selections available when they visited the quartet's record table at concerts around the country. No less than six Statesmen albums were released by four different record labels that year. Capitol issued "Something To Shout About," mentioned previously. Skylite Recording Company issued the "Statesmen Encores" and "Statesmen-Blackwood Favorites" albums. RCA Victor released two Statesmen albums—"Mansion Over the Hilltop" and "The Statesmen On Stage." RCA also issued a Statesmen album entitled "Peace, O Lord" on RCA-Camden, the company's economy label. Additionally, Skylite issued a 45 rpm EP version of "Statesmen Encores" (SREP-104), and RCA Victor released a 45 rpm EP of "The Statesmen On Stage."

RCA Victor also released the final Statesmen single in 1960. The Statesmen went into the company's Nashville studios with producer Chet Atkins on March 30. They recorded two songs, "To Me It's So Wonderful" and "I Found the Answer," with Atkins accompanying on guitar, Marvin Hughes at the organ, Ben Speer playing bass, and Hovie Lister at the piano. Both songs were packaged together and released on a 45. It was the last Statesmen release with Chet Atkins serving as producer. After the release of this single, RCA concentrated on marketing the Statesmen on album products exclusively.

The Statesmen first heard the song "To Me It's So Wonderful" during one of their appearances at an African-American church, the First Church of Deliverance, on South Wabash Avenue in Chicago. They always enjoyed singing for black congregations, and the quartet's interpretations of popular spirituals were received royally.

"They took it as a compliment instead of an insult," says Jake. "We've had a good black following down through the years. We really had a home out there at the First Church of Deliverance in South Chicago."

Dr. Ralph Goodpasteur, Minister of Music at the First Church of Deliverance, wrote "To Me It's So Wonderful." Dr. Goodpasteur and the First Church of Deliverance choir were sources of a number of Statesmen songs through the years. Goodpasteur served as a session musician on some recording projects with the group. Hovie describes him as a "very, very dear friend of mine." They have stayed in touch down through the years. "We still see each other. He's a very dear friend of my family. He's now the administrator of that whole operation and he's in his 70s."

The album "Peace, O Lord" (CAL/CAS-574), although released on RCA's economy label, was by no means a cheap record. Nine songs on the album were recorded while Cat Freeman was singing tenor with the quartet. Three songs had been recorded after Rosie Rozell replaced Cat with the group. None of the 12 songs had been released previously on any RCA album or single. Six of the songs had been recorded in the same sessions (during the June 1957-January 1958 period) that had produced the "Statesmen Quartet Sings With Hovie Lister" album (LPM/LSP-1605). These included "Jonah, Go Down to Ninevah," "Wait 'Til You See Me In My New Home," "Bring Peace, O Lord," "God Is My Friend," "Peace in the Valley," and "There's Gonna Be A Great Day," from the Broadway musical comedy "Great Day." The song was later the theme for a popular breakfast cereal commercial on television. The album also featured "I'm Looking for Jesus," "A Little Bit of Heaven" and "I Don't Want This Modern Religion" from one of Cat

Freeman's last sessions with the group. The three songs with Rosie Rozell—"It's Different Now," "Something Within" and "God Will Bless You All"—were recorded early in 1959.

Statesmen Out West

Bolstered by the motion picture industry, western music—a thriving musical genre—swept the country in the 1940s. Singing cowboys revived traditional western ballads and popularized new melodies created for the silver screen by commercial songwriters. This music was characterized by romantic imagery of the great American West and its scenery. The cowboy is one of the most cherished figures of Americana, a rugged symbol of the making of this great country, of a hard life and of elemental existence. After Gene Autry, Roy Rogers and other singing cowboys successfully made the transition from the silver screen to television, western programs inundated the new medium. Most were not of the musical variety but, nonetheless, Americans were tuning in.

Such vocal groups as the Sons of the Pioneers and Riders of the Purple Sage often served as backup vocalists for some of the top cowboy stars. The popularity of the Sons of the Pioneers was aided in no small way by the success of songwriting members Bob Nolan and Tim Spencer. Nolan had penned such western classics as "Cool Water" and "Tumbling Tumbleweeds," among others. Spencer composed "Room Full of Roses" and "The Everlasting Hills of Oklahoma." Because of the popularity of the Sons of the Pioneers and their trademark western vocal group style, many gospel quartets had held a fascination for western songs for several years. Several early quartets included cowboy selections along with gospel songs in their performances on radio and personal appearances. In 1950, the Sunshine Boys appeared in a western movie with Smiley Burnette and Charles Starrett. During the syndicated Nabisco television series, the Statesmen had filmed cowboy sequences featuring such songs as "Twilight Shadows Are Falling," "The Trail to Paradise," "At the End of the Trail" and "Cowboy Camp Meeting," among others.

In 1959, rockabilly singer Marty Robbins had a megahit on the country & western and popular music charts with his western ballad "El Paso." Not only were cowboy shows dominating TV programming, but western music continued to sell well on the commercial record market.

"I like the love songs, but, the songs I really like to do the best and listen to are songs of the west," Robbins would say years later. "It's really a big part of this country—the American cowboy, the American cowboy songs, trail drives, covered wagons. The American cowboy and that image, that is what all foreign countries think the American Yankee is—a cowboy."

Taking note of the upsurge in western music, RCA executives saw an opportunity for another departure from the standard gospel quartet recording package. They had taken note as the Statesmen had achieved success with their album of Albert E. Brumley compositions. The album combining the voices of the Statesmen and Anita Kerr Singers had also been a novel approach to a gospel record project. After recording the Statesmen in a live concert setting for an album, RCA

Western attire in a photo shoot for the "Out West" album.

A Cowboy Camp Meeting. From left: Tim Spencer, an original member of the Sons of the Pioneers and writer of "Room Full of Roses," "Cowboy Camp Meeting," "The Sea Walker," and others; Hovie Lister; Roy Rogers, "King of the Cowboys;" and Stuart Hamblen, who enjoyed commercial success with "Out on the Texas Plains" prior to his spiritual conversion. Spencer wrote the jacket notes for the RCA-Victor "Statesmen Out West" album. The photo was taken at a RCA-sponsored Gospel Sing held at Nashville's War Memorial Auditorium in conjunction with the National D.J. Convention.

turned its attention to producing the Statesmen in an album of gospel songs with a western flavor. The company called in Darol Rice, its new A&R man for religious recordings, to produce the project.

The Statesmen went to work writing and arranging appropriate material for an album to be called "The Statesmen Out West." They selected Tim Spencer's "Cowboy Camp Meeting," featuring a rousing, rap-like recitation by the Big Chief; two songs by Vep Ellis, "At the End of the Trail" and "We're Riding the Range for Jesus;" and "Look Around You," written by Melvin Morris. The Statesmen composed seven western songs for the album. Big Chief contributed "At Sundown," "A New Range in the Sky" and "Roundup in the Sky." Doy Ott also wrote three, including "My Dad," "Up the Winding Trail" and "Cowboy's Paradise." Jake Hess penned a song called "My God is Riding Beside Me." All seven selections were published by Faith Music Company along with "I'm Riding Home," a tune contributed by Blackwood bass singer J.D. Sumner.

"The Statesmen Out West" was the first Statesmen album to be recorded outside of Nashville. As Darol Rice lived in Hollywood, he scheduled the Statesmen to record the project, fittingly, out West, at RCA Victor's Music Center of the World in Hollywood, California. The entire album was recorded in one day, in three sessions on July 13, 1960.

"We went in, we knew the songs and we brought written arrangements. The musicians then learned, or sight-read, our arrangements," says Hovie.

The musicians included violinist Bobby Bruce, George Bamby on accordian, bassist Morty Corb and guitarist Neil Levang.

Released early in 1961, "The Statesmen Out West" (LPM/LSP-2281) featured a cover photo of the Statesmen in cowboy hats and western ties. The backliner notes were written by Tim Spencer, formerly of the Sons of the Pioneers. "The titles of their songs," Spencer wrote of the Statesmen, "weave a lyric pattern that paints a spiritual word picture of a western wonderland. The peaceful West, where the theme of faith, hope and charity overshadows the infamy of 'shoot 'em up cowboys,' 'scalpin' Indians' and 'cattle rustlers'."

"I Want To Tell You Something."

Once considered an exclusive province of the American Bible Belt, gospel quartet music had, by 1960, extended its scope of popularity from the South across the nation "from sea to shining sea," and into Canada. While thousands flocked to the major quartet concerts in numerous southern cities, groups like the Statesmen and Blackwood Brothers were packing the masses into several auditoriums out West, throughout the Midwest and up North. Detroit and

Indianapolis were favorite spots on the tour, but, says Hovie Lister, Chicago was like a second home to the Statesmen.

"I say this, and I don't mean to sound egotistical or to be bragging, but Chicago was just our town. When we went there for a concert, I don't care who else was on the program, they were pretty much our audience. They were most receptive, a very outgoing audience, very vocal in their applause. It mattered not if we were doing something fast, hand-clapping, foot-stomping, they'd do that. If I wanted to get serious with them and do a little bit of exorting, they were in for that. I was just myself. I always have been wherever I go. I always had a saying, 'Just be yourself wherever you go and then if you get invited back you don't have to remember what you said the last time you were there'."

Producer Darol Rice, impressed by the success of the Statesmen's live, concert recording, "The Statesmen On Stage," wanted to repeat the formula in an album to follow "The Statesmen Out West." Knowing how popular the Statesmen were in the Windy City, Rice scheduled RCA's remote recording unit to be at Chicago's Medina Temple on the night of November 15, 1960, to capture the quartet's concert performance in that setting. Brad McCuen supervised the technical end of the recording operation, with engineers Ron Steele and Dick Bain capturing the performance and audience reaction on tape.

Onstage, the quartet members vigorously plunged into their repertoire, the adrenalin feeding on the energetic enthusiasm of the thousands of appreciative fans in attendance. With each song the excitement gained momentum, exploding in thundrous applause at the conclusion of the quartet's fifth song, "I Believe in the Old Time Way," written by J.D. Sumner.

"Just a minute. Just a minute," shouted Hovie above the din. Then, adamantly, "JUST A MINUTE! Just a minute! Wait a minute! All right, listen. One minute! We'll do it again if you'll wait a minute."

But the crowd wanted an encore, and demanded it NOW! Nothing Hovie said could quell the riot at his feet.

"Just a minute," he continued. "We'll do it again. Let me say something. Let me say this and we'll sing it again!"

"Do it again!" encouraged Big Chief.

"QUIET!" shouted Hovie. "I want to tell you..." his voice trailed off. Then, with resignation, he attacked the keyboard, pounding out an introduction for the encore while shouting into the microphone: "I don't want to tell you anything!"

More than 30 years later he reflected on that triumphant moment in the quartet's recording career. "I've had I don't know how many people to ask me, 'What were you gonna tell them?' To this day I don't know!"

The song selection for the concert and subsequent album included, in addition to "I Believe in the Old Time Way:" "Just a Little While," a song the group had first heard at Chicago's First Church of Deliverance; Ralph Goodpasteur's "To Me It's So Wonderful," "Love is Why," written by Vep Ellis; and "Sorry, I Never Knew You," by Henkle Little. There were four original compositions by group members: Doy Ott contributed "Little Joe's Prayer" and "Have You Tried the Lord Today," while Big Chief penned "Our Debts Will Be Paid" and Rosie Rozell offered "He's Not Disappointed in Me." Rounding out the lineup were "Happy Am I," by J.E. Marsh; "I Believe in the Man in the Sky," by Richard Howard, Jr.; and the hymn "We'll Understand It Better By and By."

Titled "Through the States With the Statesmen" (LPM/LSP-2351) the concert album was released in the spring of 1961. The jacket art featured a cartoon bus with a piano mounted on the back motoring along a highway with a map of the United States in the distance. The members of the Statesmen were portrayed with oversized heads atop small cartoon bodies, and leaning out of the bus windows and waving, with Hovie seated at the piano behind the bus.

That Chicago concert of 1960 was one of the finest examples of what happens when everything meshes in a concert setting—singers and audience synchronized on the same electric wave of tension as amplified by God. Sometimes, however, came those rare occasions when glitches occurred.

The Statesmen once entertained at a convention for post office workers in Atlanta. They got no further than the conclusion of the opening song before Hovie began to get the idea something was amiss. Leaping from the piano bench during the applause for the opening number, he was met by a round of laughter. Thinking the quartet must be clowning behind him, Hovie looked around and said softly, "Cut it out back there, fellows."

He introduced the next song, the quartet sang it, and he stood to acknowledge the applause. Again, laughter rippled through the audience. Turning to Jake and Big Chief, convinced they were up to something, Hovie adminished, "Now you guys knock it off. I'm trying to be serious here."

After the next song, when scattered laughter again spread through the auditorium, Hovie began to lose his cool. He was in charge here. There would be no cutting-up going on behind his back. "I'm serious, you guys. Cut it out!"

"Hovie," said Chief calmly, "your pants are unzipped."

"Yeah, sure. I said to cool it!"

By now the singers were struggling to maintain their cool and suppress their own laughter. They managed to get through the next song somehow. The audience responded with equal measures of laughter and applause.

"No kidding, Hovie," said Chief. "Your pants are unzipped."

Hovie stubbornly refused to go along with Chief's joke, enraged that one of the classiest, most professional quartet men he had ever met would stoop to pull such a trick on him in front of an audience. "Chief, if you say that again I'm gonna give you this mic!"

"Say it again, Chief!" urged Jake.

"Hovie," deadpanned Chief. "Your pants are unzipped."

"Big Chief and Jake are telling me," Hovie said, turning to the audience, "that my pants are unzipped." Then, backing away from the microphone, Hovie dared to look down and discovered—to his great dismay, amid a riotous round of laughter—the evidence that it had been no joke after all.

Rosie Rozell suffered a similar fate during an encore of "Get Away Jordan" at an appearance in Birmingham. The song had long been a monstrous hit for the quartet. The audience erupted in a standing ovation at the conclusion of the song. The quartet followed with several encores. During the last of these, Rosie jumped up on the piano stool and felt his trousers rip from the crotch to the knee. At the conclusion of the number, Rosie managed to gracefully get off the piano bench, slipped behind the piano and quickly escaped behind the curtains. Just then, he heard Hovie's voice from onstage. "Come back out here, Fat Boy, and let's sing it again!"

Sticking his head out of the curtains, Rosie shook his head vigorously, "I'm not coming out there again!"

Startled, Hovie's eyebrows furrowed. "I said to come back out here!"

"I'm not coming back out there," answered Rosie, and he turned so that Hovie could see the sad state of the seat of his trousers.

Hovie, amused but determined, marched offstage, and dragged the embarrassed specimen back into the spotlight, saying, "Now sing that song one more time!"

Even on the best nights, a preacher can get tongue-tied. During one West Coast tour the Statesmen were singing to a full house. The quartet concluded a song and Hovie jumped from the piano bench. Intending to quote Scripture, he thundered, "And Jeezley said ..."

"Uh, Hovie," Jake quickly interjected to the great amusement of the audience, "His name is Jesus."

Stop, Look and Listen for the Lord

The only other Statesmen album issued in 1961 was the quartet's second release on the RCA-Camden label (CAL/CAS-663). All twelve songs had appeared previously on RCA singles, including the quartet's first release on RCA Victor. There was "This Ole House," from the quartet's first RCA recording session on August 24, 1954, and "Love Never Fails" from 1956, both with Denver Crumpler. Cat Freeman appeared on seven of the selections. "God Is God," featuring a rockabilly Chet Atkins guitar solo, was similar to early Elvis Presley releases on RCA and dated from 1957. The title song, "Stop, Look and Listen for the Lord," was written by Doy Ott and recorded in 1957. From 1958 came "At the Roll Call" (written by Big Chief), "My God Won't Ever Let Me Down," "He's Got the Whole World in His Hands," "Until Tomorrow," and "What a Happy Day." Three songs with Rosie Rozell—"Until You Find the Lord," "Get Thee Behind Me, Satan" and "God Bless You, Go With God"—were recorded in 1959. The title song and "Get The Behind Me, Satan" featured chanting solos by the Big Chief. Each member of the quartet, including Hovie Lister, enjoyed a solo on "He's Got the Whole World In His Hands."

Camp Meeting Hymns

On August 1-2, 1961, RCA's Nashville studios resounded with the melodious strains of the Statesmen as they put down tracks for a new album which was released early in 1962 as "Camp Meeting Hymns." Only three traditional hymns—"Let the Lower Lights be Burning," "There is Power in the Blood" and "Rock of Ages"—appeared on the album, however.

In selecting songs for the album, the goal of the quartet and producer Darol Rice was to evoke the image of the old-time singing conventions, camp-meeting days, the old-fashioned revival and "brush arbor" meetings. The scenario was strengthened by such songs as Joe Roper's "I Like the Old Time Way (Of Praising His Dear Name)" and "Old Camp-Meeting Days." A nostalgic touch was John W. Vaughan's "If I Could Hear My Mother Pray Again."

Newer numbers appearing on the album were "Closer To Thee," published by the Statesmen's Faith Music Company; Stuart Hamblen's "Teach Me, Lord, To Wait," and "You Can't Stop God From Blessing Me," written by Hovie Lister. Rosie Rozell rendered an especially soulful interpretation of Doris Akers' "I Cannot Fail the Lord," which Akers has said is her favorite of the songs she has written down through the years. The spiritual "I Shall Not Be Moved" rounded out the collection.

Gary McSpadden

A bout with nephritis forced Jake to take a leave of absence from the road early in 1962. Edema, or fluid retention of the lungs, a condition associated with inflammation of the kidneys, caused coughing and shortness of breath, symptoms that made singing very difficult.

To fill the vacancy created by his absence, Jake recommended to Hovie a young man from Lubbock, Texas. Gary McSpadden, although only 19 years of age, had developed an outstanding voice in the high baritone range, honing his skills as a soloist in the church his father, Rev. Boyd McSpadden, pastored. Gary was quite a quartet fan, and greatly admired the Statesmen, especially Jake Hess.

"I had always wanted to sing either with him or like him," McSpadden said years later, "so I tried like him since I thought I'd never sing with him. Jake got sick in 1962. He had heard me sing at my father's church out in west Texas. Jake thought that I had some potential, I guess. So, when he was ill, he told Hovie Lister to give me a call and a tryout. Hovie didn't really want to do it."

"I don't think I want a kid," Hovie repeatedly told Jake. He didn't think a teenager had any business trying to sing for an established group.

Gary McSpadden

But Jake prevailed. Hovie finally gave in and placed a call to the handsome youngster in Texas. But he made it clear to young McSpadden that it was very unlikely he would get the job.

"If you'll come," Hovie said on the phone, "we'll pay your plane fare and we'll let you have a tryout, but I really don't think that we want to use you."

"So, with that kind of thing hanging over my head, I went to Atlanta and stayed with them for about five months," McSpadden says, smiling. "I guess I passed the audition. Then, when Jake came back, I went to the Oak Ridge Quartet for two years."

Statesmen fans around the country accepted young McSpadden enthusiastically. Later, with the Oak Ridge Boys, he harmonized on the first gospel quartet album with full orchestration accompaniment, "The Oak Ridge Boys With the Sounds of Nashville," a Warner Brothers release. One of the highlights of that album was a song featuring Gary: "When I Come to the End of the Road." The song was written by Hovie Lister.

Later that year, as Gary and Carol McSpadden were married at the conclusion of the 1962 National Quartet Convention in Memphis, Jake served as best man and Hovie assisted Gary's father in performing the ceremony.

The Comfort of the Road

In 1960, the Statesmen, Blackwood Brothers and several other gospel quartets began appearing in California on a regular basis. Promoter Polly Grimes began booking gospel talent in California and other parts of the West. Grimes told a writer for Billboard magazine that her shows were "fast-moving programs, produced professionally."

Gospel concerts were becoming quite popular on the West Coast, Grimes said, because the music appealed to all age groups. "Teen-agers like them because the songs are jivey. Adults enjoy them because there is a lot of showmanship. The concerts are not meant to be church services, but we do try to be spiritual in nature."

By 1962, an extended Statesmen tour might keep them on the road for weeks at a time, especially the West Coast trips. When the quartet bade farewell to their families in Atlanta to begin another singing tour, that single road trip might encompass a third of all the United States and half of Canada.

For traveling comfort, The Statesmen purchased this roomy, new General Motors Flexible bus in 1962.

In four years the quartet's first bus had traveled nearly a half-million miles. And the old Silversides had been through several hundred thousand miles of hard duty with Greyhound before the Statesmen bought it.

With the Statesmen and Blackwood Brothers frequently traveling together and working many of the same concerts, it was natural that they purchase new buses together, just as they had done with their identical Silversides in

Dallas. By buying two buses instead of one, they secured a better price from the manufacturer.

In 1962, recalls Hovie, "we both went up to Ohio to the Flexible Bus Company and bought two brand-new Flexibles just alike, painted gold and trimmed in black."

Straight from the factory, the coaches cost $40,000 each. Cargo compartments, located beneath the passenger sleeping areas and accessible from the outside, provided storage space for the quartet's public address sound system and merchandise—recordings, sheet music, songbooks and photographs, etc.—to sell at their concert appearances.

The interiors of these new buses were stripped out—empty shells ready to be customized to each quartet's needs. J.D. Sumner was again in charge of custom-designing the interiors for the optimum comfort of each quartet. His design, based on the experience of the Blackwoods' two previous buses and the previous Statesmen coach, was implemented by a mobile home manufacturer in Memphis at a cost of $12,500 for each bus.

Features of these luxurious, state-of-the-art vehicles included soundproof walls, six sleeping compartments similar to a Pullman sleeper with individual air conditioning in each sleeping compartment; intercom radio from each compartment to the driver, two-way citizen's band radio for conversing with other travelers on the road, a mobile telephone for Hovie to conduct business and update bookings while traveling, and a table for writing. Other comforts included restrooms, a lavatory, refrigerated box for cold drinks, private wardrobes for each quartet member and bus driver, and a lounge area with six reclining seats, television and radio.

The roomy comfort of the new coaches provided a home-like environment in which the quartets were at ease playing games like chess, rehearsing, composing new songs, reading, making phone calls, enjoying each other's fellowship, resting and sleeping. The quality of life on the road was a far cry from the quartet's beginnings when, crammed into the old Plymouth (with the mother-in-law back seat), they had bounced along the rugged backroads of rural Georgia. Through 14 years and millions of miles the Good Lord had certainly been smiling on Hovie Lister and the Statesmen Quartet!

Hovie Lister and the Statesmen Quartet in the early 1960s. Clockwise from top left: Rosie Rozell, Jake Hess, James "Big Chief" Wetherington, Hovie Lister and Doy Ott.

16

O What a Savior

The Mystery of His Way

When Jake Hess had recuperated sufficiently to return to the road late in the spring of 1962, producer Darol Rice scheduled three RCA Victor recording projects for the Statesmen. The first album was a joint project featuring both the Statesmen and Blackwood Brothers. It was recorded in June and targeted for release in advance of the 1962 Christmas season. Entitled "James Blackwood and the Blackwood Brothers Combine With Hovie Lister and the Statesmen to Wish You a Musical Merry Christmas" (LPM/LSP-2606), the album featured several traditional favorites supplemented with tunes penned by J.D. Sumner and Jim Wetherington. Each group sang five selections on the album with the quartets singing jointly on two selections.

On August 15, 1962, the Statesmen were back at RCA Victor's "Nashville Sound" studios to record their next album project, "The Mystery of His Way" (LPM/LSP-2546). The title song was written by Bob Nolan, who had penned the western classics "Cool Water" and "Tumbling Tumbleweeds" while a member of the legendary Sons of the Pioneers.

The quartet drew upon the vast resources available through its various music publishing companies to select nine of the songs for the album. They chose "He Will Pilot Me" from the J.M. Henson Music Company collection. From Abernathy Publishing Company came "God Can" and "Who Could Ask For More." Writers for the Statesmen's Faith Music Company contributed six songs for the album. These included "That's Why I've Gotta Sing," composed by Big Chief; "I've Found A New Way," written by Doy Ott; Al Langdon's "Little Bitty Chapel," "I've Got The Corners Turned Down (In That Hymn Book of Mine)," from the pen of Marion Snider; a Joe Roper composition, "Love So Divine;" and "What Love," written by Eldridge Fox, who was business manager for the quartet's publishing interests.

They also recorded "Sweeter As The Days Go By," a song that had been pitched to them by Sing Music Company, owned by the LeFevres. The 12th song, "O What A Savior," was published by the Stamps Quartet Music Company. Marvin Dalton had written the song in 1948.

"Rosie Rozell introduced that song to the gospel quartet world," asserts Hovie. "He brought it with him to the Statesmen."

"Marvin Dalton gave the (Tulsa) Trumpeteers the original manuscript," Rosie recalled shortly before his death.

It was the type of piece that Rosie Rozell could pour himself into, and he gave it such a classic rendering that, although many other tenor singers have recorded the song down through the years, "O What A Savior" is still synonymous with Rosie. It was his signature song. Nearly two de-

Quite expressive as he sang, "O What A Savior" is an excellent example of Rosie Rozell's ability to communicate through song.

cades after the release of "The Mystery of His Way" album, the song was still so much in demand at Statesmen concerts that Hovie would tell audiences: "I think I would be doing you an injustice if we did not include this next song, a song that is legendary with Rosie Rozell wherever he has been in the last several years singing gospel music."

The entire "Mystery" album was recorded in one day during two sessions, totalling seven-and-a-half hours. The album was released early in January, 1963.

For the next album project, Rice arranged for the RCA remote recording equipment to be on location at the Long Beach, California, Municipal Auditorium on Friday, Sept. 21, 1962. The Statesmen and Blackwood Brothers were headlining one of Polly Grimes's concerts in the facility. Rice and recording engineer John Norman were on hand to capture the excitement.

For this concert and subsequent album the Statesmen continued the trend of selecting material from their own publishing companies. They sang three of Big Chief's songs: "He Will Never Let Me Down," "I'm Going There" and "Is Your Name Written There." Doy Ott contributed "Lord, I'm Coming Home To Thee." Blackwood bass J.D. Sumner wrote "A Million Years From Now" for the Statesmen's Faith Music Company. Other songs from Faith Music included Al Langdon's "Look Up" and Joe Southerland's "At Last." "The Best For You" and "There's A Sweetness Through It All" were published by the group's J.M. Henson Company. The quartet also included a number by Vep Ellis, "Something Lifted Off of Me."

The only two songs on the album the Statesmen did not publish were Wally Fowler's "Wasted Years" and a Stamps Quartet Music Company song, "I'll Be Ready To Go," by David Reese.

"A Gospel Concert by the Statesmen Quartet with Hovie Lister" (LPM/LSP-2647) was released early in 1963. The Blackwood Brothers' album of their recorded appearance at the same concert, "On Stage!" (LPM/LSP-2646), was released simultaneously.

The "Pea Picker" and ABC-TV

As a cross-over artist and network television personality, Tennessee Ernie Ford was a country music trendsetter in the 1950s. He was among the first country music artists to enjoy huge success in the popular music field. A former radio announcer, he had been signed to a singing contract with Capitol Records in 1947, a couple of years before Hovie Lister and the Statesmen Quartet were signed to that company's roster of recording artists. He enjoyed some degree of success with a series of country recordings. But with the release of "Sixteen Tons" in 1955, Ford's career kicked into high gear. Written by Merle Travis as a bluegrass tune, "Sixteen Tons" was a tribute to blue collar workers. Tennessee Ernie Ford's recording of the song became the fastest-selling record in the history of the recording industry to that time, selling the first million copies within three weeks of its release.

The song led to a TV variety series for the Bristol, Tenn., native. Sponsored by Ford Motor Company, "The Ford Show" was aired on NBC from 1956-61. Leaving NBC, Ernie found a new home on the new ABC-TV network with his "Tennessee Ernie Ford Show." Ford later said it was exciting breaking into TV in the mid-1950s when most of the country was getting acquainted with the new medium. It was a feeling he shared in common with the Statesmen who had been pioneers of television with their syndicated Nabisco program at about the time Ford was breaking into TV.

Ford, known affectionately as "the ol' peapicker" and "ol' Ern," typified the kindly country uncle. With his warm, bass/baritone voice, ingratiating manner and homespun humor, Tennessee Ernie Ford came across the TV screen as a loving member of the family. Genuinely humble and very religious, he closed nearly all of his television shows and personal appearances with a hymn. This act proved so popular with his fans that he recorded some albums of hymn collections. Sales of these recordings skyrocketed. At the time of his death in October 1991, Ford's albums of sacred music had sold nearly 25 million copies.

"Of all the singing I do," he once said, "the hymns, spirituals and gospel songs not only give me the greatest pleasure, but seem to be something that truly needs to be done. Hymns and spirituals are the finest love songs of all."

Tennessee Ernie Ford's love of gospel music led him to invite Hovie Lister and the Statesmen Quartet to appear on his ABC television program. The show featuring the Statesmen aired in

The Statesmen and Tennessee Ernie Ford pose with the quartet's new bus, 1962.

October 1962. The quartet was spotlighted for a couple of selections on their own and accompanied Ford in the show's closing number—"Where Could I Go But To The Lord." With millions of network viewers tuning in, the show offered the greatest widespread TV exposure the Statesmen had enjoyed since the days of their syndicated Nabisco program, perhaps as much as their winning appearance on Arthur Godfrey's Talent Scouts on CBS-TV in 1954.

After taping the show, the Statesmen took Ford for a ride around Los Angeles in their new Flexible bus. Ford was quite taken with the new vehicle, according to Hovie. He had a couple of bags of popcorn with him that he had brought from the studio. Ford was standing in the doorwell entrance of the bus listening to driver O'Neill Terry explain the many features of the bus as Terry wheeled around the city streets. Suddenly, Ford instructed Terry to stop at a street corner where a man was waiting for the traffic light to change. As the bus rolled to a stop, Tennessee Ernie Ford opened the door, thrust a bag of popcorn to the stranger on the corner and said, "Here, friend, have a bag of popcorn on me!" The man stared bug-eyed, reached out and took the popcorn in trembling hands. He barely had time to stammer out a "thank you" as Tennessee Ernie Ford and the Statesmen Quartet wheeled away, leaving behind a bewildered, but satisfied, fan.

Hovie Takes the Spotlight

Darol Rice, always thinking of fresh approaches to recording and presenting the sacred artists on RCA's roster of talent, posed a new idea to the Statesmen in 1963. Why not record an album including several songs spotlighting Hovie's singing talents? Hovie occasionally sang in the quartet's concerts, and occasionally was featured in a song on Statesmen albums. Although he did not possess a highly-trained voice like the members of the quartet, it was obvious the people liked to hear him sing. Rice felt an album spotlighting Hovie might also prove to be popular among gospel music fans.

"I would usually sing on one song on Statesmen albums on RCA Victor or whatever label we happened to be on," explains Hovie. "It would either be a spiritual like 'Get Away Jordan' or maybe a slow, very spiritual type song that would touch the heart strings."

From the quartet's early years Hovie had been featured on an occasional number. This included a couple of recordings with Capitol, as Mosie Lister explains: "I wrote a song called 'Reap What You Sow' that was tailored to fit Hovie's voice. I wrote an arrangement of the old standard 'Stand By Me' that had a special line in it for Hovie with the other four voices singing behind him."

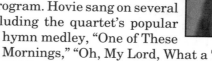

The Statesmen later re-recorded "Stand By Me" for RCA Victor. "Reap What You Sow" was popular with the group for several years, and was among the numbers they sang on their Nabisco television program. Hovie sang on several other Statesmen songs through the years, including the quartet's popular hymn medley, "One of These Mornings," "Oh, My Lord, What a Time," "The Old Landmark," "Jesus Fills My Every Need," "He's Got the Whole World In His Hands" and "What Love."

Hovie and Ethel Lister with children, Lisa and Hovie, Jr. (Chip).

Rice reserved studio facilities at RCA Victor's Music Center of the World in Hollywood, California, scheduling the Statesmen to record there in back-to-back sessions on Wednesday, June 26, 1963. He booked Dave Hassinger as recording engineer, and penciled in session musicians Lloyd Lunham, standup bass; and organist Shirley Mays to join Hovie Lister in accompanying the Statesmen. Rice was not yet ready to budget for large combos or orchestras to complement the recordings of the quartets on RCA's stable of artists. "Large orchestras aren't really necessary because this is message music we're dealing with," he told a writer from *Billboard* magazine.

Selections for the album included six songs featuring Hovie and six featuring other members of the group. Jake was spotlighted on "Worry, Who I," written by Prophets Quartet pianist Joe Moscheo. Lee Roy Abernathy penned "Lord, I'm Ready Now To Go" and "On That Judgment Day," both featuring Big Chief; and "He's A Personal Savior" on which Rosie Rozelle took the lead. Rosie also took command of Hazel Shade's "Show Me Thy Ways, O Lord," and "Goodbye, Troublesome Blues," a Doy Ott composition.

The songs featuring Hovie included two Vep Ellis tunes, "When He Calls I'll Fly Away" and "Jesus Knows;" a fourth song from Lee Roy Abernathy, "My Home;" and "Without Him." The latter was written by seventeen-year-old Mylon LeFevre, youngest son of Hovie's old friends Urias and Eva Mae LeFevre from the famous singing family of the same name. Additionally, the quartet selected two of Hovie's compositions—"Hands" and "As Time Goes By"—to be included on the album. Hovie by 1963 was quite active as a composer, following the lead of Wetherington and Ott, who had become prolific songwriters.

"Hovie Lister Sings With His Famous Statesmen Quartet" (LPM/LSP-2790) was recorded in six-and-a-half hours. Released late in 1963, the album was well accepted. "Without Him" became a gigantic success for the Statesmen, the LeFevres and eventually many other quartets as well. Today, the song can be found in numerous hymnals in churches all across the country.

Jake Hess & the Imperials

By 1963, Jake Hess felt the time had come to fulfill a personal ambition. He felt in his heart that he had already been afforded the privilege of singing in what the Gospel Music world had

perceived as the greatest gospel quartet ever—the Statesmen during the Denver Crumpler years. Now he wanted to organize his own quartet. He began to search for the best possible blend of voices he could find. He determined his new group would not build its presentation around high energy or flashy showmanship. In fact, this quartet would do no encores, thus enabling them to present more selections in their concert appearances.

"I wanted to organize a quartet and just stand flat-footed and sing," he explains. "It wouldn't be necessary to tell jokes or jump high or anything, just really enjoy singing. And I think I fulfilled that dream with the Imperials."

Jake had been taking note of talent that had impressed him down through the years. He approached several young men with his idea and eventually found four who shared his dream. Henry Slaughter, a prolific songwriter, keyboard stylist and talented arranger, had been accompanist for the Stamps-Ozark Quartet and the Weatherford Quartet, among others. At the time Jake called him, Slaughter was serving as music director of Rex Humbard's Cathedral of Tomorrow in Akron, Ohio. Another member of the Weatherfords was Armond Morales, who possessed a smooth, velvet-bass voice, with excellent blending qualities. Sherrill Nielsen, an Irish tenor from Montgomery, Alabama, was a member of the Speer Family. Gary McSpadden was still fresh in Jake's mind after his brief stint with the Statesmen. Gary had moved on to the baritone position with the Oak Ridge Boys. The Imperials were five attractive, young men, distinguished not only by their individual talents, but as experienced, established quartet men within the industry. After several months of careful planning and calculated dreaming they were ready to venture out on their own. All would leave their respective groups near the end of 1963.

"When I told him I was leaving I don't think Hovie really believed me, but there were no bad feelings," Jake says.

In retrospect, Hovie feels Jake may have become dissatisfied with the Statesmen in the early 1960s.

"Perhaps there might have been some disappointments there for him, or he felt like he wanted to go a different direction than what we were going. Maybe he felt like we had reached our peak at that time. But it was very devastating to me because Jake Hess has always been and always will be the greatest lead singer that gospel music has ever known. Not only that, he's one of the greatest men that I've ever worked with. Jake Hess is an idea man. Jake was the type of guy that if I had an idea or if he had an idea—which he had lots of them—he would call quite often and say, 'What do you think about so-and-so?' Not only about music, but Jake was always thinking ahead about sponsorship or about concert dates, or who would be a good person that would be a great ally to our group, or supporter of our group and that sort of thing. He and I, when we were at home and not on the road, we were constantly in touch by telephone or he was at the office and we were planning ahead for various things for the quartet. So, naturally, when

Jake Hess & the Imperials (from left): Armond Morales, Henry Slaughter, Gary McSpadden, Jake Hess and Sherrill Nielsen. The Statesmen have recorded several songs penned by Slaughter down through the years. McSpadden's first professional singing experience came with the Statesmen while substituting for an ailing Jake. Nielsen was to eventually succeed Rosie Rozell as tenor for the Statesmen.

Jake left I was very much devastated."

"Jake was like a member of mine and Jim's family," says Elizabeth Wetherington. "He came to us when he was just 18, so we more or less saw him grow up, and it was quite a loss to us."

Jake's last concert with the Statesmen—at least in a Statesmen lineup that included his longtime buddy James Wetherington—occurred at the Medina Temple in Chicago, on December 7, 1963. Although disappointed and maybe angered by Jake's departure, Hovie nonetheless gave his quartet partner of 15 years a sendoff befitting a hero in front of the Chicago crowd. After the concert, Jake caught a flight to Atlanta, while the Statesmen boarded their bus to continue their work. It was with mixed emotions that Jake winged his way home that night. Half of his life had been spent working together with Big Chief Jim Wetherington, first as struggling farm boys who were forced to "borrow" peaches so their starving quartet could eat, later as successful radio stars in Nebraska, and then as ambassadors of good will in the "perfect quartet." Their friendship would continue and Chief would later write songs for The Imperials. So, too, would Doy Ott. The friendship between Jake and Hovie survived this chapter in their lives. "Without Hovie Lister there would not have been a Jake Hess," Jake has often said, recalling how he had taken voice training when he joined the Statesmen because Lister felt his voice was too thin. Little did they know that December night in Chicago that Jake's departure from the Statesmen would not be permanent. They were destined (with the exception of James Wetherington) to work together again. "I know that when I die, I will be a Statesman," says Jake.

Jake Hess and the Imperials met the following week to begin rehearsals and chart their new futures together. Jake, then 36, relocated from Atlanta to Nashville, Tennessee, and the Imperials made Nashville their base of operations. They signed a recording contract first with Skylite, and later with HeartWarming Records, a new recording company organized by the John T. Benson Music Company. Jake Hess and the Imperials eventually pioneered new directions into contemporary vocal arrangements.

"Jake had desired to draw from some of the main groups a group of singers that he felt would comprise one of the best quartets that had ever been," McSpadden said in 1979. "I think we approached that and we changed the face of gospel music somewhat during those few years. I think music was changing at that time. You know, music is constantly changing. But the thing that we have to remember is the message that we have to give is very consistent. It stays the same because it's based on scripture."

The Imperials, says Jake, "had a sound that I loved. I think the Statesmen influence was evident in the Imperials. Nielsen had a Crumpler sound that I really liked. I think anybody that listened to the Imperials closely enough, they could hear a few Statesmen chord progressions and a few of the ideas. Henry Slaughter was the sound of the Imperials. He put the sound in the Imperials with his arranging. You can't minimize Henry Slaughter's influence on the Imperials."

By late 1967, however, Jake was forced to "turn a dream loose about the time it seemed to be the brightest." Still plagued by recurrent health problems which were aggravated by his diabetes, Jake visited his doctor for a series of tests. Analyzing the test results, the physician was firm in his grave assessment of the singer's condition. Jake had to retire from the rigors of the road or he would have a heart attack.

"So," says Jake grimly, "I got off the road and had a heart attack anyway."

17
The Sensational Statesmen

Jack Toney

Sand Mountain, in northeast Alabama, has produced many great gospel singers down through the years. Statesmen tenors Bobby Strickland, of Albertville, and Cat Freeman, of Fyffe, grew up there. Howard and Vestal Goodman, John Daniel, Buddy Parker, Carl Raines, Erman Slater, Seals "Low Note" Hilton, Bob Crews, and others were all from this part of the country. In later years the Sand Mountain town of Fort Payne would be the home of the award-winning country music band Alabama. The members of this group were friends of Cat Freeman in his latter years when Cat hosted a television program.

Jack Toney, born into a Southern Baptist home in Boaz in 1933, became well aware of Sand Mountain's great tradition of gospel singers during his youth. When classes at his rural school near Boaz dismissed for summer vacation, Jack looked forward to summer singing schools.

"I had two uncles that were singing school teachers so I had no other choice," he recalls. "I had to go about four weeks out of the summer to the singing schools."

Curtis and Carrie Toney also saw to it that their son took private music lessons in piano and voice the rest of the year. This training led to Jack's involvement in part-time groups around Alabama for a few years. In 1962, he sang on a program which also featured the Prophets Quartet of Knoxville, Tennessee. The Prophets were looking for someone to fill an upcoming vacancy and offered the position to Jack. Nine months later the Florida Boys were in a bind when lead singer Les Beasley fell ill. Jack filled in for five weeks with the Florida Boys until Beasley was able to return to work. When Jack was released by the Florida Boys, he got together with gospel promoter J.G. Whitfield to form the original Dixie Echoes.

"People would call me and would want a concert, because I had worked with a number of people down through the years," recalls Whitfield. "The Florida Boys would be booked. So I would put together something with my brother Joe and his wife Sue and we'd go do the show for them. At that time Jack Toney was in Pensecola and one day he came to our church. In fact, Coy Cook and Jack and myself, and I don't know who else, we sang at our church that day. Well, Jack stayed in Pensecola. He loved Pensecola so he stayed. And he kept after me, 'Whit, why don't we put a group together and just enjoy singing?' I said okay. He went to work for a radio station. So I got Joe and Sue and Jack and the other old boy was George Forbus. I don't know how many recall him but he was a good tenor."

Jack Toney

While with the Dixie Echoes, he attracted the attention in late 1963 of Hovie Lister and the Statesmen who were looking for just the right lead singer with whom to replace Jake Hess. Of course, other quartets were looking to fill some positions as well.

"There were some vacancies because of the Imperials being formed," observes Toney. "That's where the opening came for me" with the Statesmen.

The Statesmen were impressed with the tall, dark and handsome bachelor. Possessing a powerful lead voice, young Jack Toney was an up-and-coming gospel vocalist whose style was very different from that of the lead singer he would replace.

"I feel like anytime that you're offered a job after Jake leaves it you've got to have something going for you. I've always admired Jake. We have a good relationship," says Toney. "Of course, my favorite lead singer has always been James Blackwood. I guess I patterned more after James than I did anybody."

"I must say that we were fortunate in being able to secure the services of Jack Toney who was, and is, a very outstanding singer," states Hovie. "He wasn't Jake Hess. They had an altogether different style of singing. But Jack Toney had a great voice."

Jake's departure had been a great disappointment to the Statesmen. Jake had provided the strong melody around which the Statesmen had harmonized for 15 years. Even with the capable Jack Toney stepping in at the lead spot, the quartet went through a period of adjustment. But their determination, coupled with the work ethic that drove them to rehearse long hours and polish arrangements, brought them through the transition in fine style.

"There was not really a change in attitude," Hovie says of the transition from Jake Hess to Jack Toney. "Of course, we missed that particular sound and style" that the group had with Jake. "But Jack had a very magnetic personality with the people. Jack Toney had a following of his own, a big following. People loved him. He was a good mixer with the people and he had a great personality. On the stage he was a take charge type of guy, and as far as walking out when he'd have a lead and doing that sort of thing. You know, I could never minimize Jake's leaving, but at the same time I cannot say that the Statesmen didn't carry on. We went on."

Jack felt the pressure of the situation. A younger man might not have handled it well. But at age 30, Toney realized most of the pressure he felt as Jake Hess's replacement with the Statesmen was pressure that came from within.

"You know, any time you follow a person like Jake that has created his own niche in the business in the number one group in the nation, yes, there was some pressure. There was no doubt about that," he reflects. "Probably the most pressure I had was from myself. The fans were very receptive because they had accepted the fact that Jake had organized another group. So I had no real problem as far as the fans were concerned. It was the highlight of my life. It was a good opportunity. I feel I was very fortunate to be called to sing with the Statesmen Quartet. They were some good troupers: The Big Chief, Doy, Rosie and Hovie were at that time Number One!"

Doy Ott Takes the Spotlight

Don Butler, who late in the 1960s managed the Statesmen's music companies, once compared the teamwork of gospel quartet singing to that of a football team. He stressed that just as a football team must play with an effort of unity, the gospel quartet must work together as a "team effort of four voices that will blend and meld together." A football coach occasionally singles out an individual player to handle a difficult play because of that player's abilities. Butler's example of specialized team talent was the skill of punting or kicking a field goal. Likewise, individual quartet members are often assigned special tasks in certain musical arrangements.

"The Tenor singer is usually singled out to perform the lead or solo part on a song because of the tenderness of the tone or the ability to sing the high notes," Butler wrote. "The Bass singer is always easily distinguishable because of the lowness and the power of his booming tones. The Lead Tenor singer is called on to execute the signals or carry the ball so to speak; however, the Baritone is an important man in the quartet. It is the Baritone who supplies the weld that links all the parts together in beautiful rich harmony; it is the Baritone who acts as the pivot man who can either sing high or low and often has to switch parts many times during the performance of a number so that the unit will function in a pleasant easy to listen to manner."

Doy Ott handled his unpretentious role with class. His mellow baritone was key to the Statesmen's ability to blend. And blending he accomplished very well indeed. A songwriter, he provided many good songs for the quartet. Additionally, Doy wrote many of the unique arrangements that helped define the classic Statesmen style. But rarely was Ott featured on a solo part with the quartet.

On February 4-5, 1964, the Statesmen committed twelve songs to tape for their first album with Jack Toney in the lineup. For this album project the quartet leaned heavily on the vocal talents of their Indian baritone. Titled "The Statesmen Quartet Spotlights Doy Ott" (LPM/LSP-2864), the album featured Doy on seven songs. "I'll Pray For You," "Pass Me Not" and "He'll Go With Me" were among the songs that received the benefit of Doy's mellow interpretations. Eldridge Fox, who at the time continued to manage the vari-

ous publishing interests of the Statesmen, penned "Those Tender Hands" for Doy. Big Chief, Doy and Jack Toney traded solo verses on "Tell Them What It's All About," one of three songs Chief penned for the album.

The only composition Ott contributed to the collection was the poignant "Wait For Me," written after the death of his wife of more than 20 years. Joyce Ott had succumbed to cancer the previous year. Although Ira Stanphill's song "I Know Who Holds Tomorrow" had been closely identified with Doy since the early 1950s, its appearance on the album is indicative of Doy's faith in his Master during the uncertain days following his family's loss. Doy, his 21-year-old daughter Delores and nine-year-old son Joe had placed their tomorrows in the hand of God, secure in the knowledge that their beloved wife and mother would indeed be waiting "by the river of life" to meet them on the appointed day when the Lord beckoned, "Come home, we're waiting for you."

Jack Toney was given the opportunity to shine on the song "Ship Ahoy." Rosie Rozelle provided soulful interpretations of Big Chief's "I'm the Least In the Kingdom of the Lord," Doris Akers' "Sweet Jesus" and Lee Roy Abernathy's "The Greatest of All These Things." Big Chief Wetherington's commanding bass shared solo lines with Rozelle on another of Chief's compositions, "In the Name of the Lord."

Shortly after the release of the album "The Statesmen Quartet Spotlights Doy Ott," the quartet was again in the recording studio. On July 14, 1964, the Statesmen recorded four songs for a new RCA Camden release, "Songs of Faith" (CAL/CAS-843). Big Chief Wetherington was featured on the ever popular "How Great Thou Art." Doy Ott stepped to the fore on "Must Jesus Bear the Cross Alone." Rosie Rozell took the solo on "If I Can Help Somebody."

The fourth song from that session was "Beyond the Gates," a number that has become closely identified with Jack Toney down through the years. Toney had been charming audiences with his interpretation of the song for several years before recording it with the Statesmen. "Beyond the Gates" was written by Rev. Rupert Cravens. While a student at the Vaughan Music Company's music school in Lawrenceburg, Tennessee, back in 1935, Cravens had studied under G.T. "Dad" Speer. "Beyond the Gates," in fact, was published by the James D. Vaughan Music Company. Interestingly, Blackwood-Statesmen Enterprises had purchased the company in

1962.

"We didn't have what you would call any specific hits at that time, I don't think," Toney now says of his first year with the Statesmen. "We had some good songs. There was not a 'Get Away Jordan' or 'Sweeter As The Days Go By.' That was already there. But 'Beyond the Gates' has followed me for about 30 or 40 years."

The new recordings were to supplement six songs which had been released by RCA as singles during the Jake Hess era. "Songs of Faith" was released in November, 1964.

Back In Syndication

The exit of Jake Hess from the Statesmen did not significantly diminish the popularity of the quartet, if at all. In reality, they were greatly in demand in 1964. As Jack Toney had said, the fans had accepted the fact that Jake had formed another group. And as Hovie stressed, the Statesmen "went on" with their business of praising the Lord in song and entertaining all over North America. The rigorous schedule of 287 concerts in 1964 is a testament to the quartet's enormous demand for appearances. By 1963, the quartet's hectic calendar of concerts and extended road trips had forced Hovie to resign his pastorate at Mount Zion Baptist Church. No longer was he able to regularly get back to Georgia to fulfill his pulpit duties each Sunday. One concert tour to the West Coast included an extended trip into Canada for several appearances there. This tour consumed 31 days on the road.

"We did three West Coast trips to California," says Jack Toney of his years with the Statesmen, "but they were usually 21, 22 or 23 days. But this one we went on up into Vancouver, all up into Canada and came back down through."

However, the quartet didn't always sleep on the bus, Toney stresses. The Statesmen, whenever possible, checked into a motel for greater sleeping comfort. They were able to shower and feel refreshed before the evening concert or before the next day of travel.

"Of course, back in my Statesmen days, a motel room was anywhere from five, six, seven or eight dollars," says Toney.

Early in 1964, the Statesmen and Blackwood Brothers launched a new television venture which they called Statesmen-Blackwood TV Productions. The new company began production of a one-hour television program, "Singing Time In Dixie." The syndicated show was soon showing in markets throughout the country, from Maine to California. Hovie Lister and James Blackwood served as co-hosts of the program. Regulars on the show included the Speer Family, Rebels Quartet, Oak Ridge Boys and Stamps Quartet, in addition to the Statesmen and Blackwood Brothers, of course. All groups were Skylite Record Company recording artists, also owned by Blackwood-Statesmen Enterprises and managed by Blackwood bass singer J.D. Sumner. It was natural that the Blackwoods and Statesmen bring on quartets that recorded for Skylite, for TV exposure increases record sales, an economic benefit to both the Statesmen-Blackwood partnership and to the quartet selling the record.

Every two months the quartets would meet for two days at production facilities in Charlotte, North Carolina, to film eight to 10 programs on videotape. They would begin filming at 2 p.m.

on a Monday and work until 10:30 p.m. They would return to the production facilities the following day to begin filming at 9 a.m. Again they would work until 10:30 p.m. Don Butler served as producer and Bob McCollum as director for "Singing Time In Dixie."

"It was very successful," says James Blackwood of the TV program. "We had a man who had quite a bit of experience in selling syndicated programs. He sold the program to stations around the country and at the peak we were on about 100 stations."

The Sensational Statesmen

In the years since he first wrote "Lord, I Want To Go To Heaven" with Mosie Lister in the early 1950s, Big Chief Wetherington had become quite prolific as a songwriter. By the early 1960s, Chief was turning out hit songs one after another, for not only the Statesmen but other groups as well.

"Back in the early years I begged him to learn more about writing by reading," Mosie recalls, "because he read music very poorly. He happened to have an extremely good ear. But a couple of years before he died he said, 'Mosie, I wish I had taken your advice and learned to read music so I could write out all these ideas that I have.' Chief had a very good mind and he had a vivid imagination. He had some excellent ideas. He had some ideas that he was not musically sophisticated enough to write down. But he came up with some very good songs."

Elizabeth Wetherington says her late husband often used sermon texts, or drew upon illustrations preachers used as the inspiration for the songs he created. A topic or a phrase would seal itself in his mind and later germinate into an idea for a song.

Chief accompanied himself somewhat primitively with a guitar as he composed his melodies. "He really didn't play," says his daughter Diana. "He knew a few chords and 'frammed,' as he called it."

When his surroundings limited the availability of suitable writing paper on which to pen his lyrics, Chief committed his ideas to anything and everything that was handy at the time. "This Was Almost Mine" had been written on stationery from a Louisville hotel.

"I've seen him do that many times," says Hovie. "Whenever an idea would hit him he would write it down on whatever was available."

"Back in the days when each member of the group took turns driving the bus, the Chief seemed to get his biggest inspiration for the songs he wrote," recalled Don Butler, who for a time operated the Statesmen publishing interests. "Often he would be sitting in the driver's seat clad in his pajamas and as the bus rolled down the highway he would tap his ring finger to the rhythm of a new song. When the drivers would change shifts, he would get the nearest piece of paper or cardboard and write down thew new song."

"He did a lot of writing when he was traveling on the bus," says Mrs. Wetherington. "I have songs of his that are written on the backs of menus, cardboard out of his starched shirts, backs of popcorn boxes and paper towels that they had on the bus. I'd stick those in a drawer somewhere and save them, and I've still got a bunch of them. Sometimes at home, if something hit him just right, he would get up in the night and go in the den and sit in there and start writing."

She estimates that Big Chief wrote about 200 songs, including several that were never published or recorded. He wrote a number of songs which were never recorded by the Statesmen, but became very successful songs for such groups as the Oak Ridge Boys, the Speer Family, Jake Hess & the Imperials, and others. Most of his compositions were published by the quartet's Faith Music, Inc. He later formed LoDo Music which published several of Wetherington's compositions in the last seven or eight years of his life. Elizabeth Wetherington continues to operate the company today.

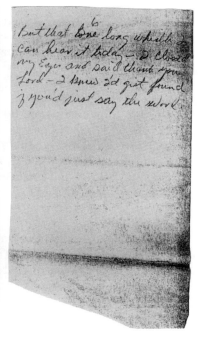

Ideas for songs often came to James "Big Chief" Wetherington while traveling on the bus. He wrote lyrics to his compositions on menus, hotel stationery, popcorn boxes, or whatever was available at the time. Shown here is the original draft of his popular narrative "Little Boy Lost" in Wetherington's handwriting on six brown paper towels.

The Statesmen usually included anywhere from one to three Wetherington compositions on each new album. After spotlighting first Hovie and Doy on RCA Victor albums, the Statesmen and producer Darol Rice agreed to feature Big Chief on an album. Not only would the quartet show off Chief's distinct bass vocals, but also his songwriting capabilities. Chief had a lineup of 12 songs ready and the Statesmen began to rehearse long hours in readying the material for the studio.

On August 11-12, 1964, nearly a month after concluding work on the "Songs of Faith" album for RCA Camden, the Statesmen were back in RCA's "Nashville Sound" studio facilities to record the new album which would be titled "The Sensational Statesmen With Hovie Lister" (LPM/LSP-2989).

Big Chief's bass vocals came shining through in solo spots on such songs as "Wake Me, Shake Me, Lord," "Till I Know," "Don't You Want To Be Saved," "How Many Times," "If You Drink This Water (You Will Never Thirst Again)," "Samson," and the popular recitation "Little Boy Lost"—about a boy who gets lost in a south Georgia swamp during a hunting trip. Somewhat autobiographical, the narrative could be perceived as a tribute to his Grandpa and Grandma Swett.

Jack Toney exhibited his vocal talent on "God's Got His Hand On You" and "It's Better To Be Late At the Pearly Gate (Than To Arrive In Hell On Time)," and shared the spotlight with Hovie Lister on "I'll Keep Walking All the Way." "Give Me A Man That Can Cry" was perfect for Doy Ott's wide vocal range. Rosie Rozell was spotlighted on the collection's closing number, "Greater Love Hath No Man."

The album was released in January, 1965, simultaneously with "The Best of the Statesmen Quartet with Hovie Lister" (LPM/LSP-2933), a collection of favorites from previous RCA Victor albums.

18

Showers of Blessing

Gospel Music Association

In an effort to promote gospel music to the masses on a major scale, several leaders in the gospel music industry gathered during the 1964 National Quartet Convention in Memphis, Tennessee, to organize the Gospel Music Association. Taking as their lead the example of the Country Music Association which had successfully promoted country music, the founders of the Gospel Music Association (GMA) envisioned an organization that would bring together all facets of Christian music—publishers, promoters, performers, recording companies, disc jockeys—to unite the gospel music business and achieve things as an association that could not be accomplished by individual groups and artists.

GMA, under a non-profit charter issued by the State of Tennessee, was to serve as a clearing house for exchanging ideas and suggestions to improve the entire industry, focus on issues and present a united front to tell the world about gospel music. GMA first focused its attention on the radio market. The organization's founders believed that by courting radio executives and disc jockeys, the broadcast people would be encouraged to play more gospel records.

The members of the original GMA Board of Directors and the facet of the industry each represented included the following: Hovie Lister and Urias LeFevre, representing radio/television broadcasters; James Wetherington and J.D. Sumner, music composers; James Blackwood and Bill Hefner, record companies; Brock Speer and Don Baldwin, artists/musicians; W.B. Nowlin and J.G. Whitfield, concert promoters; Warren Roberts and Larry Scott, disc jockeys; John T. Benson, Jr. and Meurice LeFevre, music publishers; Don Light and Charlie Lamb, trade papers; and W.F. Myers and Frances Preston, directors-at-large. Don Light, of *Billboard*'s Nashville office, was elected Chairman of the Board. Elected GMA President was Willis F. "Jim" Myers, an executive with the performance rights organization SESAC.

Golden Gospel Songs and Happy Sounds

On March 1-2, 1965, the Statesmen took a break from their busy road schedule to record an album which was released in July as "The Statesmen Quartet With Hovie Lister Sings the Golden Gospel Songs" (LPM/LSP-3392). Their old friend Ralph Goodpasteur from the First Church of Deliverance in Chicago sat in as organist on one of the sessions.

Big Chief contributed a powerful new song, "This Was Almost Mine," complete with one of his gripping recitations. Faith Music staff writer Charles Matthews offered "Walk His Way" and "If Everybody Prays." The quartet included three selections from the pen of Lee Roy Abernathy—"I'm Building A Bridge," "Meet Me Up In Heaven Someday" and "Checking Up On My Payments To The Lord." Doy Ott enjoyed the spotlight on "Praying Hands," from Alma Gray and Aileene Hanks, and Beatrice Beal's "Since Jesus Spoke Peace To My Soul." Also included were "The Heavenly Parade," by Adger M. Pace and J.T. Cook; Lucie Campbell's "Touch Me, Lord Jesus" and O.A. Parris's "Hallelujah, I'm Going Home." The "Golden Gospel Songs" album also included the first Statesmen recording of a Bill Gaither song—"O, How I Need Thee." Eventually, the Statesmen were to record several of Gaither's compositions and, in the process, build a lasting friendship.

The quartet's second record project of 1965 was a collection of new recordings for a Camden release. Earlier Camden albums had consisted mostly of previously-released songs. Camden producer Ethel Gabriel agreed with Hovie Lister's suggestion to hire the talented Goss Brothers of Atlanta to serve as instrumentalists on the project. James Goss provided the guitar licks, Lari and Ronald Goss alternated between organ and bass guitar.

Recorded in RCA's "Nashville Sound" facilities on July 1-2, the album included songs by Cleavant Derricks, "We'll Soon Be Done With Troubles and Trials" and "When God Dips His Love In My Heart;" "I Walk With Jesus" and "I'll Live In Glory," from J.M. Henson; "Get On The Happy Side of Living," by Vep Ellis; "I'm Satisfied With Jesus," written by Doy Ott; Hovie Lister's "When I Come to the End of the Road;" and the popular collaboration of Rusty Goodman and Gov. Jimmie Davis, "I Wouldn't Take Nothing for My Journey Now." Rosie Rozell arranged "Jesus Is Gettin' Us Ready for That Great Day" featuring modern harmony on the closing chorus. The arrangement of "Do Lord" also incorporated modern harmony in the closing refrain.

Although a product of RCA's economy label, the album—titled "All Day Sing And Dinner on the Ground" (CAL/CAS-916)—was among the finalist nominees for a National Academy of Recording Arts and Sciences (NARAS) Grammy Award the following year. Jack Toney remembers the album fondly and considers it one of his three favorites of the recordings he has made with the Statesmen.

Ironically, after finishing the "All Day Sing and Dinner on the Ground" album, the Statesmen appeared in an all-night sing while a number of concertgoers enjoyed picnic lunch "on the ground." Following the Friday afternoon session on July 2, the Statesmen worked a concert in Nashville. The next morning they climbed aboard the bus for a 450-mile trek to Bonifay, Florida, to appear in promoter J.G. Whitfield's big sundown to sunup sing, an event that was reported in *Billboard*. Whitfield had prepared instructions and the schedule in which the quartets would appear during the first round of singing. These were distributed to each quartet manager.

The lineup included: 1. Blue and Gray Quartet, 15 minutes; 2. Pathfinders Quartet, 15 minutes; 3. Blackwood Brothers, 20 minutes; 4. Commanders Quartet, 15 minutes; 5. Plainsmen Quartet, 20 minutes; 6. Messengers Quartet, 15 minutes; 7. Jimmie Davis, 20 minutes; 8. Conn Trio, 15 minutes; 9. Statesmen Quartet, 20 minutes; 10. Melody Men Quartet, 20 minutes; 11. Couriers Quartet, 20 minutes; 12. Florida Boys, 20 minutes; 13. Dixie Echoes, 20 minutes; 14. Happy Goodman Family, 20 minutes; 15. Jubilee Group (no time listed).

Additional instructions were: "Use this line-up for the second round. Mr. Whitfield will tell you when you go on the second time how long to stay. All managers have your group ready to go on: ON TIME."

Billboard described the Bonifay Memorial Field football stadium setting: "Excitement filled the air, as if one was about to witness a compelling drama. People were everywhere. There was a piquant flavor of a carnival-like atmosphere. People milled around stands selling hamburgers, Cokes, ice cream. The quartets set up their racks to sell albums, sheet music and songbooks.

"...Soon the seating stands on both sides of the stadium were packed full. The entire football field was filled with people who had brought lawn chairs to sit on. Some brought cots for small children to sleep on. Most brought picnic-type lunches—fried chicken, sandwiches, watermelon, cake, thermos bottles...

"The sing had started about 7:15. The sound system from the portable stage at the far end of the field carried the harmonizing voices loud and clear out over the stands and field."

"I remember being in Bonifay," recalls Jack Toney, "on the night they had probably the largest crowd that had ever attended. They said there were about 15,000 people at that time. At one time in Fort Worth we did three buildings each night during maybe the two or three times that we were out there. And, of course, the Long Beach Municipal Auditorium. The Blackwood Brothers and Statesmen, along with the Stamps and other groups would fill that up Fridays and Saturday nights two or three times a year. Those were some highlight times."

Back in Nashville on August 17-18, the Statesmen—again with Goss Brothers in tow—prepared a new album slated for release in January, 1966. "The Happy Sound of the Statesmen Quartet with Hovie Lister" (LPM/LSP-3494) included several hymns and traditional songs: "Will the Circle Be Unbroken," "Leave It There," "Lived and He Loved Me," "Back to the Dust," "Peace, Sweet Peace," "My Home, Sweet Home," "I'm a Millionaire" and "No, Not One." Also included were several new songs—Mosie Lister's latest effort that was sweeping the country, "His Grace Is Sufficient for Me;" "You'll Find Him There," "Ain't Nothing You and Me Can't Handle" and "You Gotta Live Like Jesus Every Day." The latter two were given Hovie Lister's inimitable vocal treatment. "You Gotta Live Like Jesus" was especially popular with Hovie's fans across the country.

Shortly after the release of the album, Jack Toney asked for a leave of absence. Newly married, he was having great difficulty dealing with the extensive amount of travel away from hearth and home. The replacement on whom the Statesmen finally settled was an expressive vocal stylist with several years of quartet experience—Roy McNeil.

Roy McNeil

The Prophets Quartet first hit the gospel quartet circuit in the spring of 1959. Although they never reached superstar status, the Prophets enjoyed a large following throughout the country. In their early years, the Prophets frequently played small churches and auditoriums in small towns for free-will offerings. Much of the money was used for bus repairs or to replace worn-out sound equipment. "No one could call us the 'profits' quartet because there were none," says Ed Hill, one of the founding members.

Through the years the Knoxville, Tennessee-based quartet served as gospel music's equivalent of a baseball "farm team" for the more well-known quartets. Many rising stars in the business used the Prophets as a springboard to launch them into a career with one of the major groups. Among these were baritone Duane Allen, who in 1966 went from the Prophets to the Oak Ridge Boys and remains the lead singer for the Oaks today. Original member Jay Berry left the Prophets for a short but successful career as lead singer for the Rebels. Pianist Joe Moscheo left to replace Henry Slaughter as keyboardist with Jake Hess and the Imperials. With the Imperials, Moscheo later became a member of the Elvis Presley and Jimmy Dean shows, made national television appearances on The Tonight Show and Merv Griffin Show, and enjoyed immense popularity as a pioneer in the contemporary Christian music scene. Moscheo is now an executive with Broadcast Music Incorporated (BMI). After the Prophets disbanded in 1973, founder Ed Hill became baritone with J.D. Sumner and the Stamps, traveled with the Elvis Presley Show, and became the stage announcer for Presley's concerts.

Roy McNeil

Roy McNeil was singing lead for the Prophets when the Statesmen called him to succeed Jack Toney in the spring of 1966. Ironically, Roy had followed Toney with the Prophets late in 1962. Prior to taking his spot in the Prophets' lineup, Roy sang tenor in the Rangers Trio with David Reece and Clarke Thompson. As a vocalist McNeil is one of the classic stylists of gospel quartet music and a specialist in voice control. His great dynamics and trademark variation of tone within a word or note set him apart from many lead and tenor singers of the 1960s.

During Roy's brief stay with the Statesmen, the quartet recorded two albums for RCA Victor. The first was "The Gospel Gems" (LPM/LSP-3624), recorded on May 3-4, 1966. Three songs in this collection, including "The Lord Accepted Me" written by Big Chief, had been big songs for McNeil with the Prophets. The others were "I Thank My God," written by former Prophets pianist Joe Roper, and "You Must Make Up Your Mind," from the pen of Joe Moscheo.

"Always Remember" and "River of Grace" featured the smooth baritone of Doy Ott. Doy shared the solo spotlight with McNeil on "The Lord Accepted Me," and with Big Chief on the hymn "Count Your Blessings." The Statesmen backed Hovie on "God Knows How" and "He's With Me," the latter written by Chief's uncle, Ben Swett, who years earlier had replaced Jake Hess with the Melody Masters. Swett later served as a missionary to Jamaica. Rosie Rozell provided soulful tenor treatment of "O, Yes Indeed," "Have I Done My Best for Jesus," Rusty Goodman's classic "Who Am I," and "You Gotta Walk That Road," written by Albert Brumley. RCA released "The Gospel Gems" in July 1966.

On August 15-16, the Statesmen recorded "In Gospel Country" (LPM/LSP-3703), released in February 1967. Songs in this collection included two old standards, "Brighten the Corner Where You Are" and "Just Over In The Gloryland." Big Chief contributed "In Jesus Name, I Will" and "When You've Really Met the Lord," both published by his new music company, LoDo Publishing. The Statesmen recorded three songs published by J.M. Henson Music Company, another of the quartet's music firms. These included "Watching You," written by J.M. Henson; "I Told My Lord," by Marion Snider; and "Grace for Every Need," by J.M. Henson and Byron L. Whitworth. Two songs from Faith Music, Inc., were Murray Smith's "Where the Milk and Honey Flows," and "Give Me Light," a song by the writing team of Don Butler and Larry Taylor. Butler had just succeeded Eldridge Fox as manager of the Statesmen's various music companies and served as producer of the "Singing Time In Dixie" television program. "Heaven Is Where You Belong" was penned by Lee Roy Abernathy. Duane Allen contributed a song called "No More" to the effort. "No More" was published by the Oak Ridge Boys' Silverline Music Company. The twelfth selection was Gene Autry's classic, "That Silver Haired Daddy of Mine."

Boyce Hawkins, who briefly had served as Statesmen pianist during Hovie's military service in 1950, was among the backup musicians during the "Gospel Gems" and "In Gospel Country" sessions. Joining Hawkins were guitarist Herman Wade and bassist Roy Huskey, Jr.

Jack Toney returned to the quartet shortly after the Statesmen had completed work on the "In Gospel Country" album. Roy McNeil resumed his previous role as lead singer for the Prophets.

Skylite Records, Inc.

Within a few years after Blackwood-Statesmen Enterprises formed Skylite Record Company in 1959, several new recording firms came on the scene. The gospel quartet recording industry became a very competitive field. In Atlanta, Sing Recording Company opened and soon boasted a lineup of artists that included the LeFevres (owners of Sing Recording Company and Sing Music Company), the Prophets, Blue Ridge Quartet and Johnson Sisters. In 1964, the widely-known John T. Benson Music Company formed HeartWarming Records. Leaving the Skylite fold for HeartWarming were Jake Hess and the Imperials, the Speer Family and the Weatherford Quartet. Word, in 1965, formed a subsidiary—Canaan Records—to record gospel quartets. Skylite artists, including the Florida Boys and Rebels quartets, joined several groups on the Canaan roster, including the Plainsmen, Dixie Echoes, the Harvesters, the Couriers and others.

For several years, J.D. Sumner had been sole manager of Skylite Recording Company. On top of this, Sumner had left the Blackwood Brothers in July, 1965 to join the Stamps Quartet as bass singer and manager. Sumner, however, remained a partner in the Blackwood Brothers who owned the Stamps Music organization, including the quartet. A few months later, Sumner ap-

Hovie Lister & The Statesmen, 1968 (l-r): Hovie Lister, Rosie Rozell, Jack Toney, Doy Ott and Jim Wetherington.

proached his Blackwood-Statesmen Enterprises partners about selling Skylite.

"It got to be where I had to do all the work, and it just got to be too much of a hassle to be in the back of a bus trying to run a record company," says Sumner. "It was owned by six people and I wasn't getting any more than anybody else out of it and I was doing all the work. Nobody else wanted to run it so we sold it." On March 1, 1966, they sold the company to Joel Gentry.

"J.D. Sumner had been managing Skylite from the back compartment of the Stamps Quartet bus," says Gentry. "It just became too much to handle."

"Some other gospel record companies were coming on the scene," recalls longtime Skylite producer Brock Speer. "I know that HeartWarming was. Canaan came on at about that time and (Word vice president) Marvin Norcross was a very energetic, aggressive man. So the competition was pretty strong." Concerts and their own recordings continued to be the primary focus of the Blackwoods, Statesmen and Stamps, Speer adds. "I don't think they had the time to do the marketing and production" for other quartets. "That's the reason they sold it."

Several quartets, including the Oak Ridge Boys, remained with Skylite after Gentry purchased the company. The Oaks, however, eventually migrated to HeartWarming. The Blackwood Brothers continued to record some product with Skylite while remaining under contract to RCA Victor. The Statesmen returned to the Skylite fold when their contract with RCA Victor expired in 1968.

Soon after selling Skylite, the Statesmen and Blackwoods discontinued their "Singing Time In Dixie" syndicated television program. The hour-long, black-and-white format was replaced by a half-hour program called "Glory Road." This new show from Statesmen-Blackwood TV Productions was filmed in color for syndication to most of the stations that had aired "Singing Time In Dixie."

Showers of Blessing

The first Statesmen album with Jack Toney back in the lineup was recorded in Nashville on February 15-16, 1967. On the invitation of Producer Darol Rice, Boyce Hawkins again joined the quartet in the studio, providing organ accompaniment. Henry Strzelecki and Roy Huskey, Jr., alternated sessions on bass, and Herman Wade returned on electric guitar. Released in August, 1967, the record was titled "Showers of Blessing" (LPM/LSP-3815).

The Faith Music writing team of Don Butler and Larry Taylor penned four songs—"This Great Love of Jesus" and "You'd Better Run," both of which featured Jack Toney's sparkling lead tenor; "The Hand of God" and "I've Gotta Have Jesus"—for the album. Two other songs came from the Faith stable of writers, Garnet Lindsey's "My Father's Will," and "Come On, Be Happy," a collaborative effort by M.E. Breed and Charlotte Boyd. Big Chief and Rosie Rozell shared solos on the title hymn "There Shall Be Showers of Blessing." Each vocalist in the quartet took a solo turn on "The Old Account Settled Long Ago." Doy Ott offered a tender rendering of Henry Slaughter's "Many Joys and Thrills Ago," accented by Boyce Hawkins' touch at the console organ. From the J.M. Henson Music collection came "My Lord Will Care for Me." Rosie was spotlighted on Ira Stanphill's "Unworthy." Also included in the collection was "Choose You This Day," featuring a pleasing arrangement of modern harmony as only the Statesmen could deliver. The song was written by Bob Prather who had penned such earlier Statesmen hits as "Led Out of Bondage" and "Headin' Home."

On the heels of the "Showers" album came "Sing, Brother, Sing" (LPM/LSP-3888), recorded in three sessions on July 11-12, 1967. Darol Rice hired a variety of musicians to assist Hovie Lister in providing accompaniment for the quartet on what were to be their final sessions for RCA, although they later sang backup on an album with RCA sacred artist Tony Fontane.

During the afternoon session of July 11, Boyce Hawkins at the organ, Billy Grammar accompanying on electric guitar, and Henry Strzelecki on the bass provided support for the quartet in recording four selections—"Have You Been to Calvary," "We've Come This Far By Faith," Henry Slaughter's "Jesus Said It, I Believe It," and "The Great Physician," the latter two featuring Hovie Lister.

Hawkins returned for the quartet's second session that evening, joined by bassist Joe Zinkan and a guitarist by the name of Jerry Hubbard who would in a few years become major music and film star Jerry Reed. This session produced the title song, written by Mosie Lister, and featuring a lightning-quick guitar lick from Jerry Reed. Also recorded that evening were two Vep Ellis creations: "When I Got Saved" and "I've Got a Right to Praise the Lord," and "Step By Step, Day By Day," written by Vida Nixon and Byron Whitworth.

Bassist Roy Huskey, Jr., and guitarist Herman Wade joined Lister and Hawkins for the July 12 session. The Statesmen added two more Vep Ellis compositions—"My God Can Do Anything" and "Oh My Brother, Where You Headin'?"—to the album collection. Big Chief sang an innovative interpretation of the old standard "Where Could I Go But to the Lord." Jack Toney, who contributed some of his best recorded vocal work throughout the album, was featured on "Happy Tracks," a new song written by Ray Pennington. "Happy Tracks" had been a hit on the country charts for Kenny Price, a regular on the popular "Hee Haw" television show.

Although "Sing, Brother, Sing," released in January, 1968, was the last album the Statesmen were to record for RCA, it was not the last Statesmen album released by the company. "The Best of the Statesmen Volume 2" (LPM/LSP-3925), a collection of previously-released songs, was released in April 1968. The company later issued some albums of previously-released material on the RCA Camden label.

Steve Sholes, the man who had signed the Statesmen and Blackwood Brothers to recording contracts with RCA back in the 1950s, died in 1968 shortly after being elected to the Country Music Hall of Fame. Soon, Darol Rice also was no longer active as RCA's top gospel producer. The company had changed and so had its sense of musical direction.

"All of the people that we knew or had contacts with, or that had a love particularly of gospel music, were no longer with the company," says James Blackwood of that era. "They just weren't doing anything for us anymore and we (the Blackwood Brothers and Statesmen) just didn't feel like it was to our advantage to stay."

God Loves American People

More than perhaps any decade that had come before it, the 1960s saw a rapid change of pace in international, social and cultural affairs. The world was making giant technological strides, especially in such areas as the exploration of space and in medicine with the development of heart transplant surgery. The United States stepped in to help a free people in Vietnam—a land on the other side of the world—in its quest to escape the evils of communism. A revolution in fashion, music, literature and the arts swept among the world's younger generation. Sexual and social taboos were eroded by the contraceptive pill, marijuana and hallucinogen drugs. Battles raged in the streets of America: The civil rights movement led a sometimes violent social revolution against prejudice. Other social-conscious movers and shakers demonstrated against our country's military involvement in Vietnam, Cambodia and Laos. During the spring of 1968, civil rights leader Dr. Martin Luther King, Jr., and Senator Robert F. Kennedy, a Democratic presidential aspirant, died brutally at the hands of assassins.

Amid this grim background, the Statesmen recorded a Lee Roy Abernathy song that they hoped would revive the patriotic spirit of the gospel music public. This song was to become the title song of their first album under a new contract with Skylite Records. The patriotic theme was reinforced in the album's jacket notes:

"America is a vast land of opportunity and goodness. Despite the cry of a 'sick society,' which is heard around us, America is a forerunner of individual freedom, individual rights and individual worship. These three elements don't combine to make a sick society.

"Hovie Lister and the Statesmen, long called Georgia's Ambassadors of Goodwill, have now the right to be America's Ambassadors of Goodwill. They have spent the last two decades traveling from one end of the U.S.A. to the other spreading 'good news' or in its more common term, gospel.

"This gospel decries corruption, violence, lack of brotherly love, the essences of principles this land of freedom was founded on.

"Freedom and Religion and America go hand in hand..."

Henry Slaughter's "How Long Will It Take?"—"How long will it take to realize that this old world ain't paradise? Heaven's waiting yonder beyond the blue..."—further addressed the troubled world climate. "That's Gospel, Brother" contained lyrics of a brotherhood theme—"I can't walk with you. You can't walk with me. We can't walk together except we first agree." Other songs in the collection contained more traditional themes.

Produced by Joel Gentry and recorded at Columbia Records' Nashville studios, "God Loves American People" (SLP-6080) was released in the fall of 1968.

Jack Toney

During the Christmas holiday season of 1968, Jack Toney resigned.

"I had some family problems," he says. "Just to make it plain, my wife didn't want me on the road. I have never been a good road person. That was probably my downfall in the singing business. I love to be home."

However, he was somewhat disappointed to see the end of his tenure with the Statesmen.

"I was the youngest one, but I was treated very fairly by the whole group," he says. "I have no complaints. They were very professional. That was the highlight of my singing career. There's no doubt about it. They were really disappointed I was leaving the group, seemingly. At the time I thought it was the best thing for my life, so that's what I did."

19
Thanks to Calvary

Jim Hill

Jim Hill

Although Jim Hill grew up north of the Mason-Dixon Line, he learned southern-style gospel singing in the church his family attended—the Mabert Road Baptist Church in Portsmouth, Ohio.

"In my church we had the old southern gospel music, Stamps-Baxter singing conventions," he recalls, "and we had the books that came out regularly. We formed groups. It seemed that everybody had to have a group back in those days, and I grew up singing mostly with groups in the church."

Hill later studied opera and voice. As a young man he had a chance to audition at the Cincinnati Conservatory of Music with a possible audition with the Metropolitan Opera to follow. The music of the church, however, held more appeal for him.

"When I got into gospel music I just became disinterested in the opera work and got in my local church quartet," he says. "It was a popular old weekend group. We had some good times."

This group, formed by Hill and Harold Patrick in the mid-1950s, was the Golden Keys Quartet. The Golden Keys were a widely-known, part-time quartet in the Midwest during the late 1950s and early 1960s. For several years the Golden Keys were the featured group on the Sunday morning worship service at the National Quartet Convention—quite an honor for a part-time group. In time the quartet hired a young man from Alexandria, Indiana, as lead vocalist. Danny Gaither had recently graduated from college and secured a teaching position in the Portsmouth area. Danny's older brother Bill was just beginning to write gospel songs. In time, the Golden Keys began to sing a few of these compositions.

"That's kind of how Bill's songs got started," says Jim today. "We were the first to do 'I've Been to Calvary,' and a lot of those old songs he wrote back there."

Hill also had written a song in the early 1950s—"What a Day That Will Be"—that became very popular with Golden Keys audiences around the country.

"Now I wasn't a songwriter," he says. "It was such a simple song that I didn't think anything about getting it recorded. There was nothing technical about the writing. The Golden Keys sang it and, occasionally, we would be singing together with the Speer Family there in my home town. Ben Speer really liked the song and wanted to publish it, which he did. The Homeland Harmony Quartet was the first professional group to record it. Then the Speer Family and several other groups sang it."

Eventually, the popularity of the Golden Keys proved to be the quartet's undoing. Each member held a regular job on weekdays and boarded the quartet's old bus on weekends to fill a busy concert schedule. Although they were in demand, there was not an adequate schedule to warrant the men giving up their weekday jobs for a full-time singing career. In 1962, Jim Hill received an offer to sing tenor with the Stamps Quartet. When Jim, his wife Ruth, and daughter

Taping the Thrasher Brothers' "America Sings" TV show

Susan Elaine moved to Memphis, Tennessee, for the Stamps job, the Golden Keys disbanded. Shortly thereafter, Danny Gaither moved back to Indiana to sing with his brother in the Bill Gaither Trio.

"I managed the Stamps before J.D. Sumner was with them," says Jim. "The Blackwoods, who owned the Stamps company, hired me to move down and sing the first tenor and manage the group. We had Mylon LeFevre, Roger McDuff and John Hall in the group, and Joe Roper played the piano."

Jim stayed six years as tenor singer with the Stamps Quartet. During the summer of 1965, J.D. Sumner had moved over from the Blackwood Brothers to become manager and bass singer, and the group became J.D. Sumner and the Stamps Quartet. Through various personnel changes at the lead, baritone and keyboard positions, the quartet became one of the top groups in the gospel quartet industry.

When Jack Toney left the Statesmen at the end of 1968, Jim Hill took steps to fulfill a longtime dream. The Statesmen had been his heroes for many years.

"I always dreamed of singing or working sometime with Hovie Lister," Jim recalls. "Hovie always inspired me so much onstage, and the Statesmen to me were the ultimate."

At 38 years of age, Hill felt he wouldn't be able to sing in the first tenor range for many more years. If he could sing in the lower range of a lead vocalist, he might be able to sustain his career longer in the quartet business he loved so well. Jim approached first J.D., then Hovie, with his idea. After some discussion it was agreed. Sumner hired former Statesmen lead singer Roy McNeil to sing tenor with the Stamps. Jim Hill became the new lead singer for the Statesmen.

"I thoroughly enjoyed working with J.D. Sumner and the Stamps," Jim says today. "He's the finest guy you ever could work with. I wasn't disappointed there."

Sumner had to be apprehensive about losing the Stamps' tenor singer of six years, especially when he was replacing Hill with a man who had served as lead singer for two professional quartets. "This," Sumner later said of McNeil, "to an extent, had hurt him because he has a true tenor voice, a high, smooth, easy, pleasant voice. Roy was great for us on the tenor."

Dropping from the first to second tenor (or lead) range proved to be a challenge for Jim Hill.

"It was extremely hard because you sing in such a different register," he observes. "You have to sing much lower at times. People don't appreciate the range lead singers sing in, and Jake Hess is an example of one of the best. You're singing low and next you're singing high."

Soon after getting their new lead singer settled into the Statesmen lineup, the quartet began to work up material for their next Skylite album. They resurrected two songs that had been synonymous with the Statesmen in the late 1950s—"Oh, My Lord, What a Time," featuring Hovie, and "Faith Unlocks the Door," with Jim Hill featured on the vocal and Big Chief adding the recitation. Including the traditional number "Old Time Religion" on the album proved to be a popular move as the song was well-received all over the country. From their own Faith Music, the Statesmen selected "God's Not Dead," a song that addressed a widely-publicized statement by a liberal philosopher that the Almighty had expired.

Among other new songs chosen for the new album were "Do You Really Care" and Dottie Rambo's megahit "He Looked Beyond My Fault," with new words matched to the tune of the popular Irish song "Danny Boy." Both songs contained solo verses by Doy Ott and Jim Hill. Four of the record's new songs came from the pen of Bill Gaither, including "Thanks to Calvary," "I'm

Free," "Why Should I Worry or Fret" and "Going Home." Gaither had been pitching songs to the Statesmen for several years.

"The first tune that we probably pitched to them was 'He Touched Me' which they did not record then," says Gaither. "Jake, in '63 after we wrote the song, was ready to leave to start the Imperials and the Imperials recorded it. After that we pitched the Statesmen several songs. But probably the first song that really became a major song for them that I wrote was 'Thanks to Calvary I Don't Live Here Anymore.'"

Cover photo from the "Thanks to Calvary" album, 1969

"Thanks to Calvary," featuring Hovie on the solo lines, was selected as the title song of the album (SLP-6080). It was destined to become a big hit for the Statesmen as well as solo artist Doug Oldham. Doy, Rosie and Big Chief traded solo lines on "Why Should I Worry or Fret." Chief was featured on "I'm Free."

The Statesmen also recorded "For God So Loved," a song about the crucifixion that Jim Hill had written in 1965. It had been a big song for J.D. Sumner and the Stamps when Hill worked with that group.

"That was a song," Hill recalls, "that we later sang on the last night I was with the Statesmen in Long Beach, California, at the Civic Auditorium. Elvis Presley was there sitting offstage with his crew. He loved the Statesmen, and he yelled out on the stage and wanted us to sing 'For God So Loved.' He was in tears when I went off the stage and shook his hand. I found out later through some of his bodyguards that this was one of his favorite songs. He'd had them go out and buy the record and he played it at night."

"Thanks to Calvary" (SLP-6080) was the first Statesmen recording on which the quartet was backed by strings. Producer Joel Gentry hired musicians—credited on the album as the Skylite Strings—to provide orchestral accompaniment on the selections "Thanks to Calvary," "I'm Free," "He Looked Beyond My Faults" and "Do You Really Care."

According to Gentry, the Statesmen usually sold about 100,000 copies of each album released on the Skylite label. "Thanks to Calvary," with more than 120,000 records and tapes sold, ranks as the quartet's top-selling Skylite album ever. The group's continued popularity was addressed in the album's jacket notes:

"When you are already considered the top professional group in the business, when your albums have already outsold all others, when you have reached a certain peak of success and the road still lies ahead, what do you do? Most retire from their respective business and gracefully bow out.

"But when you are the Statesmen Quartet ... you just work a little harder and consistently stay on top, become more successful and continue to turn out magnificent albums like this one."

Sherrill Nielsen

Near the end of 1969 and shortly after the release of "Thanks to Calvary," Rosie Rozell left the Statesmen. He had toured with the quartet for the better part of 12 years, met untold thousands of friends and became one of the most admired tenors ever in the quartet business. But after all that time, he was not a partner in the group, he was an employee.

"From the time he joined the group in 1958 until he left in 1969 he was promised a part ownership in the Statesmen," says Betty Rozell, his widow. "It never happened. He wasn't happy about that situation. But as far as being dissatisfied with singing with the Statesmen, he didn't feel that way."

Rosie and Betty had married on August 7, 1966. She was originally from Clermont, Georgia, where she sang in a family group, The Searchers. Even after her marriage, Betty continued to sing in the family group. When Rosie left the Statesmen, he went on the road singing with his wife's family. Lending his name to the group for better recognition within the gospel quartet music industry, the group became Rosie Rozell and the Searchers. Rosie and the Searchers sang together from 1970 through the first six months of 1973, until the Lord blessed Rosie and Betty with other opportunities in the music ministry.

To replace Rozell, the Statesmen hired young Irish tenor Sherrill Nielsen, a quartet veteran from Montgomery, Alabama. Nielsen began singing at the tender age of four in the Nazarene church his family attended, and in revivals and other meetings around central Alabama. While in the military, he was a featured soloist with the U.S. Air Force Strategic Air Command Band in Omaha, Nebraska. As a youngster he had attracted the attention of the Speer Family when they were living in Montgomery. In the early 1960s, the Speers offered him his first professional singing job in gospel quartet music. Jake Hess later hired him as the original tenor singer for the Imperials.

Sherrill Nielsen

"Nielsen had a Crumpler sound that I liked," Jake explains.

Indeed, Sherrill Nielsen's Irish tenor voice was similar to that of the late Denver Crumpler. With Nielsen in the lineup, the quartet's sound was reminiscent of the Statesmen during the Nabisco years in the mid-1950s.

"Jim Hill and Sherrill Nielsen blended well together," observes Hovie. "Of course, we can never minimize the importance of Doy Ott. Doy was a great singer, probably the best baritone singer that any quartet has ever had. He was a great musical arranger, and knew his music and how to blend. He knew how to help us keep that Statesmen sound. As long as we had Doy and Chief we had a semblance of the Statesmen sound, especially with Sherrill Nielsen and Jim Hill. We had a great group then."

Since Nielsen's tenor range was a little higher than that of Rosie Rozell, Doy Ott was able to pitch the quartet's songs a little higher for Jim Hill's comfort. It had been a little difficult for Jim to make the transition from tenor to lead, "but I was able to do it," he says, "with Sherrill Nielsen singing the first tenor. He's so high that we could pitch the songs where I didn't have to sing extremely low."

"I don't think the Statesmen handled Nielsen well," opines Jake. "I think, instead of him singing in his range or singing the type songs that he should be singing, they threw a lot of material at him that wasn't his bag. He didn't do as good a job with them as he did with the Imperials, I don't think."

However, Nielsen did have some crowd pleasers with the Statesmen. Among these were "Sweet Jesus," which had been closely identified with him during his time with the Speers and Imperials; "Walk With Me," "If To Gain the World," "Keep on Smiling," "I Wonder What My New Address Will Be" and "I Just Can't Praise Him Enough," among others.

The quartet's first album after adding Nielsen was "New Sounds Today" (Skylite SLP-6090), released late in 1969. This collection included a new version of "In the Beginning." Jim Hill sang a new Bill Gaither song, "The Cross Made the Difference." Andre Crouch was building a reputation for writing great songs in the early 1970s. His "The Blood Will Never Lose its Power" was included in "New Sounds Today." Nielsen was featured in "Tell it All to Jesus." Each group member got a solo turn in "God Put a Rainbow in the Clouds." Hovie took the spotlight for "That's What Jesus Means to Me." Other songs appearing on the album were "My Dream Home in Glory," "I'll Never Forget," "I Know the Lord Will Never Fail" and "Keep Moving."

From left: Sherrill Nielsen, Jim Hill, Hovie Lister, Doy Ott, James Wetherington.

In 1973, Skylite was invited to submit two recordings for inclusion in the record libraries of the White House and the John F. Kennedy Center for the Performing Arts. Statesmen producer Joel Gentry sent copies of the Statesmen's "New Sounds Today" album and an album by J.D. Sumner and the Stamps. Gentry accepted an invitation to the White House for ceremonies in connection with the honor. He and fellow record moguls were treated with the pomp and circumstance befitting visiting heads of state by staffers in the Richard Nixon White House. "It was one of the most fantastic things that has ever happened in my life," he says.

The next album, recorded late in 1969 but released early in 1970, was a collection of solos called "The Statesmen Featuring Hovie, Sherrill, Jim, Doy and Big Chief" (SLP-6095). Big Chief contributed two original songs: "Great is the Lord" and "When My Soul Takes its Flight." Jim Hill wrote and sang "The Road of No Return." Doy Ott revived one of his compositions previously recorded by the quartet for RCA—"Have You Tried the Lord Today." Hovie introduced "God Will Provide," a new Henry Slaughter number. Other songs included "Just Let Me Touch Him," "Unworthy," "Gonna Shout Hallelujah," "I Must Tell Jesus" and "Impossible Dream."

Hovie Lister in 1969 served as first vice president of the Gospel Music Association. That was the year the GMA first handed out Dove Awards for outstanding achievement in the Christian music industry. For several years thereafter the Doves were presented during the annual National Quartet Convention in October. That first year, awards were presented in 11 categories: Best Gospel Instrumentalist, Best Gospel Record Album Jacket, Best Gospel Television Program, Gospel Disc Jockey of the Year, Gospel Songwriter of the Year, Best Female Vocalist, Best Male Vocalist, Best Record Album of the Year, Gospel Song of the Year, Best Mixed Group and Best Male Group.

"Thanks to Calvary" was nominated for Best Record Album of the Year and Best Record Album Jacket. The Oak Ridge Boys' "It's Happening" album won in both categories. Jim Hill was nominated for Gospel Songwriter of the Year, an award won by Bill Gaither. Hill was among five nominees—Duane Allen, James Blackwood, Jake Hess and J.D. Sumner being the others—vying for Best Male Vocalist. Blackwood was the Dove recipient. Hill's "For God So Loved," from the "Thanks to Calvary" album, was among nine songs that were runners-up to R.E. Winsett's "Jesus Is Coming Soon" in the Gospel Song of the Year category. The Statesmen, Stamps, Oak Ridge Boys and Blackwood Brothers were the nominees who watched as the Imperials accepted the first Dove Award for Best Male Group of the Year. Though the Statesmen did not capture an award, it was quite an honor to have been nominated—not just once, but in six categories.

The Seventies

With the United States' military forces still firmly entrenched in Southeast Asia, antiwar feeling continued to grow in this country and abroad. As 1970 commenced there was no conclusion in sight to the hostilities in Vietnam. Each evening the national networks brought the war home to American living rooms in graphic detail.

Amid this setting, Jimmy Jones, a longtime member of the LeFevres, penned a poem that could have been the story of any one of thousands of families who lost their sons to enemy fire in the jungles of Vietnam. Jones presented the verse to the Statesmen who recorded it as the title song of their 1970 album "The Common Man" (Skylite SLP-6100). "The Common Man" was recited by Big Chief Wetherington while his cohorts provided a vocal backdrop with the song "God Bless America." In the story, the narrator, driving down a country road, is compelled to stop at a little farm home. There, an old farmer relates the story of how his wife had died years before, leaving him and a young son to carry on. He tells how he and his son would read from the Bible and pray each night. In time, the son answers the draft and vows to "do the best I can to preserve a way of life for folks like us—the common man." The young man goes to war and is killed, leaving his father to question why. In the farmer's darkest hour his son appears in a vision encouraging him to keep the faith—"if you denounce our God and country now, why Dad, I died in vain." The narration ends with the prayer: "Please help us understand that the hope of America lies in our faith in God and the common man."

"The Common Man" stirred patriotic heart strings throughout the Bible Belt and across this great country. It didn't stop the protest demonstrations. In fact, four college students died in a war protest at Kent State University in Ohio that spring. But wherever the Statesmen performed the song, and everywhere it was played on radio, "The Common Man" reminded Christians to be in prayer for our nation, its leaders, and the brave men—common men—who were fighting for the principles of freedom, including the freedom to worship.

In choosing material for "The Common Man" album, the Statesmen continued the trend—begun on the "Thanks to Calvary" album—of re-recording several hits from yesteryear. The quartet revived songs that had appeared on RCA Victor albums or earlier records on the Skylite, Statesmen or Capitol labels—records that were long out of print. This offered the group an opportunity to offer updated arrangements of some of their great hits with the current lineup of personnel. "The Common Man" included Mosie Lister's "If to Gain the World," first recorded in 1957, with Sherrill Nielsen singing the featured vocal on a song that quartet fans had identified with Cat Freeman two decades earlier. Also appearing on this album was an updated version of the "Statesmen Hymns Medley" that had first been introduced on the "Statesmen On Stage" album in 1959.

Other songs on the album were: "This is the Day," "Sin Ain't Nothing but the Blues," "I'm Going to Roll Along," "Something Happened to Daddy" and "I Just Can't Praise Him Enough."

On their 1971 Skylite album, "Put Your Hand In the Hand" (SLP-6110), the Statesmen re-recorded Henry Slaughter's "No One But Jesus Knows," first recorded with Denver Crumpler and Jake Hess back in 1956; "What a Day That Will Be," Jim Hill's great song that appeared on the "Get Away Jordan" Skylite album in 1959; and "Sweet Jesus," which had featured Rosie Rozell in the 1964 version on "The Statesmen Spotlights Doy Ott" album for RCA.

It is especially fitting that the latter two songs would be recorded with the lineup of Hovie, Sherrill, Jim, Doy and Chief. Nielsen had recorded "Sweet Jesus" with the Speer Family, and on two later albums with the Imperials. "Sweet Jesus" was his signature song. "What A Day" had been a steady seller for numerous quartets—Homeland Harmony, the Speer Family, Prophets Quartet, Oak Ridge Boys, and others—in the years since Jim Hill's Golden Keys days. It had been the title song of one of his early albums with the Stamps Quartet. Although the Statesmen had not immediately re-recorded the song when Hill joined the group in late 1968, they added it to their concert lineup. The fans were requesting it because "What a Day" was so closely identified with Hill. "We almost always presented that in every concert," he says.

Hill recalls an amusing conversation with songwriter Albert Brumley, writer of the great convention songs, "I'll Fly Away" and "I'll Meet You in the Morning."

"It was always a pleasure to be with the old gentleman, and he would squat whenever he

The Statesmen in 1972. From left are: Jim Hill, lead; Tim Baty, bass guitar; Hovie Lister, piano; Sherrill Nielsen, tenor; Doy Ott, baritone; and Jim Wetherington, bass.

would talk to you. I'll never forget him. I can see him to this day. He squatted and looked at me one day and he said, 'You know, if you hadn't written that song 'What a Day That Will Be' when you did, I was going to write it the next day.' "

Hill reflects a moment, and adds a more serious note: "It's gotten to the point that I didn't write it, you know. I couldn't write something like that. I was just chosen to be the vehicle through which God delivered it. It seems to have become a standard now and I'm thankful that I got to put my name on it. It could have been a lot of people that He could have called to write the song.

"I guess most songs like that are written during a time of tragedy. My wife's mother was 50 years of age. She had stayed home and raised her children while her husband was out holding revival meetings. He was a Baptist evangelist. When my wife's mother was 50 she was stricken and paralyzed by a stroke. We just couldn't understand it. We knew there had to be a reason why. It was during that time that I wrote this song. I went in and sang it for her and the tears rolled down her cheeks. That was the first response she had given since her stroke. Shortly after that she died. God must have wanted for that song to be written. It was a gift from Him. The songs that you write yourself just aren't blessed like the ones He gives you. Anybody who writes songs, if they're living in the right place at the right time of their walk with Him, God will give them a song like that. After a few years 'What a Day' seemed to go away but then the popularity came back and now it's a standard. Today it's used in almost every capacity in the church. A lot of churches use it for an invitation, it's sometimes used for a praise song, and I hear it's used a lot now at funerals."

Three songs which the Statesmen included on the "Put Your Hand" album came from a new youth movement that was sweeping the country in the early 1970s. This trend began with several youth musicals, such as "Good News" and "Tell It Like It Is," which were introduced in the 1960s. These musicals were written in a style similar to that of popular music in an attempt to reach young people for the Lord. Christian albums in the rock-n-roll style were introduced in 1969 by such artists as Larry Norman and Mylon LeFevre—the same Mylon LeFevre who had written the standard "Without Him" a few years before. Soon, a so-called "Jesus Movement" among youth was sweeping the country from coast to coast on the strength of the generation's favorite musical idiom—rock music. This music spawned a new genre of religious musical expression known today as contemporary Christian music.

The Statesmen reached out to their younger fans with such songs as Larry Norman's "Sweet Song of Salvation;" and two spiritually-oriented songs from the popular music charts—Simon and Garfunkel's "Bridge Over Troubled Water" and Gene MacLellan's "Put Your Hand in the Hand." Other songs appearing on the "Put Your Hand" album included "Oh What a Happy Day," "There's a Light Guiding Me," "I Know" and Bill Gaither's classic "He Touched Me."

The Statesmen's "Put Your Hand in the Hand" album was a National Academy of Recording Arts and Sciences Grammy nominee for Best Sacred Album the following year.

"Keep On Smiling," the quartet's next album for Skylite (SLP-6115), was a return to more traditional fare. The Statesmen re-recorded the Albert Brumley favorite "Turn Your Radio On" to capitalize on the popularity of the song after popular artist Ray Stevens had enjoyed commercial success with the song on the popular and country charts nationally. Although Stevens is best known, perhaps, for his novelty songs—"Ahab the Arab," "Gitarzan," "The Streak," "Shriners Convention," "Mississippi Squirrel Revival" and others—he has also written several social-conscious songs, including "Mr. Businessman" and the spectacularly successful "Everything Is Beautiful," as well as several gospel songs. Of the latter, the Statesmen selected "Can We Get to That" to appear on the "Keep On Smiling" album.

Also included on the album were "Yesterday," "Some Things I'd Change," "When We Sing Around the Throne Eternal," "I Want to Live for Him," "There's Nothing Like This Feeling" and Gordon Jenson's powerful "Redemption Draweth Nigh." "Walk With Me" had been a big song for Sherrill Nielsen when he sang tenor for Jake Hess and the Imperials. He recorded a new version with the Statesmen for the "Keep On Smiling" album. The title song, written by Joe Roper and published by the Statesmen's Faith Music, also featured Nielsen at his finest.

A remake of a Mosie Lister song on the 1972 "Let's Go Tell It" album (SLP-6120) recalled

> February 1972
>
> I am very pleased to inform you that you have been selected as a Finalist in the 14th Annual Grammy Awards. Your nomination is the result of nationwide voting by Academy members.
>
> Winners will be announced on the evening of Tuesday, March 14, 1972. Please contact the nearest NARAS office listed below if you wish further details.
>
> On behalf of the National Academy of Recordings Arts & Sciences, please accept sincere congratulations for this honor which has been bestowed upon you by your fellow creators and craftsmen in the recording field.
>
> Very truly yours,
>
> *Wesley H. Rose*
> Wesley H. Rose
> National President

Each member of The Statesmen received this notification of their 1972 Grammy nomination from Wesley Rose, President of the National Academy of Recording Arts & Sciences (NARAS).

the Denver Crumpler days. Sherrill Nielsen's treatment of "I Wonder What My New Address Will Be" was very similar to Crumpler's lyric tenor version recorded in 1956. Mosie's "Til the Storm Passes By" also appeared on this album with two songs by Lari Goss—"Precious Old Book" and the title song. Ron Hinson's "The Lighthouse" was recorded by most of the top groups, including the Statesmen, this time with a memorable recitation of the second verse by Big Chief. "Let's Go Tell It," "Higher Than the Moon" and "The Unseen Hand" were among other new songs in the collection. Chief contributed a new composition, "I Got a God I Can Recommend." In a departure from the norm, new Statesmen bass player Tim Baty (formerly of J.D. Sumner & the Stamps) sang a mellow contemporary song written by Mylon LeFevre, "You're On His Mind."

Southern gospel quartet music continued to be a very competitive business in the 1970s. Occasionally, all-night sings more closely resembled singing contests instead of concerts, as groups often appeared more interested in "putting it to" one another onstage than entertaining and ministering to the audience.

"It used to be pretty heavy," recalls Jim Hill. "We were all good friends and buddies but everybody wanted to get out there and, like a ballclub, strike the home run. And they thought more sometimes about that than they did the really important parts of it."

In the Ghetto

The Statesmen continued to sing in a variety of venues—large and small auditoriums, large and small churches; school gymnasiums, and outdoor settings, such as the annual sundown to sunup sing at Bonifay, Florida. Many quartets, the Statesmen foremost among them, were appearing regularly at state fairs across the nation in the early 1970s. The career of the Statesmen is replete with memorable performances. One such appearance stands out not because of how well the Statesmen sang or entertained, nor was it legendary for how large an audience attended or how many records were sold. Rather, Jim Hill's favorite episode of his career with the Statesmen is memorable because of the presence of the Holy Spirit.

One Saturday evening the Statesmen appeared in concert at Chicago's Medinah Temple. Don Butler, who had become a booking agent for J.D. Sumner's Sumar Talent Agency, had scheduled the Statesmen to sing the following evening at the Bostick Street Baptist Church in Chicago. That Sunday afternoon the Statesmen were driving around the city in their bus looking for the church. Everybody they asked for directions eyed the big bus. "You're going there?" they would ask incredulously. "Yes. Where is it?"

The church turned out to be a little storefront building in the ghetto in one of the roughest sections of the city. From the outside it looked to hold maybe 100 people. The Statesmen parked their shiny, big bus in front of the little street mission. The bus looked bigger than the church. Hovie eyed the rough surroundings of the neighborhood. Were they about to experience their own version of David Wilkerson's "The Cross and the Switchblade?"

"For goodness sake!," he exclaimed. "What has Don Butler gotten us into?!"

"We were just ready to leave," says Jim Hill, "when here came a little old guy with a red tie on and a black suit, just hustling up the street to meet us. It turned out he was the pastor. He was so thrilled to see us. A big smile was all across his face. He said, 'Come on upstairs to the apartment, Mama's got some cake baked for you.' So we went up there. It was right over the store—a little old place and very neat and clean. A nice, saintly, clean little lady comes out with her cake and meets us, and he said, 'How do you like Mama's dress?' And, oh, we made over Mama's dress! He said, 'She made that dress.' And, you know, they probably didn't have money to buy a new dress. He thought she was so pretty in that dress.

"Well, we just didn't know what we had gotten into, but we got into that service and the church was packed. There were guys off the street coming in with their sleeves rolled up, some wearing tank tops, until the place was packed in the back. We figured the bus would be raided before we got out of there, it was just that kind of a neighborhood. But we got to singing and the Lord got to blessing in that service. Hovie got to preaching, and I think half of the church hit the altar that night. I mean we got such a blessing out of that! People got saved! Dope addicts were there and they got saved. I mean it's the greatest service we were ever in!"

When the Statesmen climbed aboard their bus—which was still intact—they were still exalting over the visitation of the Holy Spirit in the service. "They couldn't have paid me enough to take the place of what happened here tonight! This is one of the greatest experiences I've ever had," Hovie told the quartet.

How many hours on their knees had that little preacher and "Mama" spent in that little apartment above the storefront church, agonizing in prayer over the precious lost souls in their humble mission field? How they grieved over the plight of their fellow man, daily seeing sin destroying those around them? But their faith was strong that God would help them reach a lost and dying world, and God honored that faith. On that Sunday night He led a fancy bus to their street, enticing the curious to see what that persistent little preacher was up to this time. The visitation of the Holy Spirit that night changed lives forever. For many decadent souls kneeling to make their peace with God, truly old things were passed away, all things became new.

"It's something I never will forget," says Jim Hill. "All the big places we sang, they don't seem to impress me like the little ole storefront in the ghetto. We certainly came away from there blessed. Little is much when God is in it!"

20

When I Come to the End of the Road

The commencement of a new year is usually when most people throughout the country are filled with great anticipation and resolve. New Year's Eve is party time for many. In some churches, watchnight services herald the new year with prayer and singing: Rejoicing in the blessings of the old year, and resolve for a closer walk with God in the months to come. Jim Hill approached 1973 with a heavy heart. Gospel music had been his livelihood for the better part of eleven years. However enjoyable and rewarding those years had been spiritually, the financial benefits were sometimes better than adequate, yet he was not enrolled in a retirement plan. His daughter was approaching college age and Jim knew his days as a singer with his favorite gospel quartet were numbered.

"At that time, the opportunities didn't exist that do today," he says. "I had no pension plan, and I had a daughter who was approaching 16. I just wanted to get a little better financial situation at home and more benefits. It was for economic reasons that I left because back then you just didn't make that much. And I got concerned about my own welfare in raising my family and seeing that my daughter went to college and got a good education."

During his Golden Keys days, Jim had earned a degree in Business Administration and Higher Accounting. He put this to good use by taking a job as a sales representative with a shoe manufacturing company in his hometown. He never gave up singing, however. He worked several dates as a soloist, then settled into choral work. Whenever his company relocated him, Jim was able to find a church in which he could minister as choir director. He recalls his years with the Statesmen as the highlight of his singing career, and recalls the members of the quartet fondly. He says the Statesmen were everything he expected them to be.

"They were really Statesmen. They were professional all the way—the most professional men I had ever worked with. Half of them are gone now, but I'll have to say that it was just a first-class group of men.

"It's a big letdown leaving the road. I mean nothing pleases or is so self-gratifying

Hovie Lister (seated) with The Statesmen in early 1973 (l-r): Sherrill Nielsen, tenor; Gary Timbs, lead; Tim Baty, bass guitarist; "Big Chief" Jim Wetherington, bass; and Doy Ott, baritone;

as singing full-time and ministering to people and winning friends all over the nation. Then to leave all that and walk into a business establishment where they don't care who you are, they just look at your product, was a rather traumatic change. However, the business was good for me and financially good to me and that helped. My weekend church ministering more or less filled the gap, but missing the friends and the people that you got to know and the guys you sang with was really difficult. It's like leaving your home and not coming back."

Big Chief

The life of a quartet singer can be very rewarding, especially if one is among the few who were blessed to work with highly successful groups like the Blackwood Brothers and Statesmen in the 1950s and '60s. However, to a great extent it was a life of sacrifice, as family time at home was a precious commodity. For James and Liz Wetherington, their daughter Diana, and niece, Debbie Hughey, home was a comfortable little house on Oak Grove Road in Decatur, Georgia. There, Chief raised a garden and built a playhouse for the girls in a woods on the property.

One time when Diana was in elementary school, she and her classmates were to give a report about their fathers' vocations. "I didn't know what Daddy's job was," she says. "I knew that he sang, but I thought he did that for fun. I didn't realize the Statesmen was his job." When it came time for her report, the Statesmen were home for a few days, so Big Chief drove his daughter to school in the Statesmen bus. He took her classmates for a ride most have not yet forgotten. Although many of them were children of doctors, lawyers and college professors, none of their fathers had such a neat toy. Some of her classmates still speak fondly of that episode at class reunions today.

Diana said while growing up she enjoyed going hunting and fishing with her daddy. "I was both his little girl and his little boy," she laughs. Some of her favorite memories are of spending time at Grandpa and Grandma Swett's farm in Ty Ty, Georgia. "My Dad would have to make time for me, and I would have to make time for him. We had to adjust to each other. With his road schedule the way it was and my school activities, Mother was real good about arranging our schedules when he was home for the two of us to have time especially for each other. Those occasions were like a date with my Daddy."

Three years before his death, Wetherington felt the pain of separation from his family while in a hotel room after a concert. As he did so often in quiet moments, he sat down with pencil and paper and recorded his thoughts in an essay titled "Just Thinking Out Loud To No One"...

"I venture to say that there has ever been a man
that at 47, with less to be proud of in himself
and with more to be proud of in the Loved Ones around him
that have put up with him, and all of his shortcomings,
littleness, self-centeredness, and lots more adjectives that I could use.
But, on the other hand,
All men of career have had to Sacrifice.
Not of himself so much.
But those that love him and those that he loves,
in order that things material and things intangible might be advanced.
I love my Loved Ones at home, more, I sincerely believe, than any man living.
You say — Well, why do you leave them, why not get a job
at home and be with them every night?
Then I say to you, my friend, whoever you are, and wherever you may be —
Something is nothing — without Sacrifice.
Without Sacrifice we, as Americans would not be a Free People
But bond slaves, somewhere in a still medieval land.

Without Sacrifice, we as Christians would have no Christ,
and the word <u>Christian</u> never uttered.
Without Sacrifice, there can be no love — only hate.
Without Sacrifice, there can be no progress — only stalemate.
Without Sacrifice, there can be no forward look — only present and backward.
As I write these words, I look at four walls.
Walls of loneliness, longing —
and a time that seems to stand still at 2 a.m.,
But with a thankfulness in my heart that I have
Loved Ones far away that have been willing to make
all the Sacrifices for me and what I believe in.
I thank God for you every day of my life."

In late summer or early fall of 1972, Wetherington headed back to Ty Ty for a few days of hunting and relaxation on the Swett farm. Throughout his professional career he had stayed close with his grandparents and continued to visit them at the farm as often as his schedule with the Statesmen would allow. An avid outdoorsman, Chief enjoyed hunting and fishing to his dying day. On this hunting trip Wetherington was riding in a jeep with an uncle, Vertis Swett, and an old family friend, Lonnie Register, from Ashburn, Georgia. According to Chief's nephew, Marc Wetherington, "He leaped out of the jeep to take a shot at something. His feet slipped out from underneath him and his leg slid under the jeep, causing one of the rear tires to roll over it. Although not seriously injured, the accident caused blood clots to form in his leg and pass through his body."

Chief appeared to have had a close call, as he could have been injured much more seriously. However, as time passed more serious developments were to result from Chief's near miss.

Months later, the Statesmen were a few days into one of their long tours of the West Coast when Wetherington gave the quartet cause to worry. As the motor coach breezed through west Texas, Hovie became aware that Chief was not feeling well. As the tour progressed through Long Beach, California, Chief admitted that he had been coughing up blood. When they reached San Francisco, Hovie was quite concerned.

"Why don't you catch a plane and go back home," Hovie said. "We'll finish the tour somehow."

"No, I'll make it," answered Wetherington.

"I think he had called back home to his doctor and discussed it with his wife," Hovie says. "He felt real bad. I knew something was seriously wrong with him because Chief was never sick and never felt bad. He was always ready to go and enjoyed singing as much as any man I have ever known. Never any two people ever wanted to be in a quartet all their lives no more than Big Chief and Jake Hess. But he wouldn't leave the group."

"The Chief would sing when he was sick and he would sing when he felt good," Rosie Rozell once said. "He has felt as sick as a dog but would go on stage and never complain."

Later in the tour, the Statesmen appeared in concert at the University of Oregon in Eugene. They were waiting in the wings, just about to go onstage for the second half of the concert, when Chief leaned over to Hovie.

"I tell you what," he said, "don't say anything about this until after we have sung our last song. After we have sung our last song, ask if there's a doctor in the audience and if he will come backstage."

Hovie said he'd be glad to. There was not a doctor present, however. But a lady who was the head of the Nursing Department at the University of Oregon Medical Center came back to meet with the ailing bass singer. Chief briefly told her of his symptoms.

"You call me in the morning at nine o'clock and I'll get you an appointment with a doctor," she told him.

"So Chief went," recalls Hovie. "They called me shortly thereafter and I went over and admitted him to the clinic. They found that he had a blood clot on his lung"—a result of his hunting accident in Ty Ty. "They treated him there, and then he flew back to Atlanta and spent about a week in the Georgia Baptist Hospital. They put him on blood thinning medication and if we were on a tour, about every two weeks he had to go into a emergency room or something. They would check his blood and see if he needed to lower the dose or increase it or what have you. I think he had been taken off of that medication when we were at the National Quartet Convention in October, 1973."

Only two couples—Hovie and Ethel Lister and Jim and Liz Wetherington—made the trip to Nashville aboard the Statesmen bus for the National Quartet Convention. The remaining members of the quartet—tenor Rosie Rozell, who only recently had returned to the quartet when Sherrill Nielsen left to join the Elvis Presley Show; Gary Timbs, who had replaced Jim Hill as lead singer; baritone Doy Ott and bass guitarist Tim Baty—had flown separately to Nashville. Rozell's career with The Searchers came to an end in the summer of 1973. During an appearance at the Huffman Assembly of God in Birmingham, Alabama, Rosie casually said to Bob Smith, the pastor: "If I ever get off the road I want to work in a church somewhere with a choir."

"What he meant was, sometime out in the future, 20 years or so, maybe," says Betty Rozell. "When we got back home in Marietta, there was a message on our answering machine offering him the job."

The position was part-time at first, allowing Rosie to be available when Sherrill Nielsen left the Statesmen a few weeks later.

The Wetheringtons' daughter, Diana, "had gotten married in August of that year and they had the wedding pictures," Hovie recalls. "We looked at them, enjoyed them, and had a great visit together on the way from Atlanta to Nashville. We checked into the Ramada Inn up there and everything was going fine. We sang, I think, on Tuesday night."

The Statesmen were among several groups featured during the Tuesday night program, which was Old Timers Night at the convention. They opened with the rollicking "Roll Back River Jordan," from their most recent album, "I Believe In Jesus," released earlier in 1973. They followed an encore of it with "The Lighthouse," featuring Doy, and a recitation of the second verse by the Big Chief.

"We thought we'd give you a little break and run a little youth out here for a few minutes," Hovie told the audience. "No, the trouble with us is we've outlived all the old timers."

Next was another song from the "I Believe In Jesus" album—"Why Me, Lord." This one also featured Chief, who was in fine voice that October evening. "I'm Going Higher Than the Moon," an up-tempo tune that also featured a generous helping of modern harmony, prematurely closed the set. Hovie introduced each member of the group, saving Wetherington for last. The quartet sang Rosie's signature song, "O What A Savior," to end their part of the evening.

An old-time singing convention class was held as a part of the same event, and Chief took his turn at directing a choir of his quartet peers.

On Wednesday, October 3, "we were supposed to sing that night," says Hovie. "Chief and his wife had been down in the lobby visiting with a lot of people. He and Doy and their wives had eaten together and seemingly everything was fine."

"We had a very calm day," remembers Liz Wetherington. "He got up and we had a late breakfast. Some friends came back upstairs with us and we sat and visited. After they left we looked at some television and just rested."

Chief, who had been sitting on the bed working a crossword puzzle, said to his wife, "I guess I'd better go shave. We've got to sing tonight."

"So he went to the bath. I was lying down across the bed and dozed off. I heard him fall and I jumped up. He had come back as far as the dresser and he just collapsed right there. But he had not complained. He seemed to be in good spirits. He had just had a nice visit with friends. He was supposed to go the next morning and play golf, so it was just something that we had not expected."

Wetherington had suffered a fatal heart attack, caused by a blood clot to the heart.

Hovie heard himself being paged as he relaxed in the coffee shop of the hotel. As he got to the front desk in the hotel lobby to respond to the page, the lobby elevator doors opened. Medics whisked past him, wheeling a body on a gurney from the elevator to a waiting ambulance. It was then that Hovie learned that his friend had died.

"I was at the Ramada Inn for a SESAC meeting when somebody said that Big Chief had had a heart attack," recalls Bill Gaither. "I was there in the hallway when they brought Chief's body out with a sheet over it."

"Chief and I had always been close," says Jake, who was crushed by the loss. Chief's sudden demise 28 days short of his 51st birthday threw a pall over the remaining days of the Quartet Convention, he says. "That was the end of the Convention for me. Of course, we flew to Atlanta for his funeral and it was just a bad situation. It was hard to get back into the swing of things after that. I was in a meeting with him discussing songs the day before he passed away. He had his music company, and I had a music company, and he was trying to buy one of my songs. Chief and I were together before the Statesmen and we remained friends. We don't question God about these things but wonder why this happened and that happened. Chief had so much going."

"I had always loved the Chief and it really hurt to see him die," says Mosie Lister. "He had such a marvelous voice and a marvelous way of presenting his voice."

Hovie received a series of telephone calls from Elvis Presley who was devastated by Chief's passing. He was making arrangements to fly to Atlanta for the funeral. Later, Hovie learned that Elvis had to be sedated because he was so distraught over the loss, and would not be attending the funeral after all. Elvis and Chief had spent quite a bit of time together during the six months prior to Wetherington's passing.

"A number of us," says James Blackwood, "including J.D. Sumner, Don Butler and Polly Grimes, who is a promoter out in California—I don't remember who all else—but we flew from Nashville to Chief's funeral in Atlanta. Then we flew back to the Convention after the funeral. We were very close," he says, recalling the days of the Blackwood/Statesmen team. "We shared not only our successes but also shared the griefs. The Chief enjoyed singing gospel music and had a total commitment to it."

"Of course, there is always a rivalry that exists between two people that sing the same part," observes fellow bass J.D. Sumner. He recalls that during the years of the Blackwood-Statesmen team, "we both tried to out-sing one another, but not like in the old days. He was one of the best friends I ever had. Chief was the most professional man to ever stand on stage! He just looked the part of a professional gospel singer and had the best rhythm of anybody in the world. Chief and I never in our lives had a hard word. There was a rivalry but it didn't interfere with our relationship. He was absolutely the best rhythm bass singer that's ever been in gospel music, and the most professional."

"Chief was the guy I more or less took for granted," says Hovie. "He could learn a song and learn everybody else's part. He was always on time, always there. He was one of the best rhythm bass singers I have ever heard in my life. He was so enthusiastic. He was a first-class entertainer on the stage from the word go. He was a good-looking man and the people all loved him."

"The Statesmen Quartet was one of my favorites and helped to interest me in gospel music," William Lee Golden once told a reporter. The longtime baritone singer with the Oak Ridge Boys noted that Jim Wetherington "gave more class to the business, he walked and dressed differently. He caused a lot of others to be interested in gospel music."

Hovie through the years has received numerous letters from adults who, when they were children or teenagers, would ask Chief for advice about gospel music and singing. "He would take time to stop and sit down and talk with them," he says. "That speaks well of anyone.

"He had a saying when anybody was upset and complaining or griping. He'd say, 'Aw, you've just got to roll with the punches!' We had our differences but I can't remember any real serious confrontations with Chief. He might disagree with you but he'd say, 'Well, if that's what you want to do, go on and do it.' If you were to call him up at 3 o'clock in the morning and say, 'Hey, we're going to rehearse in 30 minutes,' he'd say, 'Whereabouts?'."

"He wouldn't ask why or 'What do you want to do something like that for?'," adds Jake.

"If we had a rehearsal and had a brand-new song to learn and nobody has seen it," Hovie continues, "we'd rehearse on that thing for two or three hours, maybe four. You'd come back the next day and he knew his part and everybody else's. He'd go home after that four-hour group rehearsal and spend the rest of that day or night making sure he knew his part and yours, too."

"He'd say, 'I've got to go woodshed now,'" recalls Jake. "He was good onstage, but he was better offstage."

Wetherington "worked for the good of the whole group and never pushed to be an individual star," the late Connor Hall of the Homeland Harmony Quartet once observed.

Chief was "the best quartet man that I ever knew," declares J.D. Sumner. "I mean, when it came to something needing to be done, well, Chief was right there!"

"There's never been a greater quartet man than Big Chief," echoes Hovie.

"Yep," Jake agrees, "best quartet man that ever lived!"

When I Come to the End of the Road

The Statesmen had experienced a gradual decline from the mid-1950s, when they were at their peak, through late 1973 with Chief's passing. The Statesmen during the years of Denver, Jake, Doy, Chief and Hovie had been Hovie's model group. After Denver's passing in 1957, the Statesmen remained strong first with Cat Freeman, then Rosie Rozell providing the tenor. Even after Jake's departure the quartet had some exciting years with Jack Toney and Jim Hill. But with Chief's passing, Hovie soon found he didn't have the heart to continue.

"The world's greatest quartet had lost the one man, the one ingredient that could not be replaced," writes song evangelist and noted columnist Roy Pauley. "For Chief was the Statesmen image. Chief was bigger than life. No one performer's passing has ever devastated his group nearly to the proportions that Chief's death devastated the Statesmen."

"I think when Denver died, a little bit of Hovie died also," observes Bill Gaither. "I can't speak for him but as an outside observer I kind of saw this. When Jake left I think a lot of the heart of it went out for Hovie. I think he tried various lead singers—and here again it wasn't a matter of the lead singer being good or bad, it was just a matter that the group sound was built around Jake so much that when he left I think it was frustrating for Hovie. He just couldn't find the handle to replace Jake. But he still had Chief and that was one of the original sounds of the whole thing. So he kept going with Chief.

"Chief, of course, was a hard worker and loved what he was doing. He also evidently had an ego that was sound enough that even though they weren't number one—at that time there were some other groups coming in who were also making a big impact, the Happy Goodman Family were making a big impact, the Rambos were making a big impact. Chief's ego was evidently sanctified enough to say, 'Hey, if we're not number one, three or four ain't bad.' So I think that gave Hovie enough courage, as long as he had Chief he still had two of the originals. But I think when Chief died—I've heard Hovie say this onstage and I've heard him say it to me privately— it was just over for him."

"Needless to say," observes Hovie, "losing Chief was the last straw. There was a period of time there after Chief died that we had a mix-match of various people coming and going in the group. The group was a trio for awhile."

Only 20 days after Chief's death, Rosie Rozell left the Statesmen for the second time. The Huffman Assembly of God Church in Birmingham had offered to make his role as choir director there a full-time job. His replacement with the Statesmen was "Little Willie" Wynn, who had filled the tenor spot with the Oak Ridge Boys for 15 years. Tim Baty also left the group at that time to join a group called Voice in the Elvis Presley organization. His replacement on bass guitar was another former member of the Stamps Quartet band, Kenny Hicks. Ray Burdette joined the group as bass singer, then Elmer Cole replaced Gary Timbs.

"It just was not working out. Finally, I decided that it was best to just quit," recalls Hovie. "I told Doy somewhere around 1975 that I thought we should hang it up."

Doy enrolled in college again. Although he already held a degree in business administration from the University of Georgia, he had decided to study to become a chiropractor.

"Doy was always busy doing something," says Jake. "He studied karate and the martial arts. He was a very interesting guy to work with."

Hovie received a call in 1976 from Bill Gaither who invited him to Alexandria to record a solo album. "You have no excuse now," Bill said. "I want you to come and do a singing solo album."

"I thought he was kidding," Hovie says, laughing. "But he had some marvelous backup singers and he produced the album."

"That's when I probably became more acquainted with the real Hovie," Gaither observes. "At that time I saw the other side of Hovie—a very fragile, very sensitive, very hurt person. I think when he came out of Greenville down to Atlanta, he was a very proud young man and he put together something that nobody in our field had ever been able to put together before. I think when that train stopped with Chief's death, that was just a tough thing for him to come to grips with. And I would say that was the Hovie that I got to know and love very much, and appreciate. At that point he didn't have much of a desire to go on and do anything else. He was just tired and I understand that. There have been times in my life that I said, 'I've had all of this fun that I can take.' I'll never forget Roger Ward, the 500-mile race driver, when he said, 'I said I'd quit doing this when it wasn't fun anymore.' The day before a couple of his buddies had been killed in a wreck in a race, and he said, 'Yesterday wasn't fun, and I'm finished.' "

Taking Care of Business in Memphis

When Elvis Presley died in Memphis, on August 16, 1977, millions of popular music fans around the world mourned the passing of the man many called the "king of rock and roll." A number of gospel music fans had also been admirers of Elvis's music—especially his sacred recordings with RCA Victor. In fact, the only Grammy Awards Elvis won in his lifetime were for religious albums. Many gospel fans admired him for his use of southern gospel quartets as backup vocalists on his albums, in motion pictures and personal appearances. His first backup artists, the Jordanaires, had previously worked the gospel quartet circuit. Later came the Imperials, J.D. Sumner and the Stamps, and a group called Voice, made up of former Statesmen Sherrill Nielsen and Tim Baty, and Donnie Sumner, formerly of the Stamps.

Elvis had recorded several compositions by former Statesmen lead singer and arranger Mosie Lister, including "His Hand in Mine," which was the title song of Presley's first long-playing album of sacred music.

"I just loved his voice and I loved his approach to gospel music," says Mosie. "Whatever he did with gospel music, mostly he learned from either the Blackwoods or the Statesmen. He just loved both groups. He treated the gospel stuff like gospel. He didn't treat it like rock-n-roll, and I always appreciated that very much."

James Blackwood recalls that even after Elvis became a world-renowned entertainer, he continued to attend the all-night sings at Ellis Auditorium in Memphis.

"I would always introduce him and he would come out and sing with us," says James. "The Blackwoods or the Statesmen would back him up. I remember particularly he would do 'Peace in the Valley,' and we'd back him. Then one time he was there and I introduced him and asked him to sing. He said that Colonel Tom (Parker) had heard that he was singing at our shows and told him he couldn't do that anymore. After that I would just introduce him and have him come out and take a bow. He would attend the National Quartet Convention here in Memphis. He would come sometimes even after he was very, very popular. I remember one night in Memphis he was at the auditorium and I introduced him. The cameras looked like lightning bugs flashing. Cameras were just clicking all over the place with people taking his picture while he was out on stage taking a bow."

When the quartets were in Memphis, Graceland's doors were open to them. Jake says Elvis always enjoyed spending time with his quartet heroes. He recalls that Big Chief especially spent a lot of time with Elvis when the Statesmen were in town. Elvis's admiration for Jake was clear when he asked RCA to invite Jake and the Imperials to appear with the Jordanaires as backup vocalists on his second gospel album, "How Great Thou Art," recorded in 1966.

"When Chet Atkins' office called us and said Elvis wanted us on this gospel album, it was a compliment, I thought," Jake says. "We worked with him a week or 10 days on that album. It was really a fun thing. Nearly every night he and I would have some long conversations in the editing room about the Statesmen and Blackwood days. That's all he wanted to talk about. He wanted to talk about gospel music."

The recording studio was full of expensive musicians for these sessions. Elvis would take out an hour or two and sing quartet songs with the Jordanaires and Imperials around a piano. These were not selections that were targeted for the album they were supposed to be working on. Once, recalls Jake, one of the studio personnel came by and said, "Elvis, you've got a lot of high price musicians around here. Don't you think we ought to put something on tape?"

"Well, how do they get paid?" Elvis said.

"Well, you know how they get paid. The session pays for them."

"Then I'm paying for them, right?"

"Well, yeah."

"Well," said Elvis, "we'll sing after awhile."

"It went on and we sang for another 30 minutes after that" before Elvis got back to the business of recording, Jake says with a grin.

At the time of Presley's death, J.D. Sumner and the Stamps had been appearing regularly on Elvis's concert tours and nightclub appearances for more than six years. On the day of his son's

Reorganized version of the Hovie Lister and the Statesmen in 1979 (l-r): Ed Hill, baritone; Rosie Rozell, tenor; Tommy Thompson, bass; Hovie Lister, piano; and Buddy Burton, lead.

demise, Vernon Presley summoned J.D. to Graceland from Nashville and asked him to handle the arrangements for the funeral service. Vernon felt J.D. had an intuition of who Elvis would have wanted preaching and singing at his funeral, and what songs should be sung.

The Stamps, of course, would sing since they were so closely identified with Elvis during his last years. J.D. called Hovie, Jake, Rosie Rozell and Doy Ott, and with Sumner singing the late Big Chief's bass lines, the five men would approximate the Statesmen Quartet that Elvis had loved so dearly. J.D. also knew Elvis would have wanted James Blackwood to be a part of the service.

James recalls being in Charlie Hodge's apartment at Graceland with J.D., the Rev. Rex Humbard and Hodge, as they were firming-up final plans for the service. Charlie turned and said, "James, I think Elvis would want you to sing his favorite song, 'How Great Thou Art.' Would you do it?" Of course, James readily agreed. Later, Joe Guercio, who had been Elvis's orchestra director, came to Blackwood and said, "James, I have directed Elvis, you know, for all these years singing 'How Great Thou Art' hundreds of times. Would you let me direct you while you're singing it so I can direct it one more time?" James also was pleased to agree to this request. During the service, James recalls, "We were behind these French doors (at Graceland). The casket was right in front of the French doors. Joe stood off to the side and directed us—I did the verses and then the Stamps would sing the choruses with me. He directed and he stood over there and tears rolled down his face while we sang."

Hovie says he is often questioned about Elvis's death after stories surfaced about the star being alive. "It was definitely Elvis," he says of the corpse at Graceland. "He is dead."

Together Again

Shortly after participating at the funeral service in Memphis, Hovie accepted an invitation to preach for the annual Homecoming services at Mount Zion Baptist Church in Marietta, Georgia—the church he had pastored for 12 years. What the church members didn't tell Hovie was that they had also invited Rosie, Jake and Doy for a surprise reunion of the Statesmen.

"I was at Mount Zion," Hovie recalls, "and in comes Jake and Doy and Rosie. I went to the piano and started playing 'Oh, What A Savior' and we sang that. The church just about erupted."

They enjoyed themselves so much that they decided to make some singing appearances, on a limited basis, as a trio. Eventually, they were in so much demand that Doy Ott had to bow out.

Quite busy with his practice as a chiropractor, Doy felt he couldn't sacrifice his new career to continue singing. The Statesmen secured Jake's oldest son, Chris, to sing baritone for several months.

When Jake took a job as a featured vocalist at a large church in Los Angeles, the Statesmen reorganized in 1979 with several new personnel—lead singer Buddy Burton, baritone Ed Hill, bass singer Tommy Thompson and bass guitarist Jake Robinson—joining Hovie and Rosie. With this lineup, Hovie managed to recreate the classic Statesmen sound, as Burton had the ability to sound uncannily like Jake Hess, and Tommy Thompson provided Chief-like bass vocals on a number of the old songs. Burton is a Southern Baptist preacher who had sung with the Smitty Gatlin Trio and several other groups over the years. Hill had been the manager of the Prophets Quartet for many years before joining J.D. Sumner and the Stamps. He left the Stamps shortly after the death of Elvis.

The Statesmen recorded a live album that year at the Joyful Noise Supper Club near Atlanta. Included in the concert were a number of old Statesmen hit songs, including "I Wanna Know," "A Newborn Feeling," "Every Time I Feel the Spirit," "Let the Lower Lights be Burning" and "Closer to Thee." Other old favorites on this concert album (Skylite SLP-6225) included "Happy Rhythm," "The Lighthouse," "First Day in Heaven" and "Oh, What a Savior." The following year the quartet recorded a couple of studio albums of new material: "He Is Here" (SLP-6235) on Skylite, and "Sweet Beulah Land" (V177-1043) on Vine Records.

In the fall of 1980, Rosie, Hovie and Jake began singing with James Blackwood and J.D. Sumner in a few engagements as the Masters V. The group began as a part-time avocation but the popularity of this combination created such a demand for concert appearances that Hovie was once again forced to retire the Statesmen. But through the next decade several former Statesmen would return to the national spotlight via this all-star quartet called the Masters V.

Hovie Lister & the Statesmen at the time of the Joyful Noise concert recording. Pictured in front are (l-r): Rosie Rozell, Hovie Lister and Tommy Thompson. In back are Jake Robinson, Ed Hill and Buddy Burton.

21

The Masters V

Jake Hess and J.D. Sumner were reminiscing about old times at Sumner's office in Nashville. Jake, who had been singing with a television ministry in Los Angeles, shared with Sumner his wish to again be working in Music City. Sumner, fully recovered after open heart surgery, shared that he had been quite busy of late with his Stamps Quartet. Following the death of Elvis, J.D. and the Stamps had recorded an album of Presley's favorite gospel songs. Receiving numerous requests from Presley fan clubs for appearances, the Stamps developed a revue, featuring Presley's songs, which proved quite popular around the country. But by the fall of 1980, J.D. was tired. His first love being gospel music, he longed to return to the quartet circuit.

Their conversation was soon interrupted when LaWayne Satterfield dropped by. Satterfield was an old friend. She had served

The original Masters V (l-r): Rosie Rozell, James Blackwood, Hovie Lister, J.D. Sumner and Jake Hess.

as executive director of the Gospel Music Association in its infancy. By 1980, she was gospel editor of the *Music City News*, and frequently contributed articles to the *Nashville Banner*. After some minutes of conversation, Satterfield sensed that Hess and Sumner needed a new challenge in their careers. "What gospel music needs is somebody like you and Hovie and James and somebody else—maybe Connor Hall"—to form an all-star quartet, she suggested. "You could call it the Masters V."

The name came from a similar group of top-flight country musicians. "Floyd Cramer, Chet Atkins and Boots Randolph had what they called the Masters III," explains Sumner.

"When she left," Jake recalls, "J.D. looked at me and said, 'What do you think?' I said, 'Let's call Hovie.' "

After leaving the Imperials at the end of 1967, Jake had taken time off to recover from a heart attack. An opportunity soon presented itself that would allow Jake to take time off from the rigors of road travel, yet continue to sing for a living. This opportunity came in the form of a job as host of a daily gospel music television show with Channel 5 in Nashville.

"I was on in the early morning singing gospel songs on a country show," he says. "Then, when that show was taken off, they gave me my own show. I played gospel videotapes and I had quartets to come in when they were in the vicinity and wanted to. You don't get quartets up at 4:30 in the morning too often. I had an early morning show at 6:30 in the morning and then a noon show. Then I had one at 8 o'clock on Sunday. I had 12 shows a week. I did that for eight years."

During this time Jake signed a contract with RCA Victor as a solo artist and would eventually win three Grammy awards for solo recording projects with the label. He formed a group called Jake Hess and the Music City Singers and worked a limited schedule of engagements. Among the

Gospel music afficionados swarm the Masters V record table during a concert intermission.

members of this group was Ed Enoch who later came to prominence as lead singer with J.D. Sumner and the Stamps. Later came Jake Hess Sound, a group composed of Jake and his teenage children. In the mid-1970s, he left Nashville to sing for a television ministry in Los Angeles, California. After four years, however, he was excited about Satterfield's idea and traveling the quartet circuit again.

"J.D. and Jake and Hovie and me got together and talked about it," recalls James Blackwood. "Rosie (Rozell) wasn't in on the first talks. We really hadn't at the first settled on who we wanted to sing first tenor. But in our first talk we talked about who we'd get to sing tenor and settled on Rosie. Each of us had had our own group and had been more or less the dominant figure in our group. We decided that we would come together in this combination and people would really want to hear what we sounded like and it proved to be something that was very hot there for awhile."

James, for some time, had been singing only three or four songs a night with the Blackwood Brothers. His son Jimmy had assumed the regular role of lead vocalist in the quartet. At Blackwood Brothers appearances, James would wait offstage to join the quartet for the last few songs of the evening. He then would take the solo microphone, with the rest of the Blackwoods vocalizing in accompaniment. Because of his limited activity with the Blackwood Brothers, James was very open to the opportunity of working some dates on a limited schedule with his old friends.

Soon it was time stop talking and take action. The Masters V debuted in a series of concerts for promoter Polly Grimes on the West Coast, beginning in October, 1980.

"We all enjoyed it tremendously," James says.

At first, the idea was to fill engagements occasionally and have some fun together. In fact, Hovie announced in the January 1981 edition of *The Singing News*—gospel quartet music's premiere trade publication—that the formation of the Masters V would in no way interfere with the ministry of the Statesmen Quartet which he had reorganized only a couple of years before. The publication quoted Lister as saying the Masters V was "a special venture, by special request, for special occasions."

By April, however, the demand for appearances had become so great that the members of the Masters V decided to make the all-star quartet a full-time traveling act. J.D. had already disbanded the Stamps by 1981 and was filling a number of dates as bass with the Statesmen as Tommy Thompson had moved on. Hovie eventually retired the Statesmen for the second time in less than a decade in order to devote full attention to the Masters V. James had some obligations to fill with the Blackwood Brothers before he could join the Masters V on a full-time basis. The Masters hired Richard Coltrain to fill in for James whenever necessary.

The Blackwood Brothers, explains James, "had so many dates that were booked and the promoters were counting on me being there. Some of the dates I didn't feel like I could let them down." He finally was able to leave the Blackwood Brothers to board the Masters V bus on a full-time basis at the first of September, 1981.

The Masters V, observes Jake, was a great experience. "It was fun. For seven years there we did well. We didn't rehearse like we should. We didn't do classy arrangements like we should have done. We'd just: 'Do you remember this one?' and take off. But we had a good time."

"We worked a number of years until Rosie was stricken with a heart attack and dropped out," says Hovie. "That was a great group. Great individuals. All of them had their own following. Great men. Big names. And, of course, we had crowds, people wanting to see those men in one group. It was without a doubt probably one of the biggest happenings in gospel music, when all those five names came together as a group."

"It was something that no-body thought would ever happen," says Sumner. "There's never been a greater motivator, a greater manager, or greater emcee—a man to keep things rolling—than Hovie Lister. He's certainly one of the pros of all time. And if Jake Hess wasn't the great-est lead singer that's ever been, the only competition he ever had was James Blackwood. And they sung so much differ-ently. Jake was a stylist and James sang the old-fashioned way, right on the note the way it was supposed to be sung. But the only person that kept Jake from being the greatest lead singer that ever lived—

By 1988, four-fifths of the Masters V were former States-men including (clockwise from bottom left): Jack Toney, Ed Hill, Shaun Nielsen and Hovie Lister. Only J. D. Sumner and Hovie remained from the original group.

Shaun Nielsen, Jake Hess, James Blackwood and Hovie Lister at the record table during a concert at the Murat Temple in Indianapolis.

and he still probably is—would have been James Blackwood. They worked together the same as Chief and I."

The quartet signed a recording contract with Skylite, the company they had started in the days of the Blackwood Brothers/Statesmen Quartet partnership. Joel Gentry, who had purchased the company in 1966, served as producer for the Masters V recording projects. Their first Skylite recording, a self-titled album, was released in 1981. The record featured several selections that had been hits for the individual members when they sang with the Blackwood Brothers or Statesmen years before. A big seller, the popular album was a Grammy winner the following year in the Traditional Gospel Recording category. Subsequent albums by the group were nominated in the same category in 1983 and '84.

At the height of their popularity, the Masters V appeared in 275 engagements a year—an ambitious schedule for men who were closing in on 60 years of age. In 1981, J.D. had just turned 56, Hovie was 54, Jake 53 and Rosie 52. James Blackwood was, in fact, 61 years old. When occasional health problems prevented the elder partner in the Masters V from making a tour, Jake's son, Chris, stepped in to fill Blackwood's part with the group. The younger Hess had filled some dates with the Statesmen in the late 1970s after Doy Ott's medical practice prevented him from making appearances with the group. "He loves to sing," Jake says of his offspring. "It was a fun thing" having Chris as a member of the Statesmen and later Masters V. "I enjoy working with my son."

When a stroke forced Rosie to leave the quartet in November 1982, the Masters V hired Steve Warren to replace him as tenor. Warren had worked for several years with gospel groups in Texas, including a group called the Royals with Larry Gatlin. Gatlin later sang briefly with the Imperials en route to a successful career as a singer/songwriter in country music. Gatlin, incidentally, had written the jacket notes for the first Masters V album. Warren, too, was a songwriter and brought strong talents as a pianist and music arranger to the Masters.

The quartet's rigorous schedule took a heavy toll on personnel. Finally, in April of 1987, James was ready to slow down. He wanted to spend time at home with Miriam, his wife of 48 years, and assist in the music ministries of his two sons, Jimmy and Billy. Charles Yates, formerly of the Speer Family, Prophets, Foggy River Boys and other groups, replaced James for a few months, followed by Tommy Howe and later Ed Hill.

Tenor Steve Warren eventually departed and was replaced by Shaun (formerly Sherrill) Nielsen. When Jake bowed out in the fall of 1987, Jack Toney was hired to provide the lead vocals—the second time he had succeeded Jake as lead singer in a group. This lineup of the Masters V featured Sumner and four former Statesmen—Lister, Nielsen, Toney and Hill.

By this time, "the Masters V were not working as much as they had been working," Toney recalls, adding the group's heavy schedule, considering the ages of its members, was its undoing. "Well, you're just going to burn out, that's all. There's no way money can make up for time."

The following summer, Hovie also called it quits, leaving Sumner as the only remaining original member of the Masters V. At that point, to Sumner's thinking, the Masters V no longer existed. Subsequently, he changed the name of the group back to J.D. Sumner and the Stamps Quartet because, as Blackwood explains, the quartet was no longer "the same idea as we had in the beginning."

Had the Masters V "rehearsed like the Statesmen did or like some of the other groups," says Hovie in retrospect, "had we really not played as many dates and sung as much as we did we probably would still be going today. But that's history now. It was a great time. I have nothing but good thoughts of all the men that were involved in that group."

Doy Ott

On leaving the Statesmen in the late 1970s, Doy Ott had immersed himself in his new chiropractic practice in Roswell, Georgia. Some years after the death of his first wife, he married the former Mary Bradley. Together they had one son, Doy Ott, Jr., who in appearance is a carbon copy of his father. In the spring of 1980, more than 30 years after leaving his native state for a career in Christian music, Doy and his new family left Georgia and moved to Ardmore, Oklahoma, to establish a new practice in chiropractic medicine.

Although no one could then have known, Doy's exit from the Statesmen became his permanent retirement from gospel music. In Ardmore, Doy launched a full-time chiropractic practice, opening a clinic of his own. He specialized in the treatment and rehabilitation of athletic injuries, and gave much of his time freely to helping American Indians with their medical needs.

He was at his clinic tending to his rigorous schedule of appointments when he suffered a stroke on November 27, 1982. Weeks later his worsening condition was complicated by meningitis. Eventually, his wife brought him back to Georgia and he was admitted to a nursing home in the Atlanta area. He never recovered. Doy died on November 6, 1986, after being comatose for many months. He was 67.

"We can never minimize the importance of Doy Ott," Hovie has said. He considers Doy "probably the best baritone singer that any quartet has ever had." His strengths as a musical arranger, accompanist and businessman had been equally important ingredients in the recipe for continued success that had been attained by the Statesmen down through the years.

Although not as prolific a composer as Mosie Lister or James Wetherington, Doy's songwriting talents contributed immensely to the combined wealth of quartet music literature. Among the products of his pen were such compositions as: "When My Master Walks With Me," "I'm Satisfied with Jesus," "Little Joe's Prayer," "Have You Tried the Lord Today," "I've Found a New Way," "Lord, I'm Coming Home to Thee," "Goodbye, Troublesome Blues," "Wait for Me," "Stop, Look and Listen for the Lord," and others.

"Doy Ott," observes Jake, "was a good writer, a good keyboard man and he played the accordion well. He was just a first-class man."

New Opportunities

Although Jake and Hovie had parted company with the Masters V they were not quite ready to retire from performing. Jake began making appearances on behalf of the Genevox Music Group, a division of the Southern Baptist Sunday School Board, headquartered in Nashville. He

gathered some fine talent around him, including his son Chris, Steve Warren, his former singing partner of the Masters V; and Armond Morales, who had worked with Jake in the original Imperials. Morales, in fact, is the lone original member of the Imperials still touring with that group. But the Imperials were suffering through a rebuilding period at the time. Their schedule was not as full as in earlier years and Armond found himself available for a limited schedule of appearances with Jake.

"We'd go out and work churches, the Baptist people helped book us," Jake explains. "They paid all the expenses, all the hotels and the eats and everything. We did real well there for about four to six months."

But Armond decided against leaving the Imperials to sing with Jake full time. The Imperials had only recently taken on a couple of new members and Armond felt he owed it to the new people to

Hovie Lister &
The Palmetto State Quartet

keep the group together.

"I had an opportunity there to put a good quartet together but I could not do it," Jake laments. "The ones that had the good voices, they didn't have the life to back it up. And you just had to be squeaky clean because you were associated with the Baptist Sunday School Board."

Eventually, he returned to a television ministry on the West Coast. Hovie, meanwhile, joined forces with a long-established group from his old hometown—the Palmetto State Quartet of Greenville, South Carolina.

"Greenville, South Carolina was where I was born and reared. I went to school there, and Jack Pittman—the man who owned the Palmetto State Quartet—he and I had gone to high school together. We had known each other and our fathers were friends in the old singing convention days. Jack and I used to meet when his father, who was a very outstanding choir director and song leader, would be involved in the all-day singings. Of course, Jack would be there and I would be there with my dad and playing the piano some."

When Palmetto State needed a piano player, Hovie, no longer traveling with the Masters V, was available. It helped that they worked a limited schedule of engagements because Hovie had taken a job with the State of Georgia Department of Corrections.

"It was easy for me because we didn't go too far out. It was a pleasant experience working with the Palmetto State Quartet," who, Hovie says, were "wonderful, wonderful men. I enjoyed it very much."

Back to the Fifties

The record-buying public saw revolutionary changes in home entertainment during the 1980s. Recording companies ceased production of vinyl disc records. Albums and single releases were produced on cassette tapes and compact discs (CDs). Smaller in size than even a 45 rpm record and offering greater clarity than any previous format of recorded reproduction, CDs became the rage. Another selling point for the new technology was the durability of the discs. CDs do not get scratched during play, or wear out, because no needle or stylus touches the surface. The discs are read by a light beam from a low-powered laser.

Another important addition to the family home entertainment system has been the videocassette recorder (VCR). Motion picture companies began producing major films on videocassette for buyers to enjoy at home. Video rental stores enjoyed a thriving business. Record companies saw an opportunity to cash in on the video market, producing "videos"—video recordings of vignettes choreographed around hit songs, or concert recordings of major recording artists. Gospel record companies followed suit. Ironically, Hovie Lister and the Statesmen had pioneered the concept of videos with their Nabisco television series in the 1950s. However, videotape did not exist at that time.

A few months before Hovie had left the Masters V, Pittman and concert promoter Charles Waller were very instrumental in assisting him with the public release of a series of videotapes called "Back to the Fifties with Hovie Lister and the Sensational Statesmen Quartet."

Through the years Hovie had held onto the 16 millimeter master films of the Statesmen Quartet's Nabisco-sponsored television shows. The films were cleaned, restored and edited into a series of videos. The videos have been well-received among gospel music fans of all ages, including younger fans who were not yet born when the shows were telecast across the airwaves in the 1950s. "Recently," Hovie says, "I had a call from the Secretary of State for the state of Georgia requesting me to bring a complete set, if I would, to the state Capitol. They want to place them in the Archives. The University of Georgia has a set of those videos in their archives in the Music Department. The Georgia Music Hall of Fame is a very elaborate place. They have requested various articles, such as maybe one or two of the 16 millimeter films."

Hovie was inducted into the Georgia Music Hall of Fame some years ago. He later became a member of the Georgia Music Hall of Fame Board of Directors and the Georgia Senate Music Committee, as well as being named a Governor on the Board of Directors of the Atlanta Chapter of NARAS, the organization that annually bestows the Grammy Awards to the recording industry's top recordings.

"I try to stay current and up-to-date with anything that has to do with music," he says, "regardless of whether it's gospel, secular or what. I'm interested in what's going on in the music world."

In 1984, Hovie was inducted into the Gospel Music Association's Hall of Fame during GMA's annual Dove Awards banquet, held at the Tennessee Performing Arts Center in Nashville. "I have never sought awards," he told a writer for the *Atlanta Journal/Atlanta Constitution*. "My blessing has always come from the feeling that our music may help someone find the way to Christ. We sing to the glory of God. That is what it is all about."

Jake later joined Hovie as a member of the GMA Hall of Fame. Other former Statesmen

Certificate of Big Chief's posthumous induction into the Gospel Music Association's Hall of Fame, 1977.

who have been inducted include Mosie Lister, the late Denver Crumpler and the late James "Big Chief" Wetherington. Jake is also a member of the Alabama Hall of Fame, which displays one of his Grammys at its museum facility in Tuscumbia, Alabama.

"For a country hick like myself to have four Grammys and all these things that people have done for me all of my life is unbelievable," says Jake. "I just don't understand how one guy could be so fortunate. I've been able to stay married to one girl for 40 years and have three fine children and four fine grandchildren. I am so thankful that I have been able to keep the wolf away from the door for nearly 50 years in gospel music. But old Jake didn't do it. God has really gone before me and opened doors."

Lister and Hess reunited with Rosie Rozell and other former Statesmen, Buddy Burton and Tommy Thompson, to recreate the old Statesmen magic at Charles Waller's "Grand Ole Gospel Reunion" concert in Greenville, held in August, 1988. The concert, featuring several retired quartet personnel and other longtime personalities of the genre, was an instant hit with the fans who remembered gospel quartet music the way it used to be. The appearance by the Statesmen, complete with Jake jumping up on the piano stool, was a show stopper. As a result, Grand Ole Gospel became an annual affair, and has featured Hovie and various lineups of Statesmen personnel in the years since. The Statesmen also appeared in a so-called "final round" tour of concerts for Waller in October, 1988. But when the tour ended, Hovie and Jake were not quite ready for the Statesmen to take a final curtain call.

22

Statesmen Revival, 1992

Homecoming

During the seven years Jake traveled with the Masters V, he and Hovie often discussed the Statesmen, but the subject of reorganizing the group as a full-time entity never surfaced. "We'd often talk about what good times we'd had with the Statesmen, and we'd like to have a group that really tried to sing that was really put together for the right reasons," says Jake. But putting together a new version of the Statesmen, "was all (Bill) Gaither's idea from the beginning."

The idea, Jake says, germinated with the "Bill Gaither Remembers The Statesmen" video, released in 1990. "Bill talked with both of us a week or two after that. I guess that's where it was born. When we did the 'Homecoming' video, that's when he thought it was time to do it."

"The (Gaither) Vocal Band wanted to go back and do that 'Homecoming' record of our roots," Gaither says. "That was really a labor of love for us, something we really believed in, and to do that we wanted to bring in as many of those heroes as we could to do that one tune, 'Where Could I Go But to the Lord.' "

"I had a call from him," recalls Hovie. "He said it would be a dream to get a lot of his friends—his heroes as he put it—in gospel music to come together and do one song on that album. Finally he set a date, February 19, 1991, that he wanted to do this."

"We videoed and recorded at the same time," Gaither explains. "We had already put down the track and done the Vocal Band part, but we knew that we had one day to get those guys and we got them all there the same day. Then in the afternoon we started taking pictures around the piano and started singing. Jake came in later on in the afternoon because he'd been singing at a funeral. Larry Gatlin was there because he'd heard about it. Larry and Rudy loved those guys, too. And we did 'Homecoming,' the video, which became very big."

The setting for the recording session was a log cabin recording studio in Nashville called Masters Touch. What began as an album developed into an historic video spinoff. Although Gaither hired a video crew to tape the session, there initially were no plans to market a video of the event. When he later saw the raw footage, however, Bill was moved to share the visual experience with the gospel music public.

Joining the Vocal Band for the session—together with Gatlin Brothers Larry and Rudy, Glen Payne and George Younce of the Cathedrals, Howard and Vestal Goodman, James Blackwood, Hovie and Jake—were Speer Family members Brock, Ben, Mary Tom (Speer) Reid, and Rosa Nell (Speer) Powell; Eva Mae LeFevre, Buck Rambo and former Statesmen vocalist Jim Hill.

"I felt it a very, very high honor to be there because I was the only person no longer active in full-time gospel music on the tape," says Hill. "I just thank Bill for the opportunity to do it. I've never had a feeling like I had in that studio. It was not a competitive spirit. Everybody was glad to see each other. There were no differences in any way. It was just as close to stepping through the Pearly Gates in singing, I think, as anything I'll ever experience—a feeling that I've never gotten over and I doubt that I ever will until I get to Heaven. It was such a thrill! I just more or less stood in the background and drank it in. That was about all I could do."

After work on "Where Could I Go" was completed, the Vocal Band and their guests erupted in a spontaneous songfest, lending legendary talents to several old favorites. When Jake arrived late, his old friends at once prompted him to sing the song with which he has become synonymous—"Faith Unlocks the Door." That sterling performance was followed by an equally powerful delivery of "Until Then."

"Mike English and I were knocked out as to how well Jake sang," Gaither recalls. "We said, 'My lands! He's still singing as well as ever!' Not quite as high, maybe one note less at his top part, but that doesn't make any difference. Neither does Neil Diamond by his own admission. Gravity takes its course as you get older."

Hovie had to get back to Atlanta to be at his state job the next morning and had already left the studio when Jake joined the others to complete the session. A day or so later he received a telephone call from Gaither:

"I want to tell you something," said Bill. "You really missed it. Jake Hess came in and he started singing 'Until Then' and the whole place erupted. My guys in the Gaither Vocal Band, their eyes got so big they couldn't believe this guy with that big voice and that great singing. You ought to think about putting the Statesmen back together."

Jake was the recipient of a similar call in which Gaither said, "You guys ought to get a couple or three younger guys and put something together, because you just need the stamina of youth. Once this train gets rolling you just need some young legs to make it work."

While the three were working out the details for reviving the Statesmen, Gaither was also wrapping up production on the "Homecoming" album and companion video. When it was released, the video was telecast nationally on televangelist Pat Robertson's 700 Club program.

"The response," Gaither says, "was tremendous."

Testimonials from 700 Club viewers poured into Gaither's office. Vocalists who participated in the session, such as Jim Hill, have seen the video touch lives in unusual ways.

"I have people that are in business with me that call me and happened to see it," says Hill. "One Jewish man, a very wealthy businessman in Columbus, Ohio, called me and said, 'I saw you on this video on TV. I've never heard anything like it in my life.' He said, 'I want you to bring it to my business and play it for my employees. Let me know when you can come.' I get all kinds of reports from people who have seen that video. A lady that was dying of cancer called me. She had made contact with the Gaithers' office and located me in Evansville, Indiana. I went over and prayed with her in a nursing home and I got such a blessing out of that. She was so happy to see me. So many things have been coming in on that video it's just unbelievable."

A New Beginning

Buoyed by the response to "Homecoming," Bill Gaither vigorously moved forward with preparations for a Statesmen comeback. The first step, he decided, would be to select personnel and produce a recording for a major label. His good friend Bill Traylor was involved with both Homeland Records and Canaan Records, the southern gospel division of Word Records. "We asked Canaan Records if they would be interested. They said yes because it's a great name," Gaither says.

Having a keen ear and a genius for putting together combinations of voices that blend well, Bill began looking at available talent. Word got around among the southern gospel fraternity that the Statesmen were preparing to return. Speculation centered on previous Statesmen members Rosie Rozell, Buddy Burton and Tommy Thompson possibly rejoining Jake and Hovie. Rosie was battling various ailments and in the summer of 1990 had been forced to drop out of the James Blackwood Quartet a few months after it was organized. He later underwent open heart surgery on July 30, 1990. Tommy also had been facing open heart surgery. Several hopefuls began contacting Jake, Hovie and Gaither.

"In ensuing months," Hovie says, numerous auditions were held "of various people to be a part of the Statesmen. Most of that was done with Bill Gaither and Jake because I was in Atlanta. Gaither would come into Nashville and they would set up times to listen to various people for the quartet. Finally, along about November of 1991, it began to come together."

Gaither did not hope to find a Doy Ott, a "Big Chief" Wetherington, or an Irish tenor of the same caliber as Denver Crumpler. The three men who emerged from the auditions as members of the new Statesmen were all experienced quartet men.

Tenor Johnny Cook had been a member of the Happy Goodman Family in the 1970s during that group's pinnacle of success. Cook had been presented *The Singing News* Fan Award for Favorite First Tenor in 1974 and '75 while with the Goodmans. In later years he had left the road for an office job in the accounting department of a Memphis hospital.

Baritone Biney English had grown up singing gospel music with his family in North Carolina. In the mid-1970s he worked with a group called the Singing Samaritans, later joining the Anchormen as lead singer. A songwriter, Biney had penned several songs that the Anchormen and other quartets had recorded. Michael English, his younger brother, was a member of the Bill Gaither Trio and Gaither Vocal Band for a time.

Bass singer Bob Caldwell worked in gospel groups as a teenager in Flint, Michigan. Working full-time on the production line at a General Motors plant, Bob built pickup trucks, suburban vans and Blazer trucks for a living and honed his singing skills in his spare time. He sang for several years in a quartet with his brother and a few friends in Flint before moving to Tennessee in 1987 to join the Kingdom Heirs, host gospel quartet at the Dollywood Theme Park.

For several days in December, the New Statesmen worked recording an album at Nashville's  Suite 16 Studio. All of the group members brought songs to be considered for the album. Co-producer Gaither also brought several songs, including a few of his own compositions, for the group to hear. In the end, most of the songs that eventually appeared on the album had been suggested by Gaither. One exception was "Ride That Glory Train," an uptempo number written by Biney English. The only throwback to the Statesmen of earlier times was an updated version of "Goodbye, World Goodbye."

"That was my harmonic arrangement," says Gaither. "I wanted to get those barbershop chords in there and it really sounds good, I think."

"I've listened a lot to what they did with my old song 'Goodbye, World, Goodbye,' and they did a very, very good job in more or less recalling that old sound," says Mosie Lister.

Arrangements for some material on the album, says Gaither, "came from a combination of people. Sometimes it's dictated by the keyboard person doing the tracks. But a lot of the arrangements were probably mine."

Several older songs were among those selected for the album. Henry Slaughter's "If the Lord Wasn't Walking By My Side" had been a big song for Jake Hess and the Imperials and had been recorded by Elvis in the mid-1960s. The song served as a vehicle for a solo by Hovie. Two other songs had been popular for the Prophets Quartet in the early 1960s: "Sinners Plea," written by Joe Roper, and Joe Moscheo's "Someday."

Among the newer songs was an uptempo Bible story written by Scooter Simmons called "Come Out With Your Hands Up." "I've Been There," a solo by Jake, was the closing song of the collection. "I Lost It All To Find Everything" and "Every Eye Shall See" are among the finest of the great Gaither catalog of compositions. The most unique song of the collection belittled death. The song became a favorite of all the group members.

"Bill brought us that song when we were in the studio," remembers Hovie, "and I didn't think much of it when I read the title—'Death Ain't No Big Deal.' I thought, 'My, we don't want to record that.' I wasn't really impressed when I read through the words. But the more I listened to the men working on it in the studio, the more I realized this song was perfect for Jake. He's been through open heart surgery two times, he's had pericarditis, nephritis, he's a diabetic, and he's had two cancer operations."

The album was titled "Revival" and was rushed to release in time for the group's first live performance at the end of January, 1992.

According to Gaither, the recording business has changed tremendously since Brock Speer produced the Statesmen for Skylite 30 years ago. At that time, he points out, a group went in with the studio musicians and recorded tracks and vocals at the same time, all in one day.

"I think that says several things," he says. "Number one, it says that the groups came and basically recorded the material they were rehearsing and doing in concert. At this stage now, the recordings are more sophisticated because you do the tracks at one time and the vocals at another time. So the process is longer. I think you get better vocals that way because you don't wear them out. You can do a couple or three songs in one day. I've been to sessions where we've even gone through one section again and again and again just to get the parts totally in tune."

This technique wasn't possible in the old days, because the technology that now allows a recording engineer to "punch in"—the process of isolating and instantly editing or re-recording a certain section of the recording—did not exist. Nowadays, engineers can punch in a replacement of a few measures, a phrase, or as little as one word on a vocal track.

"In some ways the singers had to be better and they had to be better prepared in the old days—there's just no getting around it—than they do today," Gaither observes. "And that's including any current group, whether it's the Vocal Band or anybody. If we had to do it like they did it, we probably wouldn't sound nearly as good. So that makes the original group even more great than what we thought they were. They were great but they could've been even greater had they had the techniques that we have today."

Pleased with the final mixdown of the vocal tracks for the recording, Bill was more determined than ever to see the New Statesmen begin touring. But putting a professional quartet on the road on a full-time basis in the 1990s requires substantial financing. There were the salaries of the men to consider. The group would need a sophisticated sound system to accomodate the needs of auditoriums of various sizes. The procurement of a tour bus would necessitate another large expense. Gaither secured investors to get the quartet underway.

There remained the need to negotiate a booking contract with an agency to handle scheduling. Initially, the group contracted through Brentwood Talent and Marketing. Later, Spring House Associates, a division of Gaither Music, handled bookings. Finally, the Statesmen secured Century II Promotions to handle their scheduling. Sonny Simmons, a longtime gospel music promoter and talent agent, operates the company.

Gaither's next recommendation to the group was to hire a second keyboard player. At this suggestion, Hovie did a double take. Bill quickly explained that the group needed a utility person. On some songs in concert, the Statesmen would be singing to the accompaniment of sound tracks from the "Revival" album. The utility person would be responsible for keying-in the appropriate track at the appropriate time. He also would be responsible for tuning the sound system, making adjustments in volume during the concerts to ensure the correct volume for an optimum vocal and instrumental blend. Jeff Silvey, the young man Gaither had in mind, would also accompany the group on an electronic keyboard to provide strings and other synthesized instruments for a fuller sound.

Bill Gaither

The group began making preparations for their inaugural concert. Weeks of rehearsing and developing their repertoire culminated with the debut of the New Statesmen as part of a twin-bill concert with J.D. Sumner and the Stamps at Jonathan Byrd's Cafeteria, in Greenwood, Indiana, on January 30, 1992. Since the cafeteria opened late in 1988, Byrd has hosted a gospel concert every six weeks in his huge banquet hall. The walls of his office lobby are decorated with autographed photos of many of today's top gospel artists who have appeared in concert there. Byrd and his cafeteria have been featured in *Guideposts*.

The facility broke attendance records as fans of the Stamps and Statesmen poured in. Many fans traveled great distances for the inaugural appearance of the quartet who would write the next chapter of the celebrated Statesmen story. Record executive Bill Traylor, correspondents for *The Singing News*, and Bill and Gloria Gaither joined more than 500 gospel music fans for the event. The quartet not only sounded good, they were a handsome lot. Jake Hess looked great and thrilled everyone with his trademark style. At 64, he could still deliver the goods. And he was still fun to watch. "Jake even got a new wig for this special occasion," Hovie quipped as he introduced his friend of more than 40 years. It was an evening of excitement and emotion for not only the fans, but the Statesmen as well.

On the Road Again

In large, bold letters, the huge church sign facing the bustling suburban thoroughfare broadcasts the announcement: "In Concert Tonight, The Statesmen." Frisky thoroughbred colts are enjoying the warm spring air as they play in nearby Bluegrass fields, oblivious to the traffic streaming toward the church. Concert patrons line the turning lane of the Lexington highway patiently awaiting the aggravation of a delayed traffic signal. Beyond the traffic light looms the stately Colonial edifice of the huge Baptist Church. A black, Silver Eagle—a capacious royal coach gleaming regally in the late afternoon sunlight—purrs near the church entrance.

Inside the beautiful sanctuary, dressed casually, the younger members of the Statesmen are in the process of "tuning the room." This sometimes-lengthy process involves adjusting the volume, bass, treble and presence controls of the quartet's elaborate sound system to balance comfortably in the large sanctuary. Within minutes, the system is adapted to the acoustics of the sanctuary. It is time to return to the bus for a quick shave and change of clothing in readiness for the evening appearance.

In a hallway behind the sanctuary, bus driver O'Neill Terry, adds his finishing touches to the product table. All merchandise is displayed attractively. There are stacks of CDs and cassettes of the "Revival" Canaan release and two custom recordings released independently, sets of four tapes recorded by an earlier version of the Statesmen back in the 1950s, copies of the "Back to the Fifties with Hovie Lister and the Sensational Statesmen" and "Homecoming" videocassettes, full-color group photos, caps and shirts. Terry stands back to survey his work. Satisfied, he positions empty tape boxes and cargo cartons out of view. Terry knows his job well. He was the first professional bus driver hired by the Statesmen in the late 1950s, later driving Jake Hess and the Imperials to hundreds of destinations annually. Terry has been away from the quartet business for a number of years but is pleased to be working again for his old friends.

In the front lobby, Jake and Hovie make conversation with a local deacon, discussing their afternoon drive from Parkersburg, West Virginia. It is an hour before time for the service, yet people are pouring steadily through the doors.

"Do your people normally arrive for service this early?" asks Jake.

"No, they want to be sure to get a good seat for the Statesmen," answers the deacon. "They remember you fellows from being here with the Masters V. These people love good gospel singing. We'll have a full house tonight!"

On this night a full house is the equivalent of about 600 faces beaming from the pews as the Statesmen deliver in song their message of hope and cheer in Jesus Christ.

Moments before the service begins, the Statesmen gather in a small room to the left of the church platform to bow their heads and ask God to "visit this place and speak to every heart here tonight." After an opening hymn, the pastor leads the congregation in a rousing prayer, asking God's blessings on the service and the "messengers of the hour." A simple, but heartfelt, introduction brings the Statesmen quickly to the center of attention.

As the quartet sings, several members of the audience are seen nodding their heads in time with the rhythm of the music. The singers romp through several up-tempo numbers, presenting most of the songs from the "Revival" recording, with several old Statesmen classics thrown in for good measure. Throughout, Hovie remains the consummate master of ceremonies.

"I was walking down a street in a town in south Georgia the other day," he tells the audience. "I was standing on a street corner and I saw an old man crossing the street. He was all bent over and walking with a cane. He looked to be about a hundred. He was just moving along slowly, very feeble. In watching him struggle across the street there, I felt great pity in my heart for him, and I said a prayer under my breath, 'God, help him.' He walked over to me and stopped. I was dressed up, suit and tie, so I guess I was rather conspicuous. He leaned on his cane and tilted his head up and looked at me and he says, 'You're Hovie Lister, ain'tcha?' I told him I was. He said, 'First time I seen you, you and the quartet was singing over there at that county courthouse. I was 14 years old.' "

At this, the crowd erupted with laughter.

"I never wanted to slap an old man so bad in all my life," he added.

Early in the program, Hovie pauses a moment to showcase a classic Statesmen number:

The Statesmen, vintage 1992 (from left): Johnny Cook, tenor; Bob Caldwell, bass; Hovie Lister, piano; Biney English, baritone; and Jake Hess, lead.

"You know, there are certain songs that are identified with a certain artist or singer. We can't hear 'White Christmas' without thinking of Bing Crosby. I don't know how many million records of that he sold. There are certain country songs that we associate with certain artists. This next song would have to be considered Jake Hess's signature song. Jake Hess loves to sing gospel music. I've never seen anyone who loves to sing any more than Jake does. With all of his health problems he should've retired years ago, but he still hops on the bus and travels. Now that's dedication. That's being mission minded.

"Jake doesn't like pity, but there's something wonderful about our Lord and about adversity and things that happen. But Jake, I guess, is one of those who sets an example of people who have major difficult problems and yet he works hard at being well and whole. He works not only by doing the right things but by his faith. I want you to listen as Jake sings for you 'Prayer is the Key to Heaven but Faith Unlocks the Door'."

After the Statesmen have featured Hovie singing on yet another old Statesmen standard—"Oh, My Lord, What a Time"—he brings a round of laughter with another familiar line.

"I'm built more for speed than I am for comfort. I like those songs where you can get on your mule and go on downtown!"

Hovie stands and shifts into preaching gear, his voice rising in pitch and volume.

"Salvation is something to be excited about. Amen? I don't care if you're Baptist, Methodist, Nazarene—if you're born again, got salvation, and you know that you know that you've been born again, you ought to be excited. It's the greatest thing going. I happen to be Baptist but that don't keep me from having a good time. It does a lot of Baptists. (laughter) But it don't bother me none. I go to a church where once in a while I'll holler 'Amen!' (laughter) About eight or ten will have to go to the chiropractor on Monday morning to get their neck put back in shape because they'll turn it out of socket looking around to see who that idiot was that hollered amen in the main sanctuary. But this is the House of the Lord. We've come to have a good time. If you know Jesus Christ, you ought to let your light shine. You ought to talk about it, not only in the house of God but wherever you go.

"Bill Gaither brought us a song when we were in the studio. He told me what the title of it was and I had not read the words. I thought he'd lost his mind. The title of it was 'Death Ain't No Big Deal.' Now we all know we've got to die sometime but we ain't exactly in no hurry. I don't know very many people that's in a hurry to die. There's a story told about a lady over in Alabama. They used to have what they called a protracted meetin'. Do you know what a protracted meetin' is? Anybody here? One man. He must be from Alabama. That means they set no time limit. Nowadays when we're going to have revival, we Baptists have about got away from calling it revival. We say we're going to have a couple or three days of renewal. Revival's too old fashioned. Protracted meetin' means that it's going to run as long as the Lord's there and they're having a good time and souls are being saved. They said this old lady hardly ever came to church, but when she did she came during the protracted meetin'. It was an old country church — two front doors. Ever seen one of those? Usually it's a Baptist church. That crowd," he says, pointing to the left side of the church, "don't want to speak to this crowd," he motions to the right side, "and they can go out that side. This crowd can go out that door.

"This old woman, her name was Aunt Tessie Smith, and she came every time they had protracted meetin'. They said she would shout every year, down one aisle, back up the other aisle, out one front door and back in the other front door and just make a loop around like that, you know, two or three times, hollerin' and a-carryin' on. They had an old boy that lived in the community by the name of Hollister Williams, about three bricks shy of a load. He never would come into the church. He'd just lean up in one of the door casings and put his hands in the bib of his overalls and look in. And every year old Aunt Tessie would come to protracted meetin' and get happy and shout up and down the aisles and out the door. One time she made a loop past old Hollister, and she slapped him on the back and said, 'Praise the Lord, Hollister, I'm goin' to Heaven. Don't you want to go with me?!' Hollister said, 'Nope! I'll just wait'll next year, you'd be a-goin' agin!' "

The church, highly enjoying the story, erupts in loud laughter.

"We're all going sometime. Amen? The main thing is to be ready. Then, if we're ready, death really ain't no big deal."

Later, as Hovie brings the concert to a close, he relates the story of a difficult period in his life.

"You know, we've sung about salvation tonight. We've sung about joyous things. But there is something that we have to do if we want to participate in all these wonderful things. And that is to give our life to Jesus unconditionally. And sometimes it's awfully hard to really lose it all to find everything. We started the Statesmen Quartet in somewhat of a marvelous fashion in 1948. Things were great for the Statesmen. Then in 1957, at the very height of his popularity, Denver Crumpler died suddenly of a heart attack. In the early 1960s, Jake Hess left to form a great group called the Imperials. Of course, that was a great loss, but we carried on the best we could. Then in 1973 at the National Quartet Convention, Big Chief, my strongest guy in the quartet that I leaned on then, had a sudden heart attack and went home to be with the Lord.

"For awhile there I had been flying high. I thought I was doing it all. But you know God has a way sometimes of showing us that when we don't give it all up to Him, He can take it away very quickly. Bill and Gloria Gaither wrote this song at the time I was feeling my lowest. It says exactly what I was feeling at that time. I had already given up. I had just laid the Statesmen name up on a shelf and said, 'Forget it. I'll just quit.' But, no, it's not that easy. When God gets His hand on you, it's not that easy. He brought me back to my knees and showed me I had to lose everything to find Him."

Hovie then sings a powerful Gaither composition, "I Lost It All To Find Everything."

To the strains of Ira Stanphill's "Room at the Cross," the pastor gives an invitation and closes the service. Upon dismissal, everyone heads for the tape table.

One young man enjoys a reunion with Jake. He is a television producer for a Public Broadcasting System station in Lexington. He tells his young son that during his first television job in Nashville, his assignment was to produce Jake's morning gospel music TV show. His little boy asks Jake about his tie-tac which is shaped in the form of a question mark. "What's that question mark for?"

"It means where are you going when you die? I wear it for a conversation piece," drawls Jake, smiling down at the lad.

Meanwhile, Hovie is drawn aside to tape an interview with a gospel deejay who specializes in quartet music from the 1950s and '60s. All too soon the church is empty, the equipment and recordings have been stored away on the bus. The Statesmen climb aboard and dress down to casual attire—except Hovie, who is never seen in any attire except a three-piece suit. Soon, O'Neill Terry points the Silver Eagle south toward home.

The Gospel Road Today

Settling into the comfort of the bus, Jake and Hovie visit with a guest who is a longtime Statesmen fan.

"You guys are in your mid-sixties," marvels the friend. "How long do you plan to keep going?"

"Age is not a factor too much in gospel music," replies Jake. "G.T. Speer did his best singing, his best selling, when he was anywhere from 65 on up to his early 70s. Dad Carter of the Chuck Wagon Gang was enjoyed more in his later years than ever before. I was taking voice from John Hoffman in Atlanta years ago and just got married and had a little girl. And I got to thinking, 'Hey, all my life people told me you couldn't sing but for about 20 years and that was it.' So I couldn't wait to go back and see John Hoffman. I said, 'How long can one sing?' And he started laughing at me. It wasn't funny to me at all. He said, 'What do you mean, how long can one sing?' I said, 'I've spent nearly 20 years in this business now and I need to know. I've got a family to support.' He said, 'Well, how long can one talk? Don't you know we've discussed singing as talking on key with expressions? You give up your singing when you're no longer physically able to have the pressure to support the tone. But you don't go around asking people how long can one sing.' He really made a joke out of it and from then on, every time he'd see me, he'd say, 'Hey, Hess, how long can you sing?' He wouldn't let me forget it."

"I'm really thankful God has allowed us to go back into this mission work," says Hovie. "Awhile back in Columbus, Ohio, a man in his 40s came to me in the parking lot after we had sung in a service there. He said, 'I came to a Statesmen concert in Dayton, Ohio several years ago. I wasn't saved but the Holy Spirit kept speaking to me. Those songs that you sang had truth to them, they had meaning to them. I surrendered my life to Him, went to the seminary and I'm now in the ministry.' We've heard testimonies like this hundreds of times."

Another individual to whom the Statesmen were an inspiration in his youth is Bill Gaither. Hovie and Jake have high words of praise for their friend who has become a leader in almost every facet of the Christian music industry.

"I cannot ever say enough about input and how much work and how much nurturing that Bill Gaither put into the reorganization of the Statesmen Quartet," says Hovie. "I can't tell you how many hundreds of hours and I mean thousands of phone calls and how much encouragement the man has given, and how he has been so kind in encouraging every member of the group. When you've got that kind of help behind you, and that kind of love, that kind of compassion, that kind of energy and that kind of desire, it makes you want to really make things work for everybody concerned. Not just from the spiritual standpoint, but from every standpoint."

There is mutual respect between Gaither and his friends. His years of success at various levels in gospel music are evidence that his advice is to be highly valued.

Jake and Hovie acknowledge they have seen many changes in the gospel music field since the Statesmen began singing. The years have brought improvements, technically, in recordings and in onstage concert presentations. Where four men once sang to the accompaniment of a piano, today a quartet might not have a pianist, but rather may sing to full orchestral accompaniment on a sound track. Some quartets travel with a full band to accompany them onstage. Gospel music is quite diversified and more sophisticated in the 1990s, with various labels being attributed to each group's style of singing: Southern Gospel music, Contemporary Christian music, Traditional Gospel, Christian Country, etc.

"There's so many people interested in gospel music, today," Jake says. "Like I was telling a magazine writer the other day, nowadays there are talent agents, promoters, southern gospel music publications, producers, buses, and other things that we didn't have back there in the early years. And it makes things a lot easier now for us old men."

"Our industry has changed from an all-male quartet scene," observes Hovie. "You're talking to one who naturally will look back. But I also look forward and I understand that everything changes and that nothing really stands still. Coming back into the gospel quartet arena in the 1990s, I have found there's been lots of changes and rightly so, I guess, because time does change. Years ago I would not have thought about having a mouth harp on a record but now, you know, that's the thing. And I enjoy some of it. We have some on our records. It's very tasteful."

Both men agree that not all of the changes in gospel music have been good.

"I don't want to put any group down today," offers Hovie, "but I do hear groups that are supposedly professional groups, singing full time and making a living out of it, that years ago would not have been considered to be good enough for people to go pay and listen to." Some groups sell themselves short when they should be working harder. "I'm always striving to be better or to have a better group, a better sound, a better blend, to get a better arrangement."

Jake's advice to young people interested in a gospel music career is to prepare themselves.

"It really hurts me to see kids getting into gospel music and don't know what they're doing," he says. "They may have a good voice but they don't have any voice training. They don't have any musical education behind it. Sooner or later they're going to run into a tree. They don't know how to pace themselves, they don't know how to sing. They're just singing straight from their throat. They're going to wear out in five or ten years and won't know what happened. But how are you going to get that through to anyone? If they'd study the Word more and improve their singing, it's unimaginable the difference it could make."

Both men agree that the support of a loving, understanding wife is essential to maintaining both a successful marriage AND gospel music career.

"When I got married," says Hovie, "I was 30 years old. I have a very wonderful wife. She was Ethel Abbott before I married her and from a small town near Atlanta. She was quite an athlete and she had played softball and basketball with the Atlanta Tomboys and traveled herself very extensively all over the United States and Cuba and places like that to play softball and basketball. Of course, I at that time was pastoring Mount Zion Baptist Church. I told her, 'Number one, the Lord comes first in my life and my work comes second, and if you can take third place, then I'll be good to you in the third position and we've got a deal. But God's work comes first and quartet work is my life.' After five years of courting we got married and we never had any problems. She knew that that was something that I felt that I had been called to do and we were very successful in it. She was a good mother to our two children, and took them to little league ballgames, to ballet, my son was in the Atlanta Boy's Choir—all these various things—and she took them to church with her. She gets the credit. When I was at home I spent a lot of time with my kids, and vacation times. And so it was with the others. Jake's wife, there's never been a finer woman. She took care of their children. And, of course, Jake spent time with his family when we were off."

"When my daughter was born, she was eight days old before I saw her," says Jake. "I was out in Texas and California. Back then you didn't have time to sing with your kids and teach them as you'd love for them to be taught. But there's been enough good to take care of the bad."

Hovie says his wife is excited about him traveling again with the Statesmen and stands behind his decision to return to the road. "My wife has always been very supportive, because I've never been really out of the public eye, you know. I've been either in politics, or in singing—like with the Palmetto State on a limited basis—or out preaching or singing or going. So I've never really been what you would say just 'back home' every day and night. I'm not that kind of person. I've got to be on the go and doing something all the time."

Jake and Hovie are pleased by the number of old Statesmen hits that have been revived by today's artists in recent years. The Speer Family has enjoyed tremendous success with "I'll Walk Dem Golden Stairs." Carroll Roberson received a lot of radio airplay with his remake of "The Old Landmark." The Gaither Vocal Band has thrilled audiences with "First Day In Heaven." The Cathedrals have scored with such great songs as "Climbing Higher and Higher," "This Ole House," and "Oh, What a Savior." The Talleys rejuvenated "Sweeter as the Days Go By." The Heartland Boys, with former Cathedrals baritone George Amon Webster, are treating their audiences to the strains of "Glory, Glory, Clear the Road."

"Those songs are becoming hits today for those people because we have another generation coming along that didn't hear them the first time around," says Hovie. "That tells you something about the quality of material the Statesmen used back in those days. The Statesmen always tried to have good material, to be able to sing it well, and present it in a very professional and entertaining way as well as a very spiritual way. Giving the Lord the credit, those ingredients are what I consider that helped make the Statesmen an outstanding group."

"I had three ambitions in life," says Jake. "I wanted to sing with not what I would think but what the world would think was the nation's top gospel quartet. I think we arrived at that with Denver, Doy, Chief, Hovie and myself. Then, somewhere down the line, I wanted to organize a quartet and just stand flat-footed and sing. It wouldn't be necessary to tell jokes or jump high or anything, just really enjoy singing. I think I fulfilled that dream with the Imperials. And I had an ambition to win a Grammy as a soloist, and I won three Grammys as a soloist for RCA Victor. I guess anything that happens from here on out is just a bonus."

"Jake, has Hovie changed any from the early days?" the friend asks.

"I think one of Hovie's biggest assets as far as the group is concerned, he sells himself by selling others," observes Jake, "and he protects us when somebody's hoarse. Like this evening there he talked a couple of times when he hadn't planned to so we could rest."

"A lot of that's in the timing," interjects Hovie, "and being able to know when to cover up. Jake can usually say 'Talk, Hovie,' or 'Fill, Hovie,' or something like that, and people won't hear that or they won't know what's going on. Or he'll do it in some crazy way."

"Well, if Hovie has changed," Jake continues, "maybe he's changed so slowly I didn't notice it because Hovie's always been a ball of fun. He's no problem on the road to get along with. He just rolls with the punches and he's a trouper. He's a pro. Doy was very interesting to work with. Crump was the epitome of a pro in gospel music. Big Chief was one great guy. I think my life has been much fuller having known Big Chief. I'd like to think old Chief and Crump and Doy might be looking down and saying, 'Hey, that's great! Hang in there.'

"You know," says Jake thoughtfully, "I don't ever hope to sing with a quartet like that again."

Eventually, the diesel engine humming down the highway is the source of the only sound filling the somber motor coach. Through dampened eyes, Jake and Hovie stare out the windows, focusing on scenes of long ago—vignettes that are beyond the recollection of their younger colleagues. Beyond the bus windows, the tranquil Kentucky countryside flashes by—Americana at rest beneath a purple sky. The road stretches before them, an endless ribbon of asphalt that leads homeward on this spring evening. Tomorrow brings another venue, another sea of smiling faces, another opportunity to share their unique style of "Happy Rhythm."

The motor coach rolls steadily along and, gradually enveloped by the darkness, it disappears into the night.

The ledger book page at right, in Bervin Kendrick's handwriting, records Statesmen engagements for the months of July, August and most of September, 1949. Notations in the middle column indicate the concert promoter. Each man's share of earnings for the engagement are shown in the column at far right.

The Statesmen lineup that was featured in the first few gatherings of the Grand Ole Gospel Reunion in Greenville, South Carolina. From left are: Rosie Rozell, tenor; Buddy Burton, baritone; Hovie Lister, piano; Jake Hess, lead; and Tommy Thompson, bass.

The Statesmen packed Atlanta's City Auditorium (right) every month during the 1950s.

A full house in Birmingham (below) for a Wally Fowler all-night sing featuring the Statesmen.

Cover photo from a 1956 picture book about the Statesmen.

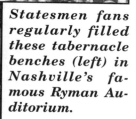

Statesmen fans regularly filled these tabernacle benches (left) in Nashville's famous Ryman Auditorium.

Epilogue
Still Sensational After Fifty Years

As this 50th Anniversary edition of **Happy Rhythm** goes to press, Hovie Lister and the Statesmen are still making news. The Statesmen continue to make singing appearances, but are being selective about the number of engagements they accept these days. Only Hovie remains of the group that organized in late 1991. Jake Hess, weak and battling increasing health problems, retired from the group on June 5, 1993. At that time Jack Toney resumed his now-familiar role as "Jake's replacement" in the lead-singing role with the Statesmen.

After leaving the Statesmen at the end of 1968, Jack worked in several jobs—working briefly as lead singer with Rosie Rozell and The Searchers, and later as a church music director, a salesman for the Proctor & Gamble Corporation, and as a public relations representative for Rev. Jerry Falwell's ministry. It would take 18 years, but quartet music would again lure him out of obscurity and into the public eye as a member of first the Masters V, then J.D. Sumner and the Stamps, and presently with the Statesmen.

"I think that any time you're in the entertainment business and you're with a top-notch group, there's always a letdown" when you step away from it to pursue a different line of work, he says. "There's very little that can fulfill that letdown, especially if you enjoy singing, which I do. I did have a large church choir. In fact, I had one church choir in Birmingham that had 125 in the adult choir. But still it's not the same as the quartet business to me. This is the biggest letdown—the people that you're used to seeing in different locations, the fans. As my wife says now it's ego. But without ego we have very little reason to be entertainers."

Jack Toney and wife Gail are now prolific songwriters, having written more than 400 songs. Many have been recorded by a number of top groups in the quartet field, including "Some Dawning," recorded by The Kevin Spencer Family and Stamps Quartet; "Twelve Gates," recorded by The Kevin Spencer Family; and "I'll Rise Up From The Grave To Meet The Lamb," a song the Kingsmen propelled to Number One on the Gospel charts. Other groups recording songs by the Toneys include the Palmetto State Quartet, Dixie Echoes (of whom Jack was an original member), and Melodyaires. Gail usually writes the lyrics and Jack writes the music, according to Toney.

"We want to write songs from the heart that reach people," Jack told a writer with *The Singing News* in 1996. "We're not interested in seeing how many songs we can write. We just want to write songs that touch people. We're here to serve the groups and provide them with good songs that will bless people's hearts."

Several personnel have worked with the Statesmen during the past few years. When Johnny Cook departed the group, the tenor role was filled for a time by Gene "Tank" Tackett. Scooter Simmons replaced Biney English as baritone, and when Bob Caldwell resigned as bass singer Roy Pauley stepped in to fill the role

Hovie Lister (seated) and the Statesmen in 1994. From left are Gene Miller, tenor; Jack Toney, lead; Buddy Burton, baritone; and Roy Pauley, bass.

whenever his revival schedule would allow. Buddy Burton returned to the group in favor of Scooter Simmons. Burton was also pastoring at the time in Maiden, North Carolina. He later accepted an opportunity to move to Austin, Texas, to sing with a new quartet, Men of Music.

Bob Caldwell, who now sings with Brian Free & Assurance, looks back on his two years with the Statesmen as a career highlight. "For two years I sang with one of my gospel music heroes, Hovie Lister," he says. "It was a real good experience for me. I've been exposed to a lot more different situations, and different people that I never would have been, I'm sure. There's not a lot of people that can look back on their life and be able to say that they sang with the Statesmen."

At this writing, the members of the Statesmen are: pianist Hovie Lister, Tucker, Georgia; tenor Wallace Nelms, Kingsport, Tennessee; lead Jack Toney, Boaz, Alabama; baritone Rick Fair, Cartersville, Georgia; and bass Doug Young, Huntsville, Alabama. Retired from Eastman Kodak, Nelms is an active member of the Gideons International. Fair previously worked with the Rebels Quartet, the Senators and the Blackwood Quartet. A successful businessman, Young operates a bus leasing service in Nashville, and a crane leasing business in Huntsville. Before taking his spot in the Statesmen lineup Doug was bass guitarist for gospel singer Aaron Wilburn, and played bass guitar and sang bass with the Regents Quartet. This lineup recently released an album—the first new Statesmen recording in more than five years—titled "Still Sensational." The new album was produced by Ben Speer, brother of former Skylite producer Brock Speer, and includes five new songs from the pen of Jack Toney. Longtime Statesmen fans will recall a couple of old favorites—"Higher Than The Moon" and "Closer To Thee"—made popular by previous Statesmen lineups of the past.

"I've worked hard at maintaining the Statesmen sound," says Hovie. "When we walk on the stage, it's still there. I'll never have another group that was as great as Denver, Jake, Doy and Chief; or Rosie, Jake, Doy and Chief. But the guys I have now are great in their own right!"

Bill Gaither continues to be a big promoter of the Statesmen. After his "Homecoming" video series became the rage among the Christian public, Gaither decided to take his Homecoming friends on the road in a series of concerts across the country. Featured regularly in the videos and concerts are former Statesmen Jake Hess, Jim Hill, Ed Hill (with J.D. Sumner & the Stamps) and Mosie Lister, and present Statesmen Hovie Lister and Jack Toney. For one taping Gaither assembled a Statesmen Quartet that included Hovie Lister, Sherrill Nielsen, Jake Hess, Jack Toney and Roy Pauley that produced a sound approximating the old magic of the Denver Crumpler years. It is a shame this lineup did not do at least one concert tour. Other Statesmen lineups have been a part of a few Gaither concerts, including Gaither's "All Day At The Dome" concert on June 27, 1998, at the 70,000-seat Georgia Dome in Atlanta.

Gaither's marketing organization, Spring House, has been responsible for the release of several Statesmen-releated products in recent years. During the 1994 National Quartet Convention in Louisville, Kentucky, Bill and Gloria Gaither released a documentary video in their "Hall of Honor" series—"Bill & Gloria Gaither Present Hovie Lister and the Sensational

Statesmen, An American Classic." Additionally, Gaither produced a series of Statesmen videos, called "What a Happy Time, 20 Illustrious Years." Three volumes, featuring vintage television clips from the Nabisco shows and the "Glory Road" television series, are on the market. Another video in the Gaither Gospel Series is "The Statesmen With Rosie Rozell," with clips from Statesmen television appearances featuring the

Rex Nelon, Bill Gaither and Hovie Lister relaxed at Gaither's booth during the 1994 National Quartet Convention while watching the video, "Bill & Gloria Gaither Present Hovie Lister and the Sensational Statesmen, An American Classic."

great tenor. In 1997, Spring House, by special arrangement with RCA Records, issued a digitally
remastered collection of songs from the RCA masters.
The 22 songs first appeared on several RCA Victor
albums from 1957 through 1963.

Rosie Rozell

A major development in the 50-year story of the
Statesmen was the passing of legendary Statesmen
tenor Rosie Rozell in February 1995. After a stroke
forced his exit from the Masters V in 1982, Rosie was
told by his physicians that his kidneys were function-
ing at 50 percent of their capability. He had undergone
numerous surgeries during the last decade of his life,
including open heart surgeries in 1982 and 1990.
Despite his numerous health complications, Rosie
continued to sing when able. In addition to working
solo dates, Rozell teamed with former Statesmen Jack
Toney and Buddy Burton, and song evangelist Roy
Pauley to work a few dates as The Legends. "We didn't
make many appearances together, but imagine what it was like to share the stage with Rosie
Rozell," Pauley wrote shortly after Rozell's death. "I will forever be grateful for that rewarding
experience."

When a new quartet was organized in 1990, Rosie came on board as the original tenor, joining
James Blackwood, Ray Shelton, Ken Turner and pianist Brad White as the James Blackwood
Quartet. "His health just kept getting worse and worse," recalls Blackwood. "On the last tour
that he did with us in the first part of March in '91 he was having to give himself some kind of
dialysis. And it just became impossible for him to travel with a group and to do what he was
having to do for himself."

By the time of his death, Rozell had lost 90 percent of the function of his kidneys. After bowing
out of the James Blackwood Quartet, Rosie was seldom seen by the gospel quartet public. Rozell
was present for the taping of Bill and Gloria Gaither's video on the Statesmen in the "Hall of
Honor" series, and shortly before his death attended a couple of taping sessions in the Gaither
Homecoming video series. When he did make an appearance, fans were alarmed by his gaunt
physique. The once rotund tenor had been reduced to a shadow of his former self. Where once
stood a showman who communicated from the stage as few others in the gospel quartet industry,
now appeared a tired old quartet warhorse with short, unsteady steps. But the great voice,
although weakened by his many physical battles, still could evoke excitement.

Rosie's last appearance with the Statesmen occurred at the 25th Anniversary Albert E.
Brumley Memorial Sing in August, 1993. He had been invited to participate in the event as a
soloist, but joined the Statesmen during their concert set to sing two songs—"Surely I Will, Lord"
and "O, What A Savior". "Rosie Rozell has been through a lot of operations," Hovie told the
audience as he brought the emaciated crowd favorite out to sing. "He has had bad diabetes, his
health has been bad, but God has allowed him to be here to sing with us one more time."

Rozell sang "Surely I Will, Lord" with Jack Toney, Tank Tackett and Nick Val in vocal support.
On "O, What A Savior," Scooter Simmons stepped in to join Toney and Val in the background
vocals. Midway through the song, Rozell stopped singing to communicate with the crowd: "In
the last few years I've come close to all that, what I'm getting ready to sing to you about," he said.
"It says, 'death's chilling waters I'll soon be crossing,' but those same nail-scarred hands you've
heard about all your life, they're gonna lead me safe home. But then the joyous part is when we
get there, in my human imagination is that I'm gonna sing for the first thousand years. And you
folks that's got tender ears, don't come around me 'cause I'm gonna clean your front door! When
we get down to our ages, you begin to wonder and count the cost. Marvin Dalton gave the
Trumpeteers the original manuscript, and when I went with the Statesmen we started doing

it. Little did I know way back then that this second verse would become so dear and such a reality to folks."

Rosie's signature song became a reality for him a year-and-a-half later. Rosie Rozelle "joined the chorus in that bright city" on February 28, 1995, crossing death's chilling waters at Birmingham's Medical Center East at 2:08 a.m. He was 66.

"Rosie Rozell had a dynamic way of singing that no other tenor ever had," wrote Roy Pauley when Rosie died. "He not only possessed a quality and style that was unique, but Rosie had something that hardly any other tenor had, and that was the ability to sing with his heart... he didn't just sing to you, but he talked to you as he sang."

"He could thrill a crowd better than anybody I ever knew," observes Hovie Lister, "by just singing 'O, What A Savior.' Rosie Rozell was a great tenor!"

Sadly, two richly deserved honors have never been bestowed upon this enormously talented man—induction into the Gospel Music Association's Hall of Fame and the Southern Gospel Music Hall of Fame.

Jake Hess

Since his retirement from the Statesmen in the summer of 1993, Jake and Joyce Hess have settled in Columbus, Georgia. The couple had resided in the Nashville area for 28 years since leaving the Statesmen to form the Imperials in 1963. When Jake and Joyce left their home in Brentwood, Tennessee, he honestly felt he was moving to Georgia to "be close to my family and die." On his last tour with the Statesmen in 1993, Jake had begun involuntarily shaking onstage so badly that he could no longer hold a microphone. He honestly felt his career was over. Tests at Atlanta's Emory University indicated his physical problems were beyond anything medical science could do for him. He was in such poor physical condition that he wasn't considered a fit candidate for a heart transplant. His children and their families had all settled in Columbus, and he had resigned himself to move there and live out the rest of his days enjoying the company of his grandchildren.

However, at Bill Gaither's urging and encouragement, Jake occasionally made some singing appearances "that I thought I could not do anymore." The more Gaither called and asked him to do, the better Jake began to feel. "I don't understand it," he says, nor do his doctors.

Jake now sings frequently at Bill Gaither's concert appearances, and occasionally works solo dates. Jake's many friends recall that he offered an unforgettable delivery of "Death Ain't No Big Deal" on the late Tammy Wynette's "Legends of Country" television show, which aired on The Nashville Network in October, 1994. Jake has kept busy with several solo recording efforts, including the albums "Jus' Jake and a Few Close Friends," "Jake Hess—I've Been There" and "Leanin;'" and his autobiography, **Nothin' But Fine**, written with Richard Hyatt. He also

recorded a duet album with football Hall of Famer Terry Bradshaw. Bill and Gloria Gaither also produced a video in their Hall of Honor Series, called "Jus' Jake," about Jake's career.

Jake continues to enjoy the accolades of his success. At Charles Waller's Grand Ole Gospel Reunion in 1994 he was the recipient of a "This Is Your Life" celebration honoring his career. In 1995 he was inducted into the Alabama Music Hall of Fame, in Tuscombia, Alabama. The museum there displays one of his Grammy awards. In 1997 he was among several luminaries inducted into the Southern Gospel Music Hall of Fame. Other Statesmen alumni inducted were Hovie Lister, Mosie Lister, the late Denver Crumpler and the late James S. "Big Chief" Wetherington. In 1998, the Gospel Music Association inducted several quartets into its Hall of Fame, a recognition that had only been open to individuals previously. Among the inductees were the Statesmen, and the group that Jake Hess organized in 1964, the Imperials.

Hovie Lister

On leaving the Masters V in 1988, Hovie went to work on the personal staff of Georgia Lt. Gov. (now Governor) Zell Miller, a close personal friend for several decades. Later, Hovie became executive assistant to the State Board of Pardons and Paroles. On March 27, 1997, both houses of the Georgia State Legislature adopted resolutions commending Hovie "for his contributions to music and service to the State of Georgia." A few weeks later, U.S. Senator Max Cleland, of Georgia, rose in the United States Senate "to recognize a man whose name has become synonymous with gospel music, Mr. Hovie Lister." Senator Cleland's comments, now public record are as follows:

"Hovie was born into music. At the age of 6, he began studying the piano and later attended the Stamps Baxter School of Music. He often accompanied his family group, the Lister Brothers Quartet, around the piano.

"His professional career began when he joined the famous Rangers Quartet and later the popular LeFevre Trio. In 1945, he came to Georgia and was the pianist for the Homeland Harmony Quartet heard over WAGA and WGST Radio in Atlanta.

"In 1948, he organized the world famous Statesmen Quartet. The Statesmen steadily rose in popularity and became the premier gospel group in the nation. Hovie, as the group's manager and pianist, soon emerged as the chief spokesman and head of the rapidly growing gospel music industry.

"Hovie was also an accomplished director and producer of radio and television shows. He became the first gospel artist to sign a national television contract and successfully directed and produced syndicated television shows for Nabisco, as well as scripted and starred in the company's commercials.

"In the early 1980s, Hovie brought together five performers who came from the top four groups in gospel music to form the Masters V. In 1982, this group won the prestigious Grammy Award and in 1986, Hovie was inducted into the Georgia Music Hall of Fame.

"Mr. President, I ask that you and all our colleagues recognize Hovie Lister, not just for the contributions he has made to the music industry and my own State of Georgia, but for bringing gospel music to the attention of all Americans."

Hovie Lister and today's Statesmen Quartet. From left are: Jack Toney, Doug Young, Hovie Lister, Rick Fair and Wallace Nelms.

Hovie's home is a storehouse of accolades that continue to be heaped on him. Burton College and Seminary has conferred upon him the degree of Doctor of Divinity. During a recent concert in Atlanta, Bill Gaither presented him with several gold video awards for his participation in the wildly successful Homecoming video series.

Like Jake, Hovie has experienced his share of health problems in recent years. Hovie has battled back from a bout with throat cancer. During the summer of 1993 he struggled with a hacking cough that wouldn't go away. Doctors at Emory University Hospital in Atlanta found and removed a lesion from his throat during surgery on September 17, 1993—Hovie's 67th birthday. Following a regimen of radiation therapy, he was on the road to recovery. By the spring of 1994, Hovie was back to work politicking, making appearances on behalf of Governor Miller, singing and playing piano, talking, shouting and preaching. "I can do 'em one at a time or all at once!" he quipped in his typical, flamboyant way. At the end of 1995 he began having back pain, and went to the doctor for a checkup. A CT scan revealed a lymphoma which was pressing against his right kidney. Following extensive tests Hovie was given chemotherapy treatment. He underwent another regimen of chemotherapy treatments in the summer of 1997. As a result of the periodic chemotherapy treatments, he loses his hair regularly, and can often be seen wearing a cap.

Ethel Lister has survived a bout with breast cancer recently. The Listers have a home in St. Simon's Island, Georgia, and a condominium in Tucker, Georgia, a suburb of Atlanta. Their children, Lisa and Hovie, Jr., live in the Atlanta area with their families.

Hovie was surprised with a "This Is Your Life" tribute at Charles Waller's Grand Ole Gospel Reunion in 1997. A special treat for Hovie was the appearance of orchestra leader Wade Craeger, his old friend from the Nabisco Show days, whom he had not seen for 40 years. For a sequel, Waller pulled out all the stops in producing the highlight event of the 1998 Grand Ole Gospel Reunion—a 50th Anniversary Tribute to the Statesmen.

Post Script

The Statesmen most quartet fans remember were the "state of the art" vocal group during an era when gospel quartet music was in its most exciting period of development. There are various divisions by which we characterize Christian music today—southern gospel, black gospel, traditional gospel, Christian country, contemporary Christian, etc. In the 1950s, the Statesmen were the equivalent of today's DC Talk or 4 Him. The Statesmen were the contemporary Christian music giants of another era. They refused to limit themselves to fit a mold. Their repertoire included songs from the singing conventions, the black tradition, blues, Dixieland jazz, country and, yes, even rock and roll—and they did it all extremely well! Very few "southern gospel" groups of today are versatile enough to be considered in the same league as the group many believe to be the "perfect quartet"—Denver Crumpler, Jake Hess, Doy Ott, James Wetherington and Hovie Lister. Their work ethic, professionalism and dedication to their art should serve as an inspiration to all who pursue music as a ministry or vocation.

For every Hovie Lister, Jake Hess, Jack Toney, Rosie Rozell, Cat Freeman, Denver Crumpler, Doy Ott or James Wetherington, there are hundreds of talented wannabes who dream of being in the greatest singing group in the world. But God hand-picked only one very select group of men to become "Statesmen." He blessed them with the perfect singing job and in the process crowned them kings of the gospel music world.

The rest of us are merely pretenders to their throne.

DISCOGRAPHY
The Statesmen Quartet with Hovie Lister
The following pages contain an exhaustive listing of Statesmen recordings. Extensive re-
search resulted in a reasonably accurate, albeit incomplete, summary.

Capitol Records
Singles ...
Record number/Selection/Composer/Selection/Composer/Release Date
40242 "Hide Me, Rock of Ages" (George C. Brentley) b/w "Heaven's Joy Awaits" (Vep Ellis) October, 1949
40256 "Satan's Boogie" b/w "A Newborn Feeling" November, 1949
40263 "The Santa Claus Song" b/w "White Christmas" (Irving Berlin) November, 1949
40289 "Land Where Living Waters Flow" (Mosie Lister) b/w "If You've Never Learned to Pray" January, 1950
40296 "Happy Am I" (J.E. Marsh) b/w "Stand By Me" (C.A. Tindley) June, 1950
1189 "Wait 'Til You See Me In My New Home" (Joe Parks) b/w "Led Out of Bondage" (Bob Prather) August, 1950
1211 "Something to Shout About" b/w "Happy Rhythm" (Mosie Lister) November, 1950
1416 "You're Gonna Reap What You Sow" (Mosie Lister) b/w "When I Got Saved" February, 1951
1467 "Hide Me, Rock of Ages" (George C. Brentley) b/w "Heaven's Joy Awaits" (Vep Ellis) April 2, 1951
1489 "Peace in the Valley" (Thomas Dorsey) b/w "Sho' Do Need Him Now" (Thomas Dorsey) April 16, 1951
1582 "I Wanna Be Ready" (G.T. Speer) b/w "Listen to the Bells" (Lee Roy Abernathy) June 16, 1951
1917 "I'm Gonna Take a Ride" (G.T. Speer) b/w "Standing Outside" (J.A. McClung) December 24, 1951
2016 "On Revival Day" (public domain) b/w "Bound for the Kingdom" (Mosie Lister) March 17, 1952
"Happy Am I" (J.E. Marsh) b/w "Stand By Me" (C.A. Tindley) November 26, 1951
2115 "Rock-A My Soul" (public domain) b/w "Sunday Meetin' Time" (Mosie Lister) June 2, 1952
2303 "The Love of God" (Vep Ellis) b/w "Trouble" (Mosie Lister) December 8, 1952
2469 "How Many Times" (Thomas Dorsey) b/w "Someone to Care" (Jimmie Davis) May 11, 1953
2566 "One of These Mornings" (Herbert Brewster) b/w "When You Travel All Alone" (Mosie Lister) August 17, 1953

Albums ...
T-1508 "Something to Shout About" (Compiled from previously released singles recorded 1949-53) Producer: Ken Nelson.
"Something to Shout About;" "Bound for the Kingdom" (Mosie Lister); "On Revival Day" (public domain); "Standing Outside" (J.A. McClung); "Gonna Reap Just What You Sow" (Mosie Lister); "When You Travel All Alone" (Mosie Lister); "Happy Rhythm" (Mosie Lister); "Heaven's Joy Awaits" (Vep Ellis); "Land Where Living Waters Flow" (Mosie Lister); "Rock-A My Soul" (public domain); "Peace in the Valley" (Thomas Dorsey); "I'm Gonna Take a Ride" (G.T. Speer); "Sunday Meetin' Time" (Mosie Lister); "Listen to the Bells" (Lee Roy Abernathy); "Everybody's Gonna Have a Terrible Time Down There" (Lee Roy Abernathy), 1960
DT-2539 "Happy Land" (Compiled from previously released singles recorded 1949-53) Producer: Ken Nelson. "Led Out of Bondage" (Bob Prather); "Sho' Do Need Him Now" (Thomas Dorsey); "The Love of God" (Vep Ellis); "How Many Times" (Thomas Dorsey); "Happy Land [Happy Am I]" (J.E. Marsh); "Stand By Me" (C.A. Tindley); "If You Never Learn to Pray;" "I Want to Be Ready" (G.T. Speer); "When I Got Saved;" "Wait Till You See Me In My New Home" (Joe Parks); "Someone to Care" (Jimmie Davis); "A Newborn Feeling;" "Trouble" (Mosie Lister); "Hide Me, Rock of Ages" (George C. Brentley); "One of These Mornings" (Herbert Brewster), 1968
4XL9776 "Sunday Meetin' Time" (Compiled from previously released singles recorded 1949-53)

Statesmen *(custom label)*
Singles ...
101 "Sunday Meetin' Time" (Mosie Lister) b/w "Bound for the Kingdom" (Mosie Lister)
103 "The Love of God" (Vep Ellis) b/w "I'll Leave it All Behind"
105 "Lord, I Want to Go to Heaven" (Mosie Lister/James Wetherington) b/w "Everytime I Pray"
107 "Jubilee's A-Comin' " (public domain) b/w "Listen to the Word of the Lord"
109 "Cowboy Camp Meeting" (Tim Spencer) b/w "Riding the Range for Jesus" (Vep Ellis)
1011 "Mother's Prayers Have Followed Me" (Mosie Lister) b/w "Shouting Hallelujah"
1013 "In the Sweet Forever" (Luther Presley) b/w "An Old Log Cabin for Sale"
1015 "Talk About Jesus" (Littlefield/Robey) b/w "If God Didn't Care" (Lee Roy Abernathy)
1017 "Oh, My Lord, What a Time" (public domain) b/w "When You Travel All Alone" (Mosie Lister)
1019 "White Christmas" (Irving Berlin) b/w "Silent Night" (Joseph Mohr/Franz Gruber)
1021 "My God Is Real" (Kenneth Morris) b/w "I'll Meet You by the River" (Albert Brumley)
1023 "One of These Mornings" (Herbert Brewster) b/w "Just a Closer Walk With Thee" (public domain)
1025 "How Many Times" (Thomas Dorsey) b/w "Someone To Care" (Jimmie Davis)
1027 "Get Away Jordan" (public domain) b/w "I Bowed On My Knees and Cried Holy"
1029 "Nothing Can Compare" (Mosie Lister) b/w "Sin Ain't Nothing But the Blues"
1031 "Crying in the Chapel" (Artie Glenn) b/w "Somebody Bigger Than You and I" (Lange/Heath/Burke)
1033 "I Believe" (Drake/Graham/Shirl/Stillman) b/w "Belshazzar" (Mosie Lister)
1035 "His Hand In Mine" (Mosie Lister) b/w "When the Sun Goes Down"
1037 "Walking in the Garden" b/w "I Know it Was the Lord" (Herbert Brewster)
1039 "I Have a Desire" b/w "The Old Landmark" (Herbert Brewster)
1041 "I Believe in the Man in the Sky" (Richard Howard, Jr.) b/w "Jesus Knows What I Need" (Mosie Lister)
1043 "In My Father's House" (Aileene Hanks) b/w "I Just Can't Make it By Myself" (Herbert Brewster)
1045 "I Got News" (Lee Roy Abernathy) b/w "When I Move" (Buford Abner)
1047 "The King and I" (Mosie Lister) b/w "One Night"
1049 "The Fourth Man" (Arthur Smith) b/w "Known Only To Him" (Stuart Hamblen)

1049 "There Are Two New Voices in the Heavenly Choir" (Mosie Lister) b/w "Known Only To Him" (Stuart Hamblen)
1051 "Can't Help Talking About My Lord" b/w "I'm Climbing Up the Mountain"
1053 "Heavenly Love" (Mosie Lister) b/w "Jesus Fills My Every Need" (Vep Ellis)
1055 "Rusty Old Halo" b/w "The Carpenter's Son"
1057 "Rock Love" b/w "Church Twice on Sunday" (Traditional)
1059 "I Saw A Man" (Arthur Smith) b/w "Happy Rhythm" (Mosie Lister)
1061 "Some Glad Day" b/w "Where No One Stands Alone" (Mosie Lister)
1063 "Goodbye, World, Goodbye" (Mosie Lister) b/w "I Know Who Holds Tomorrow" (Ira Stanphill)
1065 "I've Found a New Friend" (Mosie Lister) b/w "I've Got That Old Fashioned Love"
1067 "Down Old Log Cabin Lane" b/w "All Alone" (Mosie Lister)
1069 "On Revival Day" (public domain) b/w "I've Found it in Mother's Bible" (Stamps-Baxter)
1071 "I Won't Turn Back" b/w "Way Over the Blue"
1073 "I'm Gonna Walk Dem Golden Stairs" b/w "Twilight Shadows Are Falling"
1075 "I Wanta Know" (public domain) b/w "My Heavenly Father Watches Over Me"
1077 "I'm Living With Jesus" (Barnett/Henson) b/w "These Are the Things That Matter" (Arthur Smith)

Albums ...

Statesmen-1198 "Hymns By The Statesmen" (Same album as "Hymns By The Statesmen," Skylite label SRLP-1198) Recorded in Atlanta's Biltmore Hotel Ballroom for Nabisco television show. Personnel: Hovie Lister/Denver Crumpler/ Jake Hess/Doy Ott/James Wetherington. "Softly and Tenderly" (Thompson); "Leaning on the Everlasting Arms" (Showalter); "I Am Thine, O Lord" (Doane); "There Is a Fountain" (Cowper-Mason); "Sweet Hour of Prayer" (Bradbury); "I Surrender All" (Weeden); "Near to the Heart of God" (McAfee); "The Old Rugged Cross" (Bennard); "Have Thine Own Way, Lord" (Pollard-Stebbins); "Just As I Am" (Bradbury); "My Jesus, I Love Thee" (Gordon); "Let the Lower Lights Be Burning" (P.P. Bliss), 1957
Statesmen K80P-5966-612S-5965 (Same album as Skylite SRLP/SSLP-5965 "Get Away Jordan") Personnel: Hovie Lister, Rosie Rozell, Jake Hess, Doy Ott, James Wetherington. "How Many Times" (Thomas Dorsey); "Get Away Jordan" (public domain); "Hide Thou Me" (L.R. Tolbert/Thoro Harris); "When You Travel All Alone" (Mosie Lister); "Happy Rhythm" (Mosie Lister); "Jesus Fills My Every Need" (Vep Ellis); "Where No One Stands Alone" (Mosie Lister); "In the Sweet Forever" (Luther G. Presley); "I Bowed On My Knees and Cried Holy;" "What A Day That Will Be" (Jim Hill); "On Revival Day" (public domain); "Sho' Do Need Him Now" (Thomas Dorsey), 1958

RCA-Victor

Singles ...

5850 "This Ole House" (Stuart Hamblen) b/w "I've Been With Jesus" (Arthur Smith) 1954
5911 "Move That Mountain" (Joe Thomas) b/w "If God Didn't Care" (Lee Roy Abernathy) 1954
6020 "Taller Than Trees" (Lee Ferebee) b/w "In The Beginning" (Cochran/Twomey/Wise/Weisman) 1955
6066 "I'm Climbing Higher and Higher" (Herbert Brewster) b/w "My Brother's Keeper" (Twomey/Wise/Weisman) 1955
6100 "A Man Called Peter" (Tobias/Stein/Sloan) b/w "The Bible Told Me So" (Pat Ballard) 1955
6191 "Headin' Home" (Bob Prather) b/w "Poor Old Adam" (public domain) 1955
6583 "No One But Jesus Knows" (Henry Slaughter) b/w "Your First Day In Heaven" (Stuart Hamblen) 1956
6658 "How Long Has It Been" (Mosie Lister) b/w "I'm Gonna Walk With My Friend Jesus" (Ernie Newton) 1956
6723 "Faith Unlocks the Door" (Samuel Scott/Robert L. Sande) b/w "My Heart Is a Chapel" (Mack David/Roy Carroll) 1956
6760 "A Brand New Star" (Greiner/Greiner/Greiner) b/w "Practice What You Preach" (Albert Brumley) 1956
6876 "I've Found A New Friend" (Mosie Lister) b/w "Love Never Fails" (Charles Matthews) 1956
6962 "God Is My Partner" (Forrell/Stein/Thall) b/w "Stop, Look and Listen for the Lord" (Doy W. Ott) 1957
7053 "Till The Last Leaf Shall Fall" (Sonny James/Jack Rhodes) b/w "Every Hour and Every Day" (Marshall Pack) 1957
7103 "God Is God" (Donald M. Love) b/w "Mansions Can't Be Bought" (Lee Roy Abernathy) 1957
7131 "Up Above My Head" (Rosetta Tharpe) b/w "Oh What a Friend He is to Me" (Mosie Lister) 1957
7152 "Who Do You Think" (J.D. Sumner) b/w "Look Up" (Al Langdon) 1958
7198 "A Terrible Time Down There" (Lee Roy Abernathy) b/w "My God Won't Ever Let Me Down" (J.D. Sumner) 1958
7253 "He's Got the Whole World In His Hands" (Linden/Henry) b/w "At the Roll Call" (James Wetherington) 1958
7347 "Until Tomorrow" (Wallace Varner) b/w "What A Happy Day" (Joe Roper) 1958
7476 "Light of Love" (Charles Singleton) b/w "Until You Find the Lord" (Jay Green) 1959
7531 "Something Lifted Off of Me" (Vep Ellis) b/w "There's Room at the Cross" (Ira Stanphill) 1959
7579 "Get Thee Behind Me, Satan" (Bob Prather) b/w "God Bless You, Go With God" (Warren Roberts) 1959
7631 "He Set Me Free" (Jerry Berry) b/w "He's Already Done" (Roberta Martin) 1959
7691 "Message In the Sky" (John D. Smith/Bonnie Smith) b/w "I Follow Jesus" (James Wetherington) 1959
7751 "To Me It's So Wonderful" (Ralph Goodpasteur) b/w "I Found the Answer" (Johnny Lange) 1960

Extended Play Singles ...

45EP EPA-1 1411 "I Wonder What My New Address Will Be" "He's Everywhere" "One of These Mornings" "Everybody Will Be Happy Over There" (EPA-1,2 & 3 1411 all released in 1957)
45EP EPA-2 1411 "Glory, Glory Clear the Road" "Led Out of Bondage" "My Journey's End" "Guide My Feet"
45EP EPA-3 1411 "I Know It Was the Lord" "Lord, I Want to Go to Heaven" "Hide Me, Rock of Ages" "My God is Real"
45EP EPA-4358 "The Statesmen With Hovie Lister Recorded in Performance at the Ryman" "Thanks to Calvary" "It's Worth More" "Hymn Medley" 1960
45EP EPA-5090 "Faith The Statesmen Quartet" "Up Above My Head" "How Long Has It Been" "Faith Unlocks the Door" "Who Do you Think" 1959

Albums ...

LPM/LSP-1411 "The Statesmen Quartet With Hovie Lister" Producer: Steve Sholes. Personnel: Hovie Lister/ Denver Crumpler/Jake Hess/Doy Ott/James Wetherington. "Glory, Glory, Clear the Road" (Willis/Hancock/Matthews); "Journey's End" (Ted Brooks); "Lord, I Want To Go To Heaven" (James Wetherington); "My God Is Real" (Kenneth Morris); "Led Out Of Bondage" (Bob Prather); "Guide My Feet" (J.D. Sumner); "I Wonder What My New Address Will Be" (Mosie Lister); "One Of These Mornings (Herbert Brewster); "He's Everywhere" (Arthur Smith); "Everybody Will Be Happy Over There" (public domain); "Hide Me, Rock Of Ages" (Brentley George); "I Know It Was The Lord" (Herbert Brewster), 1957

RCA-Victor Albums *(continued)* ...

LPM/LSP-1605 "The Statesmen Quartet Sings With Hovie Lister" Producer: Steve Sholes. Personnel: Hovie Lister/ Cat Freeman/Jake Hess/Doy Ott/James Wetherington. "Nicodemus" (Berni Barbour); "God Is My Shepherd" (Country Earl); "It's A Wonderful Feeling" (Charles Matthews); "Wonderful Is The Lord" (Jay Greene); "The Sea Walker" (Tim Spencer); "I Know He Heard My Prayer" (Vep Ellis); "Ransomed Millions" (Wendy Bagwell); "My Lord's Been A-Walkin' " (Luther Presley); "When My Master Walks With Me" (Doy Ott); "If To Gain The World" (Mosie Lister); "Stand By Me" (Thomas Dorsey); "The Gentle Stranger" (Mosie Lister), 1958

LPM/LSP-1683 "The Bible Told Me So" Producer: Steve Sholes. Personnel: Hovie Lister/Denver Crumpler/Jake Hess/ Doy Ott/James Wetherington. "My Heart Is A Chapel" (Mack David/Roy Carroll); "No One But Jesus Knows" (Henry Slaughter); "The Bible Told Me So" (Pat Ballard); "Taller Than Trees" (Lee Ferebee); "Move That Mountain" (Joe Thomas); "If God Didn't Care" (Lee Roy Abernathy); "Brand New Star" (Greiner/Greiner/Greiner); "Known Only To Him" (Stuart Hamblen); "In The Beginning" (Cochran/Twomey/Wise/Weisman), "Your First Day In Heaven" (Stuart Hamblen), "My Brother's Keeper" (Twomey/Wise/Weisman); "I'm Climbing Higher and Higher" (Herbert Brewster) 1958

LPM/LSP-2065 "I'll Meet You By The River" Producer: Chet Atkins. Recorded in Nashville. Personnel: Hovie Lister/ Rosie Rozell/Jake Hess/Doy Ott/James Wetherington. All songs composed by Albert E. Brumley. "Jesus Hold My Hand," "Did You Ever Go Sailin'," "Surely I Will, Lord," "If We Never Meet Again," "Turn Your Radio On," "I'll Meet You By the River," "I'll Meet You in the Morning," "There's a Little Pine Log Cabin," "He Set Me Free," "Her Mansion Is Higher Than Mine," "I'll Fly Away," "I've Found a Hiding Place" 1959

LPM/LSP-2127 "Mansion Over the Hilltop" The Statesmen with Hovie Lister accompanied by the Anita Kerr Singers (Courtesy of Decca Records) Producer: Chet Atkins. Recorded in Nashville. Personnel: Hovie Lister/Rosie Rozell/Jake Hess/Doy Ott/James Wetherington. "I've Got That Feeling" (Wally Varner); "No Greater Love" (C. Westover); "He Will Show You the Way" (Jake Hess); "Provided by His Love" (D. Douglas); "Tenderly" (James S. Wetherington); "God's Got His Eyes on You" (Cleavant Derricks); "I Can Call Jesus Anytime" (Brock Speer); "The Love of God" (Frederick Lehman); "Go Down to the Jordan" (Bennie Triplett); "He Knows Just What I Need" (Mosie Lister); "Heaven's Joy Awaits" (Vep Ellis); "Mansion Over the Hilltop" (Ira Stanphill) 1960

LPM/LSP-2188 "The Statesmen On Stage" Producer: Chet Atkins. Recorded in concert at the Ryman Auditorium, Nashville, TN, November 6, 1959. Personnel: Hovie Lister/Rosie Rozell/Jake Hess/Doy Ott/James Wetherington. "I Wanna Know" (public domain); "Thanks To Calvary" (Vep Ellis); "Something Within" (John T. Benson); "Room at the Cross" (Ira Stanphill); "The Amen Corner" (Vep Ellis); "He's Already Done" (Roberta Martin); "Wade On Out" (Mosie Lister); "Gonna Open Up All My Doors" (Charles Singleton); "It's Worth More" (Henry Slaughter); "He Set Me Free" (Jerry Berry); Hymn Medley: "Oh, How Much He Cares for Me," "He's My Friend," "Jesus is the Sweetest Name I Know," "Somewhere in the Shadows," "Jesus is the One;" "Get Away Jordan" (public domain) 1960

LPM/LSP-2281 "The Statesmen Out West" Producer: Darol Rice. Recorded at RCA-Victor's Music Center of the World, Hollywood, CA. Personnel: Hovie Lister/Rosie Rozell/Jake Hess/Doy Ott/James Wetherington. "Look Around You" (Morris); "Cowboy Camp Meeting" (Tim Spencer); "I'm Riding Home" (Rosie Rozell/J.D. Sumner); "Cowboy's Paradise" (Doy Ott); "At Sundown" (James Wetherington); "Riding the Range for Jesus" (Vep Ellis); "At the End of the Trail" (Vep Ellis); "A New Range in the Sky" (James Wetherington); "Up the Winding Trail" (Doy Ott); "My Dad" (Doy Ott); "Roundup in the Sky" (James Wetherington); "My God is Riding Beside Me" (Jake Hess) 1961

LPM/LSP-2351 "Through the States with the Statesmen" Producer: Darol Rice. Recorded in concert at Medinah Temple, Chicago, IL, Nov. 15, 1960. Personnel: Hovie Lister/Rosie Rozell/Jake Hess/Doy Ott/James Wetherington. "Just a Little While" (E.M. Bartlett); "It's So Wonderful To Know He Is Mine" (Ralph Goodpasteur); "Love Is Why" (Lakey/Ellis/ Ellis); "Sorry, I Never Knew You" (Branch/Little); "I Believe in the Old Time Way" (J.D. Sumner); "Little Joe's Prayer" (Doy Ott); "Happy Am I" (J.E. Marsh); "Our Debts Will Be Paid" (James S. Wetherington); "Have You Tried the Lord Today?" (Doy Ott); "I Believe in the Man in the Sky" (Richard Howard, Jr.); "He's Not Disappointed in Me" (Rosie Rozell); "When the Morning Comes" (traditional) 1961

LPM/LSP-2440 "The Statesmen Quartet with Hovie Lister sing Camp-Meeting Hymns" Producer: Darol Rice. Recorded in Nashville. Personnel: Hovie Lister/Rosie Rozell/Jake Hess/Doy Ott/James Wetherington. "I Shall Not Be Moved" (traditional); "Closer to Thee" (Steele/Chapman/Little); "Standing on the Promises" (R.Kelso Carter); "Old Camp-Meeting Days" (Adger M. Pace); "Let the Lower Lights Be Burning" (Phillip Bliss); "I Cannot Fail the Lord" (Doris Akers); "If I Could Hear My Mother Pray Again" (James Vaughan); "You Can't Stop God From Blessing Me" (Hovie Lister); "Teach Me, Lord, to Wait" (Stuart Hamblen); "Power in the Blood" (L.E. Jones); "I Like the Old Time Way" (Joe Roper); "Rock of Ages" (Toplady/Hastings) 1962

LPM/LSP-2546 "The Mystery of His Way" Producer: Darol Rice. Recorded in RCA Victor's "Nashville Sound" Studio, Nashville, TN. Personnel: Hovie Lister/Rosie Rozell/Jake Hess/Doy Ott/James Wetherington. "I've Got the Corners Turned Down In That Hymn Book of Mine" (Marion Snider); "What Love" (Eldridge Fox); "Little Bitty Chapel" (Al Langdon); "God Can" (Lee Roy Abernathy); "I've Found a New Way" (Doy Ott); "That's Why I Gotta Sing" (James S. Wetherington); "The Mystery of His Way" (Bob Nolan); "He Will Pilot Me" (Whitworth/Bailey); "O, What A Savior" (Marvin Dalton); "Sweeter As the Days Go By" (Smith); "Love So Divine" (Joe Roper); "Who Could Ask for More" (Lee Roy Abernathy) 1963

LPM/LSP-2606 "James Blackwood and the Blackwood Brothers combine with Hovie Lister and the Statesmen to wish you a Musical Merry Christmas" Producer: Darol Rice. Recorded in RCA Victor's "Nashville Sound" Studio, Nashville, TN. Personnel: Hovie Lister/Rosie Rozell/Jake Hess/Doy Ott/James Wetherington & Wally Varner/Bill Shaw/James Blackwood/Cecil Blackwood/J.D. Sumner. "O Come, All Ye Faithful" (John Francis Wade); "Silver Bells" (Jay Livingston/Ray Evans); "Go Tell It on the Mountain" (John W. Work II); "Praises to Our King" (J.D. Sumner); "White Christmas" (Irving Berlin); "Christmas Means Christ to Me" (J.D. Sumner); "Joy to the World!" (Isaac Watts/George Frederick Handel); "Christmas Time is Here" (James S. Wetherington); "O Little Town of Bethlehem" (Phillips Brooks/ Lewis H. Redner); "Away in a Manger" (Martin Luther); "O Holy Night!" (Adolphe Adam); "Silent Night, Holy Night!" (Joseph Mohr/Franz Gruber) 1962

LPM/LSP-2647 "A Gospel Concert by the Statesmen Quartet with Hovie Lister" Producer: Darol Rice. Recorded in concert at Municipal Auditorium in Long Beach, CA. Personnel: Hovie Lister/Rosie Rozell/Jake Hess/Doy Ott/James Wetherington. "He Will Never Let Me Down" (James S. Wetherington); "I'll Be Ready to Go" (David Reese); "A Million Years from Now" (J.D. Sumner); "The Best for You" (C. Ramsey); "I'm Going There" (James S.Wetherington); "Something Lifted Off of Me" (Vep Ellis); "Wasted Years" (Wally Fowler); "Look Up" (Al Langdon); "There's a Sweetness Through It All" (J.M. Henson); "Lord, I'm Coming Home to Thee" (Doy Ott); "At Last" (Joe Southerland); "Is Your Name Written There?" (James S.Wetherington) 1963

RCA-Victor Albums *(continued)* ...

LPM/LSP-2790 "Hovie Lister Sings With His Famous Statesmen Quartet" Producer: Darol Rice. Recorded in RCA Victor's Music Center of the World, Hollywood, CA. Personnel: Hovie Lister/Rosie Rozell/Jake Hess/Doy Ott/James Wetherington. "My Home" (Lee Roy Abernathy); "Goodbye, Troublesome Blues" (Doy Ott); "Without Him" (Mylon LeFevre); "Worry, Who I" (Joe Moscheo); "Lord, I'm Ready Now to Go" (Lee Roy Abernathy); "As Time Goes By" (Hovie Lister); "When He Calls I'll Fly Away" (Vep Ellis); "Show Me Thy Ways, Oh Lord" (Hazel Shade); "Jesus Knows" (W.F. Lakey/Vep Ellis); "On That Judgment Day" (Lee Roy Abernathy); "He's a Personal Saviour" (Lee Roy Abernathy); "Hands" (Hovie Lister) 1964

LPM/LSP-2864 "The Statesmen Quartet Spotlights Doy Ott" Producer: Darol Rice. Recorded in RCA Victor's "Nashville Sound" Studio, Nashville, TN. Personnel: Hovie Lister/Rosie Rozell/Jack Toney/Doy Ott/James Wetherington. "Those Tender Hands" (Eldridge Fox); "Tell 'em What It's All About" (James S.Wetherington); "Wait For Me" (Doy Ott); "Ship Ahoy" (Cartwright/Towner); "Sweet Jesus" (Doris Akers); "I'll Pray for You" (Aileene Hanks); "Pass Me Not" (Crosby/Doane/Huddleston), "I'm the Least in the Kingdom of the Lord" (James S. Wetherington); "I Know Who Holds Tomorrow" (Ira Stanphill); "In the Name of the Lord" (James S. Wetherington); "The Greatest of These Things" (Lee Roy Abernathy); "He'll Go With Me" (Ellis/Belknap) 1964

LPM/LSP-2933 "The Best of The Statesmen Quartet with Hovie Lister" Producer: Darol Rice. Personnel: Hovie Lister/Rosie Rozell/Jake Hess/Doy Ott/James Wetherington. (All songs previously released) "The Mystery of His Way" "I'm Saved" "Surely I Will, Lord" "Sweeter As the Days Go By" "Look Around You" Statesmen Hymn Medley "I Shall Not Be Moved" "Without Him" "Sorry, I Never Knew You" "Wait For Me" "A Million Years from Now" "Mansion Over the Hilltop" January, 1965

LPM/LSP-2989 "The Sensational Statesmen Quartet with Hovie Lister" Producer: Darol Rice. Recorded in RCA Victor's "Nashville Sound" Studio, Nashville, TN. Personnel: Hovie Lister/Rosie Rozell/Jack Toney/Doy Ott/James Wetherington. (All songs written by James S. Wetherington) "Don't You Wanna Be Saved" "God's Got His Hand on You" "It's Better to be Late at the Pearly Gate (Than to Arrive in Hell on Time)" "Till I Know" "Wake Me, Shake Me, Lord" "Little Boy Lost" "I'll Keep Walking All the Way" "How Many Times" "If You Drink This Water You Will Never Thirst Again" "Give Me a Man That Can Cry" "Samson" "Greater Love Hath No Man" January 1965

LPM/LSP-3392 "The Statesmen Quartet with Hovie Lister Sings the Golden Gospel Songs" Producer: Darol Rice. Recorded in RCA Victor's "Nashville Sound" Studio, Nashville, TN. Personnel: Hovie Lister/Rosie Rozell/Jack Toney/Doy Ott/James Wetherington. "The Heavenly Parade" (Adger Pace/J.T. Cook); "Touch Me, Lord Jesus" (Lucie Campbell); "Walk His Way" (Charles R. Matthews); "Since Jesus Spoke Peace To My Soul" (Beatrice Beale); "Hallelujah, I'm Going Home" (O.A. Parris); "This Was Almost Mine" (James S. Wetherington); "O, How I Need Thee" (William J. Gaither); "Meet Me Up In Heaven Someday" (Lee Roy Abernathy); "If Everybody Prays" (Charles R. Matthews); "I'm Building A Bridge" (Lee Roy Abernathy); "Checking Up On My Payments" (Lee Roy Abernathy); "Praying Hands" (Alma Gray/Aileene Hanks) July, 1965

LPM/LSP-3494 "The Happy Sound of The Statesmen Quartet with Hovie Lister" Producer: Darol Rice. Personnel: Hovie Lister/Rosie Rozell/Jack Toney/Doy Ott/James Wetherington. "Lived and He Loved Me" (traditional); "Ain't Nothing You and Me Can't Handle" (James S. Wetherington); "Leave It There" (C. Albert Tindley); "I'm A Millionaire" "Will The Circle Be Unbroken" (Habersbon/Gabriel); "You'll Find Him There" "You Gotta Live Like Jesus Every Day" "Back To The Dust" (traditional); "Peace, Sweet Peace" "My Home, Sweet Home" "His Grace Is Sufficient For Me" (Mosie Lister); "No, Not One" (Johnson Oatman, Jr.) January, 1966

LPM/LSP-3624 "The Statesmen Quartet with Hovie Lister Sings the Gospel Gems" Producer: Darol Rice. Recorded in RCA Victor's "Nashville Sound" Studio, Nashville, TN. Personnel: Hovie Lister/Rosie Rozell/Roy McNeil/Doy Ott/James Wetherington. "You've Got to Walk That Lonesome Road" (Albert Brumley); "I Thank My God" (Joe Roper); "River of Grace" (Roger Kling); "He's With Me" (Ben Swett); "The Lord Accepted Me" (James S. Wetherington); "Who Am I" (Rusty Goodman); "Count Your Blessings" (Oatman/Excell); "You Must Make Up Your Mind" (Joe Moscheo); "O, Yes Indeed" (Dutto/Montroy); "Always Remember" (Al Langdon); "Have I Done My Best" (Harry E. Storrs); "God Knows How" (Hovie Lister) July, 1966

LPM/LSP-3703 "The Statesmen Quartet with Hovie Lister In Gospel Country" Producer: Darol Rice. Recorded in RCA Victor's "Nashville Sound" Studio, Nashville, TN. Personnel: Hovie Lister/Rosie Rozell/Roy McNeal/Doy Ott/James Wetherington. "Watching You" (J.M. Henson); "When You've Really Met The Lord" (James S. Wetherington); "Give Me Light" (Butler/Taylor); "I Told My Lord" (Marion Snider); "Where the Milk and Honey Flows" (Murray L. Smith); "In Jesus Name, I Will" (James S. Wetherington); "Grace For Every Need" (Henson/Whitworth); "That Silver Haired Daddy of Mine" (Autry/Long); "Heaven Is Where You Belong" (Lee Roy Abernathy); "No More" (Duane Allen); "Brighten the Corner Where You Are" (Gabriel/Ogdon); "Just Over In Gloryland" (Acuff/Dean) February, 1967

LPM/LSP-3815 "Showers of Blessing" Producer: Darol Rice. Personnel: Hovie Lister/Rosie Rozell/Jack Toney/Doy Ott/James Wetherington. "You'd Better Run (Butler/Taylor); "There Shall Be Showers of Blessing" (Nathan/McGranahan); "My Lord Will Care for Me" (Henson/Whitworth); "My Father's Will" (Garnet Lindsey); "I've Gotta Have Jesus" (Butler/Taylor); "The Hand of God" (Butler/Taylor); "The Old Account Settled Long Ago" (F.M. Graham); "Many Joys and Thrills Ago" (Henry Slaughter); "This Great Love of Jesus" (Butler/Taylor); "Come On, Be Happy!" (Breed/Boyd); "Choose You This Day" (Bob Prather); "Unworthy" (Ira F. Stanphill) August, 1967

LPM/LSP-3888 "Sing Brother Sing" Producer: Darol Rice. Recorded in RCA-Victor's "Nashville Sound" Studio, Nashville, TN. Personnel: Hovie Lister/Rosie Rozell/Jack Toney/Doy Ott/ James Wetherington. "Sing Brother Sing" (Mosie Lister); "Jesus Said It, I Believe It, It's Really So" (Henry Slaughter); "The Great Physician" (Stockton/Hunter); "We've Come This Far By Faith" (H. Goodson); "When I Got Saved" (Vep Ellis); "I've Got a Right To Praise the Lord" (Lakey/Ellis); "Have You Been to Calvary" (Doy Ott/Patricia Turner); "My God Can Do Anything" (Vep Ellis); "O My Brother, Where You Headin' " (Vep Ellis); "Happy Tracks" (Ray Pennington); "Where Could I Go" (J.B. Coats); "Step By Step" (Nixon/Whitworth) January, 1968

LPM/LSP-3925 "The Best of The Statesmen Quartet Volume 2" (Compiled from previously-released albums) "Brighten the Corner Where You Are" "Nicodemus" "Just A Little While" "If I Could Hear My Mother Pray Again" "O How I Need Thee" "Will the Circle Be Unbroken?" "My Home" "There Shall Be Showers of Blessing" "He Will Never Let Me Down" "Count Your Blessings" "Don't You Wanna Be Saved" "Those Tender Hands" April, 1968

RCA Camden

Albums ...

CAL-574 "Peace, O Lord" Personnel: various. "Great Day" (Rose/Eliscu/Youmans); "Jonah, Go Down to Ninevah" (Mosie Lister); "Bring Peace, O Lord" (Brown Bolte); "Peace in the Valley" (Thomas Dorsey); "Something Within" (John T. Benson); "A Little Bit of Heaven" (James D. Walbert); "I'm Looking for Jesus" (Wansley Lee); "I Don't Want This Modern Religion" (Henry Tarver); "God Is My Friend" (Lee Evans); "Wait 'Til You See Me In My New Home" (Joe Parks); "God Will Bless You All" (Ned Parker); "It's Different Now" (David Beatty) 1960

CAL-663 "Stop, Look and Listen for the Lord" Personnel: various. "Stop, Look and Listen for the Lord" (Doy Ott); "This Ole House" (Stuart Hamblen); "What A Happy Day" (Joe Roper); "At the Roll Call" (James S. Wetherington); "Get Thee Behind Me, Satan" (Bob Prather); "Until Tomorrow" (Wally Varner); "He's Got the Whole World In His Hands" (Linden/Henry); "My God Won't Ever Let Me Down" (J.D. Sumner); "Until You Find the Lord" (Jay Green); "God Is God" (Donald Love); "Love Never Fails" (Charles Matthews) "God Bless You, Go With God" (Warren Roberts) 1961

CAL-743 ... "Message In The Sky" Personnel: various. "Message in the Sky" (Smith/Smith); "Every Hour and Every Day" (Marshall Pack); "A Man Called Peter" (Tobias/Stein/Sloan); "Oh What a Friend He is to Me" (Mosie Lister); "Practice What You Preach" (Albert Brumley); "Everybody's Gonna Have a Terrible Time Down There" (Lee Roy Abernathy); "I've Found a New Friend" (Mosie Lister); "I Found the Answer" (Johnny Lange); "Mansions Can't Be Bought In Heaven" (Lee Roy Abernathy); "I Follow Jesus" (James S. Wetherington); "God Is My Partner" (Forrell/Stein/Thall); "Headin' Home" (Bob Prather) 1963

CAL/CAS-843 "Songs of Faith" Producer: Ethel Gabriel. Personnel: various. Recorded in part at Sing Studios, Atlanta, GA. "How Great Thou Art" (Stuart Hine); "Til the Last Leaf Shall Fall" (James/Rhodes); "Must Jesus Bear the Cross Alone?" (Shepherd/Allen); "There's Room at the Cross" (Ira Stanphill); "Beyond the Gates" (Rupert Cravens); "How Long Has It Been?" (Mosie Lister); "If I Can Help Somebody" (Hazel Androzzo); "He Set Me Free" (Jerry Berry); "I'm Gonna Walk With My Friend Jesus" (Ernie Newton); "To Me It's So Wonderful" (Ralph Goodpasteur) November, 1964

CAL/CAS-916 "All Day Sing and Dinner on the Ground" Producer: Ethel Gabriel. Recorded at RCA Victor's "Nashville Sound" Studio, Nashville, TN. Personnel: Hovie Lister/Rosie Rozell/Jack Toney/Doy Ott/James Wetherington. "We'll Soon Be Done With Troubles and Trials" (Cleavant Derricks); "I Walk With Jesus" (Whitworth); "Do Lord" (public domain); "Get on the Happy Side of Living" (Vep Ellis); "Jesus Is Gettin' Us Ready" (Arr. Rozell); "I'm Satisfied With Jesus" (Doy Ott); "I'll Live in Glory" (J. M. Henson); "When God Dips His Love in My Heart" (Cleavant Derricks); "I Wouldn't Take Nothin' for My Journey Now" (Rusty Goodman/Jimmie Davis); "When I Come To the End of the Road" (Hovie Lister) October, 1965

CAL/CAS-2151 "My God Is Real" Producer: Ethel Gabriel. (All material previously released) Personnel: Hovie Lister/Denver Crumpler/Jake Hess/Doy Ott/James Wetherington. "My God Is Real" "My Heart Is A Chapel" "Everybody Will Be Happy Over There" "The Bible Told Me So" "I Wonder What My New Address Will Be" "Known Only To Him" "Hide Me, Rock of Ages" "No One But Jesus Knows" "Glory, Glory, Clear the Road" "First Day In Heaven" July, 1967

CAL/CAS-2314 "Taller Than Trees" (All material previously released) Personnel: various. "One of These Mornings" "Taller Than Trees" "Till I Know" "I'm Climbing Higher and Higher And I Won't Come Down" "Little Boy Lost" "Wait For Me" "I've Got the Corners Turned Down" "What A Savior" "Lord, I Want To Go To Heaven" "Surely I Will, Lord" May, 1969

CAL/CAS-2361 "O Come All Ye Faithful" (Reissue of RCA-Victor LPM/LSP 2606) "O Come, All Ye Faithful" "Silver Bells" "Go Tell It on the Mountain" "Praises to Our King" "White Christmas" "Christmas Means Christ to Me" "Joy to the World!" "Christmas Time is Here" "O Little Town of Bethlehem" "Away in a Manger" "O Holy Night!" "Silent Night" May, 1969

CAL/CAS-2419 "No Greater Love" Personnel: Hovie Lister/Rosie Rozell/Jake Hess/Doy Ott/James Wetherington. (All material previously released) "That's Why I've Gotta Sing" "Love So Divine" "Little Bitty Chapel" "No Greater Love" "I've Found A New Way" "He Will Pilot Me" "What Love" "Who Could Ask for More" "The Love of God" "God Can" May, 1970

Skylite

Extended Play (EP) Singles ...

SREP-102 "Get Away Jordan" "Get Away Jordan" plus 3 selections from SRLP/SSLP-5965 "Get Away Jordan" 1959
SREP-104 "Statesmen Encores" Four selections from SRLP/SSLP-5968 "Statesmen Encores" 1960

Albums ...

SRLP-1198 "Hymns By The Statesmen" (Same album as "Hymns By The Statesmen," Statesmen label #1198) "Softly and Tenderly" "Leaning on the Everlasting Arms" "I Am Thine, O Lord" "There Is a Fountain" "Sweet Hour of Prayer" "I Surrender All" "Near to the Heart of God" "The Old Rugged Cross" "Have Thine Own Way, Lord" "Just As I Am" "My Jesus, I Love Thee" "Let the Lower Lights Be Burning" 1959

SRLP/SSLP-5965 "Get Away Jordan" (Same album as "Statesmen Quartet" label K80P-5966-612S-5965) Personnel: Hovie Lister/Rosie Rozell/Jake Hess/Doy Ott/James Wetherington. "How Many Times" (Thomas Dorsey); "Get Away Jordan" (public domain); "Hide Thou Me" (L.R. Tolbert/Thoro Harris); "When You Travel All Alone" (Mosie Lister); "Happy Rhythm" (Mosie Lister); "Jesus Fills My Every Need" (Vep Ellis); "Where No One Stands Alone" (Mosie Lister); "In the Sweet Forever" (Luther G. Presley); "I Bowed On My Knees and Cried Holy" "What A Day That Will Be" (Jim Hill); "On Revival Day" (public domain); "Sho' Do Need Him Now" (Thomas Dorsey) 1959

SRLP/SSLP-5968 "Statesmen Encores" Producer: Brock Speer. Personnel: Hovie Lister/Rosie Rozell/Jake Hess/Doy Ott/James Wetherington. "Something to Shout About" "I'm Gonna Walk Dem Golden Stairs" "His Hand In Mine" (Mosie Lister); "In My Father's House" (Aileene Hanks); "Heavenly Love" (Vep Ellis); "A Newborn Feeling" (Lee Roy Abernathy); "I Have a Desire" "Everybody Ought to Know" "I Just Can't Make It By Myself" "I'll Leave It All Behind" "Jubilee's A-Comin' " (public domain), "Oh, My Lord, What a Time" (public domain) 1960

SRLP/SSLP-5980 "Statesmen-Blackwood Favorites" Producer: Brock Speer. Recorded in RCA Studio, Nashville. Personnel: Hovie Lister/Rosie Rozell/Jake Hess/Doy Ott/James Wetherington & Wally Varner/Bill Shaw/James Blackwood/Cecil Blackwood/J.D. Sumner. "Lead Me To That Rock" (Arr. Varner-Hall); "My Heavenly Father Watches Over Me" (Arr. Wetherington); "I'm Bound for the Kingdom" (Mosie Lister); "Goodbye, World, Goodbye" (Mosie Lister); "This World Is Not My Home" (Arr. Sumner); "Somebody Bigger Than You and I" (Lang); "He'll Understand and Say Well Done" (Lucy Campbell); "The Love of God" (Vep Ellis); "Rolling, Riding, Rocking" (Wally Varner); "Just a Closer Walk With Thee" (Arr. Ott); "What a Friend We Have In Jesus" (Scriven/Converse); "When the Saints Go Marching In" (Arr. Sumner) 1960

Skylite Albums *(continued)* ...

SRLP/SSLP-6000 "Singing Time In Dixie" Producer: Brock Speer. Recorded in RCA Studio, Nashville. Personnel: Hovie Lister/Rosie Rozell/Jake Hess/Doy Ott/James Wetherington. "Church Twice on Sunday" (traditional); "Living With Jesus" (Barnett/Henson); "I Saw A Man" (Arthur Smith); "Someone To Care" (Jimmie Davis); "When I Move" (Buford Abner); "I've Got News" (Lee Roy Abernathy); "These Are the Things That Matter" (Arthur Smith); "Nothing Can Compare" (Mosie Lister); "All Alone" (Mosie Lister); "The Old Landmark" (Herbert Brewster); "Sunday Meetin' Time" (Mosie Lister); "Mother's Prayers Have Followed Me" (Mosie Lister) 1962

SLP-6070 "God Loves American People" Producer: Joel E. Gentry. Recorded in Columbia Studios, Nashville, TN. Personnel: Hovie Lister/Rosie Rozell/Jack Toney/Doy Ott/James Wetherington. "Until You've Known the Love of God" (Rusty Goodman); "God Loves American People" (Lee Roy Abernathy); "Life Is Worth Living" "How Unworthy I've Been" "Who Cares" "It Won't Be Long" "Higher Ground" "That Somebody Is Jesus My Lord" (traditional); "How Long Will It Take" (Henry Slaughter); "Jesus" (William J. Gaither); "That's Gospel, Brother" 1968

SLP-6080 "Thanks To Calvary" Producer: Joel E. Gentry. Recorded in Columbia Studios, Nashville, TN. Personnel: Hovie Lister/Rosie Rozell/Jim Hill/Doy Ott/James Wetherington. "Thanks to Calvary" (William J. Gaither); "Oh My Lord, What a Time" (public domain); "Why Should I Worry Or Fret" (William J. Gaither); "I'm Free" (William J. Gaither); "He Looked Beyond My Faults" (Dottie Rambo); "Faith Unlocks the Door" (Scott/Sande); "Old Tim Religion" (public domain); "Going Home" (William J. Gaither); "For God So Loved" (Jim Hill); "Do You Really Care" (Cates); "God's Not Dead" 1969

SLP-6090 "New Sounds Today" Producer: Joel Gentry. Personnel: Hovie Lister/Sherrill Nielsen/Jim Hill/Doy Ott/James Wetherington. "That's What Jesus Means to Me" "The Blood Will Never Lose Its Power" (Andre Crouch); "Tell it All to Jesus" (Aikens/Woods); "I Know the Lord Will Never Fail" "My Dream Home in Glory" "The Cross Made the Difference" (William J. Gaither); "I'll Never Forget" "Keep Moving" "God Put a Rainbow" "In the Beginning" (Cochran/Twomey/Wise/Weisman) 1969

SLP-6095 "The Statesmen Featuring Hovie, Sherrill, Jim, Doy and Big Chief" Producer: Joel Gentry. Personnel: Hovie Lister/Sherrill Nielsen/Jim Hill/Doy Ott/James Wetherington. "God Will Provide" (Henry Slaughter); "Gonna Shout Hallelujah" "Just Let Me Touch Him" "Have You Tried the Lord Today?" (Doy Ott); "Great is the Lord" (James S. Wetherington); "I Must Tell Jesus" (Elisha A. Hoffman); "Unworthy" (Ira Stanphill); "The Road of No Return" (Jim Hill); "Impossible Dream" "When My Soul Takes Its Flight" (James S. Wetherington) 1970

SLP-6100 "The Common Man" Producer: Joel Gentry. Personnel: Hovie Lister/Sherrill Nielsen/Jim Hill/Doy Ott/James Wetherington. "The Common Man" (Jimmy Jones); "Something Happened to Daddy" "This Is the Day" (N. Harmon); "I Just Can't Praise Him Enough" (C. Taylor); "Sin Ain't Nothing But the Blues" "If to Gain the World" (Mosie Lister); "I'm Going to Roll Along" Statesmen Hymn Medley 1970

SLP-6110 "Put Your Hand in the Hand" Producer: Joel Gentry. Personnel: Hovie Lister/Sherrill Nielsen/Jim Hill/Doy Ott/James Wetherington. "Sweet Song of Salvation" (Larry Norman); "Oh, What A Happy Day" (Jack W. Campbell); "There's a Light Guiding Me" (Newton); "Put Your Hand in the Hand" (Gene MacLellan); "Bridge Over Troubled Water" (Paul Simon); "What a Day That Will Be" (Jim Hill); "I Know" (Lavern Tripp); "No One But Jesus Knows" (Henry Slaughter); "He Touched Me" (William J. Gaither); "Sweet Jesus" (Doris Akers) 1971

SLP-6115 "Keep On Smiling" Producer: Joel Gentry. Personnel: Hovie Lister/Sherrill Nielsen/Jim Hill/Doy Ott/James Wetherington/Tim Baty. "Keep On Smiling" (Joe Roper); "Redemption Draweth Nigh" (Gordon Jenson); "Some Things I'd Change" "When We Sing Around the Throne" "Turn Your Radio On" (Albert Brumley); "I Want to Live for Him" (Mylon LeFevre); "Yesterday" (George Younce); "Can We Get to That?" (Ray Stevens); "Walk With Me" "There's Nothing Like This Feeling" 1972

SLP-6120 "They That Sow" Producer: Joel Gentry. Recorded in DBM Studios, Nashville, TN. Personnel: Hovie Lister/Sherrill Nielsen/Jim Hill/Doy Ott/James Wetherington/Tim Baty. "Let's Go Tell It" (R.Jordan); "Higher Than the Moon" (D. Young); "They That Sow" (Lari Goss); "You're On His Mind" (Mylon LeFevre); "I Got a God I Can Recommend" (James S. Wetherington); "The Unseen Hand" (A. Sims); "I Wonder What My New Address Will Be?" (Mosie Lister); "Precious Old Book" (Lari Goss); "The Lighthouse" (Ron Hinson); "Til The Storm Passes By" (Mosie Lister) 1972

SLP-6133 "A Time To Remember Big Chief Wetherington" Producer: Joel Gentry. (Compiled from previously released albums) "This Is the Day" "The Common Man" "When My Soul Takes Its Flight" "How Long Will It Take" "I'm Free" "Until You've Known" "No One Cared for Me Like Jesus" "Great is the Lord" "Faith Unlocks the Door" "That Somebody Is Jesus" 1973

SLP-6180 "Get Away Jordan" Producer: Joel Gentry. (All. songs previously released) "Oh, My Lord, What a Time" "That's What Jesus Means" "Why Should I Worry Or Fret" "Old Time Religion" "Have You Tried the Lord Today" "Sho' Do Need Him Now" "Get Away Jordan" "I Wonder What My New Address Will Be" "Til The Storm Passes By" "Faith Unlocks the Door" 1977

SLP-6190 "Oh What A Savior" Producer: Joel Gentry. (All songs previously released) "For God So Loved" "He Looked Beyond My Faults" "Sweet Jesus" "I've Got a God I Can Recommend" "I Saw A Man" "Living With Jesus" "Jesus Fills My Every Need" "God Put a Rainbow In the Sky" "Tell It To Jesus" "I Just Can't Praise Him Enough" 1978

SLP-6200 "Gospel Gems" Producer: Joel Gentry. (All songs previously released) "The Old Rugged Cross Makes the Difference" "Let's Go Tell It" "God Will Provide" "In My Father's House" "His Hand In Mine" "What a Day That Will Be" "Keep On Smiling" "There's a Light Guiding Me" "Turn Your Radio On" "Do You Really Care" 1979

SLP-6225 "Hovie Lister and the Sensational Statesmen" Producer: Joel Gentry. Recorded live at the Joyful Noise Christian Supper Club, Atlanta-East Point, GA. by Prestige Studios, Birmingham, AL. Personnel: Hovie Lister/Rosie Rozell/Buddy Burton/Ed Hill/Tommy Thompson/Jake Robinson. "I Want To Know" (traditional); "Happy Rhythm" (Mosie Lister); "A Newborn Feeling" (Lee Roy Abernathy); "My Home" (Lee Roy Abernathy); "Everytime I Feel the Spirit" (traditional); "The Lighthouse" (Ron Hinson); "Let the Lower Lights Be Burning" (Philip P. Bliss); "First Day In Heaven" (Stuart Hamblen); "Closer to Thee" (Steele/Chapman/Little); "Oh, What a Savior" (Marvin Dalton) 1979

SLP-6235 "He Is Here" Producer: Joel Gentry. Recorded at Young'un Sound Studios, Nashville, TN. Personnel: Hovie Lister/Rosie Rozell/Buddy Burton/Ed Hill/Tommy Thompson. "I Love My Jesus" (Roger Beshears); "He Is Here" (Shirley Windsor); "I'll Never Turn Back" (Bill Carver); "When Morning Comes" (Barbara Miller); "He Shall Reign Forever" (Vern Sullivan); "He Was There All the Time" (Gary Paxton); "I Have a New Song" (Christine Starling); "I'm In This Church" (Joel Hemphill); "How Great Thou Art" (Stuart Hine); "We Are All Going Home" (Pete Harris) 1980

SLP-6274 "Live at the Joyful Noise" Producer: Joel Gentry. (Reissue of SLP-6225) 1982

SLP-6294 "How Great Thou Art" Producer: Joel Gentry. (Compiled from previously-released albums) 1983

SLP-6307 "He Touched Me" Producer: Joel Gentry. (Compiled from previously released albums) 1983

Temple

Albums ...
Temple 7707 "They That Sow" (Compiled from previously-released Skylite material)
Temple 8305 "Precious Old Book" (Compiled from previously-released Skylite material) "For God So Loved" "Sweet Jesus" "Precious Old Book" "Jesus Fills My Every Need" "Tell it to Jesus" "He Looked Beyond My Faults" "I've Got a God I Can Recommend" "Living With Jesus" "God Put a Rainbow in the Sky" "I Just Can't Praise Him Enough" 1985
Temple 8522 "Faith Unlocks the Door" (Previously-released Skylite material) "O, My Lord, What a Time" "Why Should I Worry or Fret" "Have You Tried the Lord Today" "Get Away Jordan" "Til the Storm Passes By" "That's What Jesus Means to Me" "Old Time Religion" "Sho' Do Need Him Now" "I Wonder What My New Address Will Be" "Faith Unlocks the Door"

HeartWarming

Album ...
HW-1940 "Hits of the Decade" (Recorded in Atlanta's Biltmore Hotel Ballroom for Nabisco television show, 1953-57) Personnel: Hovie Lister/Denver Crumpler/Jake Hess/Doy Ott/James Wetherington. "I Found It In Mother's Bible" (Stamps-Baxter); "Church Twice on Sunday" (Mosie Lister); "I Saw a Man" (Arthur Smith); "The Man Upstairs" "Do Right and Come Smilin' Through" (Stamps-Baxter); "The Fourth Man" (Arthur Smith); "Old Landmark (public domain); "Roll On Jordan" (Bob Prather); "I'll Tell It" "Blow Your Trumpet, Gabriel" (Mosie Lister); "When the Saints Go Marching In" (Arr. Benson); "The King and I" (Mosie Lister) 1968

Artistic

Albums ...
Artistic-20312 "Hits of the Decade" (Reissue of HeartWarming 1940) Personnel: Hovie Lister/Denver Crumpler/Jake Hess/Doy Ott/James Wetherington. "I Found It In Mother's Bible" "Church Twice on Sunday" "I Saw a Man" "The Man Upstairs" "Do Right and Come Smilin' Through" "The Fourth Man" "Old Landmark "Roll On Jordan" "I'll Tell It" "Blow Your Trumpet, Gabriel" "When the Saints Go Marching In" "The King and I" 1972
Artistic-20711 "Hits of the Decade, Vol. 2" (Recorded in Atlanta's Biltmore Hotel for Nabisco television show, 1953-57) Personnel: Hovie Lister/Denver Crumpler/Jake Hess/Doy Ott/James Wetherington. "When I Move" "Some Glad Day" "Trouble" "Old Fashioned Love" "I've Been With Jesus" "Way Over the Blue" "Down Old Log Cabin Lane" "Trail to Paradise" "This Ole House" "Headin' Home" 1972
Artistic-1601 "I Believe In Jesus" Recorded at LeFevre Sound, Atlanta, GA. Personnel: Hovie Lister/Sherrill Nielsen/ Gary Timbs/Doy Ott/James Wetherington/Tim Baty. "I Believe In Jesus" (Mac Davis); "Why Me, Lord" (Kris Kristoferson); "Do You Understand" "No One But the Lord" "When He Calls, I'll Fly Away" (Vep Ellis); "Roll Back River Jordan" "After Calvary" (Laverne Tripp); "I'm Depending On Jesus" "Since Then" "That's Enough" (Whitey Gleason) 1973

Cam

Albums ...
CAM TS-1407 "The Sensational Statesmen In Memory of Jim 'Big Chief' Wetherington and Denver 'Crump' Crumpler" (Recorded in Atlanta's Biltmore Hotel for Nabisco television show, 1953-57) Personnel: Hovie Lister/Denver Crumpler/Jake Hess/Doy Ott/James Wetherington. "I'm Gonna Walk Dem Golden Stairs" "Lord, I Want to Go to Heaven" "Gonna Reap What You Sow" "I Believe in the Man in the Sky" "Get Away Jordan" "His Hand in Mine" "Cowboy Camp Meeting" "Sunday Meetin' Time" "Sho' Do Need Him Now" "Hide Me, Rock of Ages" 1973
CAM TS-1422 "Ain't That What It's All About" Personnel: Hovie Lister/Willie Wynn/Gary Timbs/Doy Ott/Ray Burdette/Kenny Hicks.. "You're the One" "Ten Thousand Years" "Poor Carpenter's Son" "Gentle Shepherd" "Free to Go Home" "What a Time" "Touring That City" "Restore My Soul" "Ain't That What It's All About" "My God Is Real" 1973
CAM TS-1423 "Precious Memories" Personnel: Hovie Lister/Willie Wynn/Gary Timbs/Doy Ott/Ray Burdette/Kenny Hicks.. "Precious Memories" "Old Rugged Cross" "Rock of Ages" "Let the Lower Lights Be Burning" "I'll Fly Away" "What a Friend" "How Great Thou Art" "There's Power in the Blood" "Amazing Grace" "Leaning on the Everlasting Arms" 1974
CAM TS-1494 "The Statesmen Feature Doy Ott" Personnel: Hovie Lister/Willie Wynn/Elmer Cole/Doy Ott/Ray Burdette/Kenny Hicks. "Everybody Has the Blues" "The Morning Prayer" "Wait for Me" "Mercy Lord" "Don't Give Up On Me" "Something I Can Feel" "That's Just Like Jesus" "More and More" "Three Crosses" "I Live On" 1974

Artco

Albums ...
ARTCO 1146 "Hovie Lister and The Statesmen Sing Gospel Songs Elvis Loved" Personnel: Hovie Lister/Rosie Rozell/Jake Hess/Doy Ott. "Memories of Love" "How Great Thou Art" (Stuart Hine); "Jesus Knows" (Mosie Lister); "Until Then" (Stuart Hamblen); "Down By the Riverside" "It Is No Secret" (Stuart Hamblen); "Known Only to Him" (Stuart Hamblen); "Where No One Stands Alone" (Mosie Lister); "I Believe In The Man In The Sky" (Richard Howard, Jr.); "Cryin' In The Chapel" (Artie Glenn); "His Hand In Mine" (Mosie Lister) 1977

Vine

Albums ...
Vine LPG-V-1004 "The Legendary Statesmen Return" Recorded at Associated Recording Artists Studios, Oklahoma City, OK. Personnel: Hovie Lister/Rosie Rozell/Jake Hess/Doy Ott. "All Day Singing" "Life is Worth Living" "Will He Be There" "Leave it There" "Story of Christ" "When We All Get to Heaven" "It's Not All Over" "I'm Singing His Praise" "Soon and Very Soon" "Oh, What a Savior" 1977

Vine Albums *(continued)* ...
Vine VI-77-1013 "His Love Put a Song In My Heart" Recorded at Associated Recording Artists Studios, Oklahoma City, OK. Personnel: Hovie Lister/Rosie Rozell/Jake Hess/Doy Ott. "His Love Put a Song in My Heart" "Come to Jesus" "Hold On" "Sweet, Sweet Spirit" "All God's Children" "Every Time I Feel the Spirit" "Jesus Loves Me" "Life Begins at Calvary" "A Very Special Grace" "Just Wait Till You See My Brand New Home" 1978
Vine "Silent Night" Recorded at Associated Recording Artists Studios, Oklahoma City, OK. Personnel: Hovie Lister/ Rosie Rozell/Jake Hess/Doy Ott. "It Came Upon the Midnight Clear" "Oh Little Town of Bethlehem" "Joy the the World" "Silent Night" "The First Noel" "Away In a Manger" "Hark, the Herald Angels Sing" "O Come All Ye Faithful" "Go Tell it on the Mountain" "O Holy Night" 1978
Vine VI-77-1020 "Glory, Glory Clear the Road" Recorded at Associated Recording Artists Studios, Oklahoma City, OK. Personnel: Hovie Lister/Rosie Rozell/Jake Hess/Chris Hess. "Glory, Glory, Clear the Road" "He Was There All the Time" "Songs Mama Sang" "I've Never Seen the Righteous Forsaken" "He's Got It All In Control" "I've Already Been To the Water" "Your First Day In Heaven" "Sunshine and Roses" "God Takes Good Care of Me" "You Gave Me Joy In My Heart" 1978
Vine VI-77-1043 "Sweet Beulah Land" Recorded at Associated Recording Artists Studios, Oklahoma City, OK. Personnel: Hovie Lister/Rosie Rozell/Buddy Burton/Ed Hill/Tommy Thompson. "Sweet Beulah Land" "Standing on the Solid Rock" "I Want to Go to Heaven" "Thank You, Jesus" "Jesus Is Right" "Just A Little While" "One Day at a Time" "Freedom In My Soul" "He Touched Me" "The Great Physician" 1981

Chime

Albums ...
Chime 604 "Hits of the Decade" (Reissue of HeartWarming 1940) 1977
Chime 605 "Hits of the Decade, Vol. 2" (Reissue of Artistic 20711) 1977
Chime "I Believe In Jesus" (Reissue of Artistic 1601) 1977

Power Pak *(a division of Gusto / Starday)*

Albums ...
PG-712 "Sunday Meetin' Time" (Reissue of Skylite SRLP/SSLP-6000 "Singing Time in Dixie")
PG-717 "Statesmen-Blackwood Favorites" (Reissue of Skylite SRLP/SSLP-5980 "Statesmen-Blackwood favorites")

Miracle Music Corporation

Cassette Album ...
LPI-C1039 "Statesmen Encores" (Reissue of Skylite SRLP/SSLP-5968 "Statesmen Encores") "Something to Shout About" "I'm Gonna Walk Dem Golden Stairs" "His Hand In Mine""In My Father's House" "Heavenly Love" "A Newborn Feeling" "I Have a Desire" "Everybody Ought to Know" "I Just Can't Make It By Myself" "I'll Leave It All Behind" "Jubilee's A-Comin' " "Oh, My Lord, What a Time" 1988

The Landmark Group

Cassette Albums ...
HLSQ-1001 "The Bible Told Me So" (Recorded in Atlanta's Biltmore Hotel Ballroom for Nabisco television show, 1953-57) Personnel: Hovie Lister/Denver Crumpler/Jake Hess/Doy Ott/James Wetherington. "When We All Get to Heaven," "Belshazzar," "I Found a New Friend," "An Old Log Cabin for Sale," "I'm Climbing Higher and Higher," "Lord, I Want To Go To Heaven," "He Knows Just What I Need," "The Bible Told Me So," "Your First Day in Heaven," "At the End of the Trail" 1992
HLSQ-1002 "Get Away Jordan" (Recorded in Atlanta's Biltmore Hotel Ballroom for Nabisco television show, 1953-57) Personnel: Hovie Lister/Denver Crumpler/Jake Hess/Doy Ott/James Wetherington. "I Believe in the Man in the Sky," "Happiness," "Get Away Jordan," "Journey's End," "Taller Than Trees," "There's a Little Pine Log Cabin," "I Know Who Holds Tomorrow," "Sunday Meeting Time," "If God Didn't Care," "Sho' Do Need Him Now" 1992
HLSQ-1003 "Jubilee's A Coming" (Recorded in Atlanta's Biltmore Hotel Ballroom for Nabisco television show, 1953-57) Personnel: Hovie Lister/Denver Crumpler/Jake Hess/Doy Ott/James Wetherington. "I'm Gonna Walk Dem Golden Stairs," "Mercy Lord," "Gonna Reap What You Sow," "Led Out of Bondage," "Cowboy Camp Meeting," "I've Got a Newborn Feeling," "Twilight Shadows Are Falling," "Peace in the Valley," "Mother's Prayers Have Followed Me," "Jubilee's A Coming" 1992
HLSQ-1004 "I Surrender All" "Rescue the Perishing," "I Am Thine, O Lord," "Near to the Heart of God," "Sweet Hour of Prayer," "The Old Rugged Cross," "Softly and Tenderly," "Just As I Am," "Must Jesus Bear the Cross Alone," "Have Thine Own Way, Lord," "I Surrender All" 1992

Canaan

Cassette and Compact Disc Albums ...
Canaan-9501 "Statesmen Revival" Producer: Bill Gaither and Mike English. (Tracks recorded at Suite 16. Vocals recorded at Classic Recording/Pinebrook/Skylab Studio/Suite 16) Personnel: Hovie Lister/Johnny Cook/Jake Hess/Biney English/Bob Caldwell. "Goodbye, World, Goodbye" (Mosie Lister); "Glory Train" (Biney English); "Death Ain't No Big Deal" (Lee Domain); "Sinners Plea" (Joe Roper); "Come Out With Your Hands Up" (Scooter Simmons); "If the Lord Wasn't Walking By My Side" (Henry Slaughter); "Someday" (Joe Moscheo); "Every Eye Shall See" (William J. & Gloria Gaither); "I Lost It All To Find Everything" (William J. & Gloria Gaither); "I've Been There" (Dave Clark) 1992
Canaan 9525 "O, My Lord, What A Time" Producer: Bill Gaither. (Reissue of Spring House GTP002) Personnel: Hovie Lister/Johnny Cook/Jake Hess/Biney English/Bob Caldwell. "Blood Bought Church" "What A Lovely Name" "God Takes Good Care of Me" "Forgiven Again" "O, My Lord, What A Time" "Just A Little While" "Faith Unlocks The Door" "Lord, Feed Your Children" "Your First Day In Heaven" "More Of You" 1993

Spring House

Cassette and Compact Disc Albums ...

Spring House GTP002 "O, My Lord, What A Time" Producer: Bill Gaither. (Tracks recorded at Suite 16, Nashville, TN. Vocals recorded at Pinebrook, Alexandria, IN.) Personnel: Hovie Lister/Johnny Cook/Jake Hess/Biney English/Bob Caldwell. "Blood Bought Church" (Nancy Harmon); "What A Lovely Name" (Charles B. Wycuff); "God Takes Good Care of Me" (Henry Slaughter); "Forgiven Again" (Gloria Gaither/Wm. Benjamin Gaither); "O, My Lord, What A Time" (public domain); "Just A Little While" (E.M. Bartlett); "Faith Unlocks The Door" (Samuel Scott/Robert Sands); "Lord, Feed Your Children" (David Binion); "Your First Day In Heaven" (Stuart Hamblen); "More Of You" (Gloria Gaither/Wm. J. Gaither/Gary Paxton) 1992

Spring House GTP003 "O, What A Savior" Producer: Bill Gaither. (Tracks recorded at Suite 16, Nashville, TN. Vocals recorded at Pinebrook, Alexandria, IN.) Personnel: Hovie Lister/Johnny Cook/Jake Hess/Biney English/Bob Caldwell. "Glory, Glory, Clear The Road" (Monty Matthews/Vic Willis/McMahon Hancock); "If It Had Not Been" (Margaret P. Douroux); "I'm Gonna Keep On" (William J. Gaither); "Who Am I" (Rusty Goodman); "O, How I Love Jesus" (Frederick Whitfield); "I Wanna Know" (public domain); "O, What A Savior" (Marvin P. Dalton); "Where Could I Go" (James B. Coats); "We Are So Blessed" (Wm. J. and Gloria Gaither/Greg Nelson); "Jesus Is Lord Of All" (William J. and Gloria Gaither) 1992

Gaither Gospel SeriesSHD4904 "Hovie Lister & the Statesmen" Producer: Bill Gaither. (Digitally remastered from original RCA Victor recordings) Personnel: various. "This Ole House" "Move That Mountain" "I've Been With Jesus" "Everybody Will Be Happy Over There" "I'm Climbing Higher and Higher" "Your First Day In Heaven" "How Long Has It Been" "Led Out of Bondage" "Hide Me, Rock of Ages" "My Heart Is A Chapel" "Faith Unlocks The Door" "Let the Lower Lights Be Burning" "Up Above My Head" "Light of Love" "Something Within" "To Me It's So Wonderful" "Sweeter As the Days Go By" "Without Him" "When He Calls I'll Fly Away" "My Home" "O What A Savior" "Get Away Jordan" 1997

BRG Music

Cassette and Compact Disc Album ...

BRG98064 "Still Sensational" Producer: Ben Speer. Executive Producers: Charles Waller and Bobby Ross. (Recorded at Suite 16, Nashville, TN.) Personnel: Hovie Lister/Wallace Nelms/Jack Toney/Rick Fair/Doug Jones. "I Wanna Rock My Soul" (Jack Toney); "Grace Marches On" (Jack Toney/Gail Toney); "Higher Than The Moon" (David Young); "Closer to Thee" (Steele/Chapel/Little); "If I Had Only Known" Jack Toney/Bill Landers);"Sweeter Every Day" (Jack Toney); "Sweet Beulah Land" (Squire Parsons);"The Wind Is Like The Spirit" (Jack Toney); "In The Garden" (C. Austin Miles); "I Lost It All To Find Everything" (William J. Gaither/Gloria Gaither) 1998

Memory Lane Gospel

Cassette and Compact Disc Album ...

MLG1010 "Happy Rhythm" (Same album as "Statesmen Quartet" label K80P-5966-612S-5965 and Skylite SRLP/SSLP 5965) Personnel: Hovie Lister/Rosie Rozell/Jake Hess/Doy Ott/James Wetherington. "How Many Times" "Get Away Jordan" "Hide Thou Me" "When You Travel All Alone" "Happy Rhythm" "Jesus Fills My Every Need" "Where No One Stands Alone" "In the Sweet Forever" "I Bowed On My Knees and Cried Holy" "What A Day That Will Be" "On Revival Day" "Sho' Do Need Him Now" [release pending]

Note: Most of the recorded Statesmen product, with the exception of the most recent Canaan, Spring House and Landmark releases, are no longer available in music and book stores. However, many of the older releases may be obtained through companies who specialize in older recordings. The author has personally conducted transactions with the following reputable businesses:

Gospel Gallery	**Harold's Record Outlet**
P.O. Box 140571	**P.O. Box 141**
Nashville, TN 37214-0571	**Louisburg, NC 27549**

Send your inquiry, along with a stamped, self-addressed envelope for an immediate reply.

VIDEOGRAPHY
The Statesmen Quartet with Hovie Lister

Gaither Videos

"Bill & Gloria Gaither Present Hovie Lister & the Sensational Statesmen Quartet, An American Classic" (Hall of Honor Series, Vol. 3) 1994

"Hovie Lister & the Sensational Statesmen Quartet, What A Happy Time 20 Illustrious Years" (Vols. 1-3) 1994

"The Statesmen With Rosie Rozell" (The Best of Glory Road Television series) 1997

Reel to Real Video Productions

"Back to the 50's With Hovie Lister & the Sensational Statesmen Quartet" (Vols. 1-5) 1988-1990

Gospel Gallery

"Video Memories of the Sixties. Vol. 11 The Statesmen" (12 songs with Hovie Lister/Rosie Rozell/Jake Hess/Doy Ott/James "Big Chief" Wetherington)

Hovie Lister & the Statesmen Quartet
Roll Call of Members

1. **Hovie Lister**, pianist, 1948-present
2. **Mosie Lister**, lead, 1948
3. ***Bobby Strickland**, tenor, 1948-1950
4. ***Bervin Kendrick**, baritone, 1948-1951
5. **Gordon Hill**, bass, 1948-1949
6. ***Aycel Soward**, bass, 1949
7. **Jake Hess**, lead, 1948-1956; 1957-1963; 1977-79; 1988-1993
8. ***James Wetherington**, bass, 1949-1973
9. ***Claris Garland "Cat" Freeman**, tenor, 1950-1953; 1957-1958
10. **Boyce Hawkins**, pianist, 1950-1951
11. ***Doy Ott**, pianist, 1951; baritone, 1951-1978
12. **Troy Posey**, baritone, 1951
13. **Earl Terry**, tenor, 1951
14. ***Denver Crumpler**, tenor, 1953-1957
15. **Les Roberson**, lead, 1956-1957
16. ***Roland D. "Rosie" Rozell**, tenor, 1958-1968; 1973; 1977-1981; 1988-1989
17. **Gary McSpadden**, lead, 1962
18. **Jack Toney**, lead, 1963-1966; 1967-1968; 1993-present
19. **Roy McNeil**, lead, 1966-1967
20. **Don Butler**, lead, 1957
21. **Jim Hill**, lead, 1969-1973
22. **Sherrill Nielsen**, tenor, 1969-1973
23. **Tim Baty**, bass guitar, 1971-1973
24. **Gary Timbs**, lead, 1973-1974
25. **Ray Burdette**, bass, 1974-1975
26. **Kenny Hicks**, bass guitar, 1973-1975
27. **Willie Wynn**, tenor, 1973-1975
28. **Elmer Cole**, lead, 1974-1975
29. **Chris Hess**, baritone, 1978-1979
30. **Buddy Burton**, lead, 1979-1981; baritone, 1988-1989; 1994-1995
31. ***Tommy Thompson**, bass, 1979-1981; 1988-1989
32. **Ed Hill**, baritone, 1979-1981
33. **Jake Robinson**, bass guitar, 1980-1981
34. **J.D. Sumner**, bass, 1981
35. **Johnny Cook**, tenor, 1991-1992
36. **Biney English**, baritone, 1991-1992
37. **Bob Caldwell**, bass, 1991-1993
38. **Jeff Silvey**, keyboards, 1991-1993
39. **Gene "Tank" Tackett**, tenor, 1993-1994
40. **Scooter Simmons**, baritone, 1993-1994
41. **Jerry Chandler**, 1994
42. **Nick Val**, bass, 1993-1994
43. **Steve Warren**, tenor, 1994
44. **Gene Miller**, tenor, 1994-1995
45. **Roy Pauley**, bass, 1994
46. **Doug Young**, bass, 1994-present
47. **Mike LoPrinzi**, baritone, 1995-1997
48. **Wallace Nelms**, tenor, 1995-present
49. **Rick Fair**, baritone, 1997-present

> *Note: Many personnel listed here sang with the Statesmen for a rather limited amount of time. Some, such as Gary McSpadden, temporarily filled in during an illness of a regular member. Others, such as J.D. Sumner and Don Butler, were temporary replacements until a permanent replacement could be found.*

*-deceased

About the Author

As a child Dave Taylor dreamed of singing with the best gospel quartet in the world. Raised in a Wesleyan pastor's home, he grew up listening to gospel music on the hi-fi and singing solos in church.

"Dad wouldn't have a television in the house," he says, "so my favorite entertainment—aside from play—took the form of reading books or singing with quartet records. All I ever wanted to do in life was write books and sing. I was wearing a cape long before Elvis. There is a picture in our family album of me at about the age of five—wearing a cowboy hat with a towel tied around my neck—singing with my Mom accompanying me on the piano. I guess I couldn't make up my mind whether I wanted to be Superman or Gene Autry!"

At age 46, Dave serves as Minister of Music at Hanover Baptist Church in Hanover, Indiana. He spent the better part of 15 years singing with weekend quartets, while making a living in construction, broadcasting, newspaper journalism, public relations and now full circle to construction again. He presents solo concerts for churches and civic functions whenever asked. "Singing opportunities can't happen often enough to suit me," he says.

Dave's pastor, the Rev. J.D. Traylor, says: "On numerous occasions, God has blessed us through Dave's musical presentations. He has sung solos, put on concerts for us, and served three times as our Interim Minister of Music before taking the job permanently. I have heard countless favorable remarks from our people as to how they were inspired by Dave's songs, and I too am among the multitudes who have been blessed. The quality of Dave's voice is superb, and he desires to use it for the King."

"I have wanted to write a book about the Statesmen ever since I first read the Blackwood Brothers' story in the book **Above All** back in the 1960s," Dave says. "I first approached Hovie Lister about it while the Masters V were in full swing. He was quite open to the idea then, but it wasn't until Hovie, Jake Hess and Bill Gaither reorganized the Statesmen that things began to happen. Bill was really the catalyst to get my idea beyond the proposal stage."

Since the **Happy Rhythm, A Biography of Hovie Lister and the Statesmen Quartet** was published in 1994, Dave has been collecting facts, recordings and memorabilia pertaining to the Statesmen with the intent of updating the book with a deluxe, 50th anniversary souvenir hardback edition. The product of that labor is in your hands. Dave has also written a book about Confederate General John Hunt Morgan's cavalry raid in Indiana during the Civil War (see facing page). **With Bowie Knives & Pistols** has been well-received among Civil War buffs nationwide. Two other books are in the research stage.

Dave and his wife, Cheryl, who operates a cake decorating business and sings in Dave's choir at church, are raising three gospel music fans. Daughters Merilee (trumpet) and Melody (flute) are very active in their high school marching band. Son David plays trumpet in the elementary school band. They have been known to play their instruments at church, also.

Dave says he hasn't given up on his dream of singing with the best gospel quartet in the world, "but I'll probably have to borrow Jake's hairpiece and promise Hovie that I'll leave my cowboy hat and cape at home!"